Praise for *Light from Light*

"An outstanding achievement. Centuries of thought and vision, of strenuous debate and complex argument, are here distilled in a language of bell-like clarity. For those among our contemporaries who reject the faith, or for those among us who only half understand it, this study of the Creed is so wonderfully insightful, and so telling in its authority and freshness, it may well in time be regarded as a classic. Intellectually rigorous it certainly is, but it has not got a dull page."

—**Paul Murray, OP**, Professor, Angelicum University (Rome)

"Familiarity breeds contempt! Familiar we are indeed with the Nicene Creed, as we rattle through it at every Sunday Mass. Bishop Barron, with his attractive blend of depth and ease, helps us pray it again for the first time, realizing the dramatic and radical claims we profess!"

—**Timothy Cardinal Dolan**, Archbishop of New York

"The elements of the Creed are the grammar of our faith; without them we are theologically rudderless. Bishop Barron presents these essential theological building stones in a manner that is both intellectually rich and spiritually inspiring. There is no legalistic treatment, no dry presentation of dogmas, but an unveiling of each 'gemstone' in the collection with literary finesse and insights dredged from the whole two-thousand-year-old treasury of Catholic scholarship and tradition."

—**Tracey Rowland**, John Paul II Chair of Theology, University of Notre Dame (Australia)

"This is Bishop Barron at his very best. With his characteristically dialogical and vigorous style, Barron here synthesizes the fruits of his astonishing erudition, drawing upon the best biblical scholars, the Church Fathers, Thomas Aquinas, and many of the greatest minds of the past century. More than a mere synthesis, however, this book is also a highly personal account of why Barron himself professes the Creed. In a manner that is both inviting and invigorating, Barron shows that the answer is because Christianity is true, good, and beautiful. To see how this is so, read this book!"

—**Matthew Levering**, James N. Jr. and Mary D. Perry Chair of Theology, Mundelein Seminary

"A beautifully written and illuminating presentation of the Catholic faith. This book is both a brilliant introduction to the Catholic faith and a sound initiation to the practice of theology."

—**Thomas Joseph White, OP**, Rector Magnificus, Angelicum University

"Bishop Barron's *Light from Light* is to be warmly welcomed. This new book on the Nicene Creed brings the faith that this most central of all Christian creeds articulates into a fresh, lively, and poignant dialogue with classical and contemporary theologians, a conversation that unlocks the Nicene Creed and allows Catholics, Orthodox, Protestants as well as 'nones' to (re-)discover the unheard-of novelty, yet utter credibility, of this ancient condensation of the Gospel of Jesus Christ. This engagingly written book will be a rewarding reading for anyone open to (re-)discover and (re-)claim the Nicene Creed."

—**Reinhard Hütter**, Ordinarius Professor of Fundamental and Dogmatic Theology, The Catholic University of America

"In a time of crisis, it is essential to get back to basics, which is just what Bishop Barron does in this remarkable book. Instead of attempting to attract people to the faith by 'dumbing it down,' Bishop Barron presents it here in all of its glorious intelligibility, which is just what our age needs. He does so, however, with his usual knack for making difficult matters simple and luminous. I expect that this book will open many eyes."

—**D.C. Schindler**, Professor of Metaphysics and Anthropology, The John Paul II Institute

"It is very rare to find a synthesis of the Catholic faith that is *truly learned* and also *truly accessible*, but Bishop Barron's splendid book on the Creed presents that rare accomplishment. It will be equally at home in college courses and in parish discussion groups. Plus, the evangelical zeal, powerful though not overpowering, that animates the book from the first page to the last ensures that it will be as appealing to the heart as it is to the mind. Highly recommended!"

—**John C. Cavadini**, Director of the McGrath Institute for Church Life, University of Notre Dame

LIGHT *from* LIGHT

LIGHT *from* LIGHT

A THEOLOGICAL REFLECTION ON THE NICENE CREED

ROBERT BARRON

WORD ON FIRE ACADEMIC

Published by Word on Fire Academic, an imprint of
Word on Fire, Park Ridge, IL 60068

Printed in the United States of America

Cover design, typesetting, and interior art direction
by Rozann Lee and Cassie Pease.

24 23 22 21   1 2 3 4

ISBN: 978-1-943243-84-6

Library of Congress Control Number: 2020925929

THE NICENE-CONSTANTINOPOLITAN CREED

I believe in one God, the Father almighty, maker of heaven and earth, of all things visible and invisible.

I believe in one Lord Jesus Christ, the Only Begotten Son of God, born of the Father before all ages. God from God, Light from Light, true God from true God, begotten, not made, consubstantial with the Father; through him all things were made. For us men and for our salvation he came down from heaven, and by the Holy Spirit was incarnate of the Virgin Mary, and became man.

For our sake he was crucified under Pontius Pilate, he suffered death and was buried, and rose again on the third day in accordance with the Scriptures. He ascended into heaven and is seated at the right hand of the Father. He will come again in glory to judge the living and the dead and his kingdom will have no end.

I believe in the Holy Spirit, the Lord, the giver of life, who proceeds from the Father and the Son, who with the Father and the Son is adored and glorified, who has spoken through the prophets.

I believe in one, holy, catholic, and apostolic Church. I confess one Baptism for the forgiveness of sins and I look forward to the resurrection of the dead and the life of the world to come. Amen.

CONTENTS

PREFACE

For the past twenty years, I have been involved in the work of evangelizing the culture. In the course of this effort, I have indeed encountered an openness of spirit on the part of many, but also, I must admit, on the part of many more, an enormous antipathy toward religious belief in general, and Christianity in particular. Largely, the objections that the critics present are standard ones, on offer at least from the time of the Enlightenment: God is a wish-fulfilling fantasy, Jesus is a mythic figure, God's goodness is irreconcilable with the suffering of the innocent, the Church is hopelessly corrupt and its moral teaching unreasonable, etc.

But these have taken on a new intensity, due to a number of factors. First, the culture of self-invention, with its roots in the speculations of Friedrich Nietzsche, Jean-Paul Sartre, and Michel Foucault, has now become the default position of armies of young people in the West. By this phrase, I mean the view that goodness and truth are not objective values, but only the result of the private decisions of individuals. Hence, again especially among the young, a radical relativism tends to hold sway, and this means that the Church's claim to speak the truth about anything is construed, automatically, as oppressive and exclusive.

A second factor is the influence of the so-called new atheists, who had a vogue in the first decade of the twenty-first century.[1] Though their influence has significantly waned, they have had a rather major impact on the minds of a generation of young people in the West. I know this from direct experience, for the arguments, language, and prejudices of Christopher Hitchens, Richard Dawkins, Sam Harris, and their colleagues are unmistakably present in the rhetoric of the audience that I often engage. What these figures have

1. See, for example, Christopher Hitchens, *God Is Not Great: How Religion Poisons Everything* (New York: Hachette, 2007); Richard Dawkins, *The God Delusion* (London: Bantam, 2006); and Sam Harris, *The End of Faith: Religion, Terror, and the Future of Reason* (New York: W.W. Norton, 2004).

communicated, besides their particular perspectives, is a general sense that religious belief is irrational, a holdover from a primitive age. So time and again, my interlocutors, echoing Harris, Dawkins, and Hitchens, characterize the faith as "bronze-age mythology" or the musings of prescientific people who did not understand the basics of biology or chemistry.

A third factor—and I am afraid it falls under the category of "we've met the enemy and it is us"—is the dumbing down of the faith that has occurred for over fifty years, at least in the Catholic Church.[2] How prevalent this tendency is in other Christian denominations I will not venture to comment. But certainly within the Catholic context, we have presented a highly emotional and experiential version of religion—and this has left us largely helpless before the opponents of the faith. Tragically, our own de-emphasis on the intellectual substance of our faith coincided with a tendency within the academy to denigrate religion. Some of the saddest statistical studies that I have read are those that detail the number of young Catholics who enter the university as believers and exit as nonbelievers. But given the dovetailing of a dumbed-down Catholicism with a religiously skeptical professoriate, this phenomenon is hardly surprising.

The saddest consequence—at least for faith leaders—of this cultural and intellectual situation is the rise of the religiously unaffiliated. In the early 1970s, only about 3% of Americans identified themselves as unreligious, but that number has risen, astonishingly, to 26% today. And among those under thirty, the figure rises to almost 40%, which bodes ill indeed for the future of religious practice in our country.[3] In many other countries in the West, the numbers are even more disheartening.

---

2. See Robert Barron, "The Trouble with Beige Catholicism," in *Bridging the Great Divide: Musings of a Post-Liberal, Post-Conservative Evangelical Catholic* (Lanham, MD: Rowman & Littlefield, 2004), 11–21; Robert Barron and John Allen Jr., *To Light a Fire on the Earth: Proclaiming the Gospel in a Secular Age* (New York: Image Books, 2017), 89–95; and Robert Barron and Brandon Vogt, "#034: Don't Be a 'Beige' Catholic," *Word on Fire Show* podcast, August 2, 2016, https://www.wordonfireshow.com/episode34/.

3. Pew Research Center, "In US, Decline of Christianity Continues at Rapid Pace," Washington, DC, October 17, 2019, https://www.pewforum.org/2019/10/17/in-u-s-decline-of-christianity-continues-at-rapid-pace/; Public Religion Research Institute (PRRI), "America's Changing Religious Identity," Washington, DC, September 6, 2017, https://www.prri.org/research/american-religious-landscape-christian-religiously-unaffiliated/.

What has become crystal clear to me in my twenty years of work in the field of evangelization—and all of the factors mentioned above have contributed to it—is that the overwhelming majority of the critics of Christianity do not have a firm grasp of what thoughtful Christians actually believe. Fulton Sheen made a remark seventy years ago that is, if anything, truer today: "There are not over a hundred people in the United States who hate the Catholic Church. There are millions, however, who hate what they wrongly believe to be the Catholic Church—which is, of course, quite a different thing."[4]

And this is why I have written this book, a theological interpretation of the Nicene Creed. The twentieth-century Protestant theologian Karl Barth, a man deeply appreciative of the Christian theological tradition, once commented that every generation has to tell the story again, as though for the first time. He was by no means advocating liberalism or relativism, but he was acknowledging that the Good News should always sound both good and fresh. The canny evangelist has to know what is blocking the hearing of the Gospel in his own time and present the message accordingly. So I have composed this study of the Christian basics for those of my contemporaries who are ignorant of them and/or hostile to them.

I have chosen to focus on the Nicene Creed for a number of reasons. A peculiar quality of Christianity is that, among all the major religions of the world, it is most concerned with doctrinal clarity. Unlike a number of faiths that emphasize orthopraxis (right behavior) more than orthodoxy (right belief) and unlike others that cultivate a more open-ended and less defined theology, Christianity has, from the beginning, been massively interested in laying out its beliefs clearly, succinctly, and articulately. This instinct has found expression in creeds—which is to say, formal statements of doctrinal belief. Of the many such documents that emerged in the first centuries of the Church, the most theologically developed is the one that came forth from the deliberations of the Council of Nicaea in 325 and which was slightly

4. Fulton Sheen, preface to *Radio Replies*, vol. 1, by Charles Carty and Leslie Rumble (Charlotte, NC: TAN Books, 2012).

elaborated at the Council of Constantinople in 381. Called the "Nicene" or "Nicene-Constantinopolitan" Creed, it has provided the foundation for the theological systems of most of the great spiritual teachers of both Eastern and Western Christianity and is also used in a liturgical setting in many of the churches, again both East and West. It is fair to say that most Christians would subscribe to this ancient statement of our faith.

Now, if my reader is looking for a detailed study of the historical and cultural circumstances surrounding the Council of Nicaea or a careful analysis of the debates of the Nicene fathers, I suggest he or she stop reading right now. I will focus not so much on the historical but the theological. My purpose is to bring out the meaning of this beautiful and venerable Creed so as to engage especially the skeptical and/or searching audience of today. Though I have tried to avoid technical theological jargon as much as possible and though I do not descend, for the most part, into the fussy fine points of the issues I discuss, nevertheless, I have written this book at a fairly high intellectual level. A simplistic presentation of the faith, as I said, has been, demonstrably, a pastoral disaster. Dumbing down our religion most certainly has not brought more people to us—just the contrary. Catholicism is a smart religion, and I make no apologies for it.

In a number of studies undertaken in just the past five years or so, people who have left the practice of religion were asked why they disaffiliated. They offered a number of reasons, but one of the most prominent was simply that they no longer believed in the teachings of Christianity. This book, which tries to explicate those teachings in a compelling way, is written especially for those who have wandered away from the faith.

CHAPTER 1

I Believe

"I Believe in One God"

There is an eloquent ambiguity in the way in which the opening word of the Nicene Creed has come down to us. Our best evidence suggests that in the formula that goes back to the Nicene Fathers themselves, the word is *pisteuomen* (we believe), but as the Creed has been passed on, translated, and used in liturgical settings, *pisteuomen* often became *pisteuo* (I believe). The ancient Latin translation indeed begins with *Credo* (I believe). For the first several decades of my life, the Church commenced the Creed at Mass with "we believe," but about ten years ago, it switched back to a rendering of the standard Latin version: "I believe." I say that the ambiguity is eloquent, for there is value in both forms.

On the one hand, "we believe" effectively emphasizes the communal and corporate dimension of the Church's faith: we are in this Christian project together and never individualistically. Moreover, it indicates how, in a sense, we believe not only *with* others but in some cases *for* others. Perhaps my conviction regarding an article of the Creed is wavering, but yours is strong, and mine is firm with respect to another article, and yours is weak. The "we believe" allows us to find mutual support in our faith.

However, the "we believe" also allows us to escape, at least to some degree, personal responsibility. Do *I* truly believe this? What is at stake in agreeing to this ancient statement is not a triviality or even a matter of purely epistemic interest. Rather, the issues raised by the Creed have to do with where a person stands most fundamentally. And therefore, in another sense, it is altogether appropriate that the one who recites the Creed commence by saying unequivocally, "I believe." Again, I think it is something of a desideratum not to eliminate this tension.

The verb itself is of crucial importance: "believe." Especially mindful of the army of the unaffiliated, those who have either never been exposed to a serious presentation of the faith or have actively left religious practice behind, I want to stress, as strongly as I possibly can, that authentic faith or belief has not a thing to do with naïve credulity or accepting claims on the basis of no evidence. Faith, in a word, is never below reason, never infra-rational. The Church has absolutely no interest in encouraging superstition or intellectual irresponsibility. Rather, and this will become clearer when we examine the principal object of our belief, real faith is supra-rational, above what reason can grasp. If we must speak of a certain darkness in regard to the matters of faith, it is the darkness that comes from too much light, rather than from defect of light.

Since this matter is so basic and since a misunderstanding of faith is such a consistent block for so many, I should like to approach this issue with some care and from a number of angles. I will first employ the aid of St. John Henry Newman, a man who wrestled mightily all his life with the question of the relationship between faith and reason. Newman wanted to preserve the epistemological legitimacy of Christian faith in the teeth of the rationalist critique coming out of the Enlightenment. At a time when some serious Christian thinkers—Friedrich Schleiermacher comes most readily to mind—were proposing a nonrational approach to Christianity, a retreat into an elevated sentimentality, Newman insisted on the intellectual integrity of faith. He made his argument over and against one of the titans of the English Enlightenment and one of his own philosophical heroes, John Locke. Locke argued, commonsensically enough, that the quality of one's assent to a proposition ought to be in strict correlation to the quality of the inferential support that one could muster for said proposition. Thus, if your argument for a claim is practically airtight, your assent should be strong; if your argument is moderately good, your assent should be moderate; if your argument is weak, your assent should be tentative at best; etc.[1]

1. John Henry Newman, *An Essay in Aid of the Grammar of Assent* (London: Longmans & Green, 1903), 157–187.

Newman stood completely athwart this position, taking it to be a kind of angelism. Perhaps in some perfected and abstract realm we would think this way, but here below, this is hardly ever the case. Very occasionally, for example in regard to self-evident states of affairs or mathematical indubitables, the correlation between assent and inference is absolute. But frequently, even typically, we give unconditioned assent to propositions for which there is no unconditioned inferential support. Newman's famous example is the unrestrained and unhesitating assent we give to the claim that Great Britain is an island. Our agreement with this proposition is grounded not in airtight syllogisms or self-evident sense perception, but rather in a whole congeries of hunches, intuitions, testimonies, historical records, etc. In short, with regard to this proposition and the overwhelming majority of assents we make, the operative word would be, strictly speaking, *believe* rather than know. What Newman is trying to show is that the rationalistic dichotomy between supposed knowledge and belief is largely a chimera. In point of fact, we assent to religious claims in the same way that we assent to practically any other kind of claim: through a combination of arguments, gut feeling, the testimony of others, intuition, and personal experience, a range of evidences both rational and nonrational. The object of religious assent is different than the object of nonreligious assent, but the manner of thinking in both cases is fundamentally the same. Thus, Newman can conclude that faith is just a word we use to describe "the reasoning of a religious mind."[2] Newman's approach here is, to use a phrase from classical rhetoric, a *tu quoque* (you as well) argument. He tells his enlightened interlocutors to drop their pretentious claim to sheer rationality, indeed to remove the plank in their own eye before attempting to remove the speck in the eye of the religious believer.

Another way to illumine this matter of belief is to look at it from the other side—which is to say, in regard to the radical difference between relating epistemically to God and relating epistemically to anything else.

2. John Henry Newman, "The Nature of Faith in Relation to Reason," in *Oxford University Sermons* (London: Longmans & Green, 1909), 203.

We will explain all of this in greater detail anon, but suffice it to say for the moment that God is not anything in the world—that is to say, not any kind of being among others. Both because God is infinitely actual and because he subsists as the Creator of the world, he, by definition, cannot be known in any ordinary acceptation of that term. The knowing faculty is ordered, by its nature, to things that appear and to those truths that can be deduced from things that appear. Even mathematical objects and sheer abstractions show up for the viewing of the mind, which is suggested by Plato's term *eidos* (form). But God cannot be seen, and he cannot be known through even the highest abstraction. Therefore, knowing, certitude, perception—all of which convey the sense of control—are necessarily inappropriate when talking about God. As Paul Tillich said, echoing the entire Christian tradition, God is not provisionally unknown, but unknown and unknowable through his very nature. Augustine implied the same when he said "*Si comprehendis, non est Deus*" (If you understand, that is not God).[3] And even Thomas Aquinas, who presents a very rationally informed theology, can say, "*Quidquid potest intelligi vel cogitari minus est ipso Deo*" (Whatever can be known or understood is less than God himself).[4]

To say with respect to such a reality that we have a commanding or controlling knowledge would be, if I might put it this way, epistemically impious. Belief in this context is not a concession, a settling for second best; rather, in this life at least, it is all we can or should hope for. Like the bear in Faulkner's famous story of a young man's initiation into the ways of the hunt, God is seen only in the dappling and only after the hunter has abandoned his compass and gun, the instruments of navigation and control. As we shall see shortly, the eager mind can, to a degree, track down the truth about God, but at the end of the day, God has to disclose himself—and the response to such a disclosure is, necessarily, *belief* rather than knowledge. If I might propose a somewhat homely analogy, the play between reason and faith in regard to

3. Augustine, *Sermones de scripturis* 117.3.5 (PL 38:663).

4. Thomas Aquinas, *Expositio in symbolum apostolorum* 1, in *Opuscula theologica*, vol. 2, ed. Raymundus M. Spiazzi (Turin: Marietti, 1954). For a recent English translation of this work, see *The Sermon-Conferences of St. Thomas Aquinas on the Apostles' Creed*, trans. and ed. Nicholas Ayo (Eugene, OR: Wipf & Stock, 2005).

God is something like the play between reason and faith in regard to coming to know another human being. To be sure, investigation, examination, research, and observation all play a role in this process, but finally, if one wishes to know the heart of another person, he has to wait until that other *reveals* himself, and then he has to decide whether he *believes* what he has been told. An aggressive reason that seeks always to grasp on its own terms will never come to know deeper dimensions of reality, including and especially the personal. Such depths can be plumbed only through something like a faith that accepts and receives.

It is worth noting that in Thomas Aquinas' religious epistemology, faith is a rare case of the will commanding the intellect. Typically, in Aquinas' account, it is just the opposite: will is a function of the intellect, responding to what the intellect presents to it. But when it comes to faith, the will, in a way, comes first, for it commands the intellect to assent, and it does so out of love.[5] Because the will loves God, it directs the mind to accept what God has revealed about himself, even though the mind cannot clearly see or understand it. Again, lest this sound anomalous, much the same dynamic obtains in an interpersonal relationship. Is she telling me the truth about what is in her heart? I cannot possibly know directly, but my will, which loves her and has come to trust her, commands my intellect to assent.

At this point, we might consider the dilemma proposed by Paul Tillich. One can easily enough say that God can neither deceive nor be deceived and therefore the word of God is reliable. But this begs the question whether the Bible is in fact the word of God. Many theologians, especially in the Protestant tradition, speak of the self-validating power of the Scripture. The texts are, in the Bible's own lovely self-description, "God-breathed"; God's wisdom blows through these pages, and hence we have come through experience to appreciate the one whom we have found there. We have come to trust him and hence to believe what he has said.

These last examples reveal that there is inevitably a subtle play between intellect and will, between analysis and acceptance, whenever we are dealing

5. Thomas Aquinas, *Summa theologiae* 2-2.2.

with authentic faith. In the great story of the beginnings of humanity, we find Adam and Eve walking in easy fellowship with God, listening to his command, "obeying" him, trusting him. When they grasp at the fruit of the tree of knowledge, they are arrogating to themselves the determination of right and wrong, turning themselves into gods. The rescue operation that the Lord inaugurates with Abram is primarily a matter of teaching a people how to listen to him again. Abraham's "faith" is tantamount to his willingness to attend to a voice that transcends his own. The rationalist, naturally, will object that there is no warrant for such a surrender, and we will take up this matter in the next section. But for now, let us be content with understanding that faith is a trusting surrender that there is a reasonability on the far side of reason. It is, therefore, an openness to adventure.

Having examined the term "believe" in some detail, we must attend to the little word "in," which actually carries a good deal of spiritual significance: "*Credo in unum Deum*" (I believe in one God). In Latin, *in* with the accusative case has the sense of motion toward, while *in* with the ablative case, *in urbe* (in the city) for example, has the sense of location. Our believing does not place us firmly and certainly in the space of God; rather, it moves us toward him, into him. St. Bonaventure's searching and seminal text *Itinerarium mentis in Deum* (*The Soul's Journey into God*) has a similar connotation: it is an account of how we make our way into or toward the mystery of God.[6] This clues us into a very important dimension of creedal language. We ought never to think that acceptance of the truth of the propositions contained in the Creed is tantamount to Christian experience in its totality. On the contrary, creedal formulas are guides, guardrails, indicators on the side of the road that is leading us into God. They point us in the right direction and prevent us from going completely off the path. So, for example, if you do not believe in the Trinitarian God or in the Incarnation of the Logos or in the activity of the Holy Spirit, you are certainly in dangerous territory, and you will not tell the Christian story correctly. But the "content" of these

6. Bonaventure, *The Soul's Journey into God*, in *Bonaventure: The Soul's Journey into God, The Tree of Life, and The Life of St. Francis*, trans. Ewert Cousins (Mahwah, NJ: Paulist, 1978), 51–116.

great mysteries is not fully given in the formulas themselves; we approach that completeness only through repeated narrating of the tale and through the concrete living of the Christian life. Thomas Aquinas could say in this context that faith terminates not in the *enuntiabile* (proposition) but in the *rem* (thing).[7]

"One God"

So, what is this "thing" that is the principal object of the act of faith? Perhaps the most basic observation we could make is that it (he) is not really a thing at all. Whatever we mean by the word "God," we do not intend one finite reality among many, not the "supreme being" in any conventional sense of that term. We intend that which brought (and brings) the whole of finite reality into being, that which transcends even as it remains intimately close to all that can possibly be seen or measured. I have found that many skeptical questions concerning God are generated by this fundamental misunderstanding of the meaning of the word. Or to state it more positively, many dilemmas and conundrums are cleared up the moment a person comes to grasp what serious Christians mean by "God." But even if we accept the correct definition of the word, is there any rational warrant for believing in the existence of this peculiar reality?

For much of human history, the existence of God was more or less taken for granted. Indeed, as many cultural analysts have observed, our contemporary Western culture is perhaps the first ever seriously to entertain the possibility of subsisting apart from belief in God. In this context, Charles Taylor can speak of the "buffered self"—which is to say, the ego cut off from any real connection to what transcends its immediate experience.[8] Prior to, say, 1500, Taylor contends, practically no one thought that a satisfying life

7. Thomas Aquinas, *Summa theologiae* 2-2.1.2 ad 2 in *Sancti Thomae de Aquino Opera Omnia*, Leonine ed. [hereafter Leon.] (Rome, 1882–) 8:11. See also Thomas Aquinas, *Faith (2a2æ. 1–7): Latin Text, English Translation, Introduction Notes, Appendices and Glossary by T.C. O'Brien*, vol. 31 of *St. Thomas Aquinas Summa Theologiæ* (Cambridge: Cambridge University Press, 2006), 12–13.

8. Charles Taylor, *A Secular Age* (Cambridge, MA: Belknap Press of Harvard University Press, 2018), 37–42.

could be had in abstraction from God; but now, happiness apart from God, happiness derived entirely from this-worldly goods, is seen as a very lively option. Thus, we have to make a case for the transcendent; we have to find a way to break through the buffered self.

The Catholic Church has long maintained that the existence of God can be known through the light of natural reason. There is indeed biblical warrant for this: "The heavens are telling the glory of God" (Ps. 19:1) and "his eternal power and divine nature, invisible though they are, have been understood and seen through the things he has made" (Rom. 1:20). And some of our greatest theologians and philosophers have formulated arguments for the existence of God, most famously St. Anselm and St. Thomas Aquinas. Furthermore, the First Vatican Council (1870) clearly teaches that God's existence can be known with certitude through the exercise of our rational faculties.[9] The best of our tradition has known—as I tried to indicate in the preceding section—that this knowledge has nothing to do with controlling God or with reducing him to an easily understood object of the mind. Thomas Aquinas speaks, for instance, not of "proofs" for God, but rather of *viae* or "paths" to God,[10] and of *manuductiones,* "leadings by the hand,"[11] by which a mind is brought toward a consideration of God's existence. No one of our great masters ever taught that these "demonstrations" provide anything like an exhaustive or adequate account of God. But they do, nevertheless, point us in the right direction—and that is no small thing.

The principal challenge to religious belief is coming, today, from a materialist and secularist ideology that often claims the warrant of the physical sciences.[12] This is the view that reality is simply coterminous with the realm of changeable matter. So, clearly on these grounds, belief in God is ruled out

9. First Vatican Council, *Dei Filius* 2, in Denzinger et al., *Compendium of Creeds, Definitions, and Declarations on Matters of Faith and Morals*, 43rd ed. (San Francisco: Ignatius Press, 2012), nos. 3000–3007.

10. Thomas Aquinas, *Summa theologiae* 1.2.3 (Leon. 4:31–32).

11. Thomas Aquinas, 1.1.5 ad 2 (Leon. 4:16).

12. See Robert Barron, *Arguing Religion: A Bishop Speaks at Facebook and Google* (Park Ridge, IL: Word on Fire, 2018), 17–26; Robert Barron and John Allen Jr., *To Light a Fire on the Earth* (New York: Image Books, 2017), 103–105; and Robert Barron, *Renewing Our Hope: Essays for the New Evangelization* (Washington, DC: The Catholic University of America Press, 2020), 12–18.

of court as fantastic. As a first response, we might observe that this sort of ideological materialism is self-refuting, for the claim that reality is reducible to the material cannot be justified on purely scientific grounds. One cannot determine through the scientific method that the scientific method is the only way to access reality. Nonetheless, many people, especially the young, are beguiled by the undoubted success of the physical sciences into accepting a "scientistic" epistemology and worldview. Therefore, in approaching the question of God today, it might be wise to seek points of overlap and connection between a religious and scientific *Weltanschauung.*

I would certainly not recommend, in this context, the embrace of so-called "intelligent design" speculation, whereby God is construed as an intervening cause required to account for certain forms of irreducible complexity in some living things. Not only is the biology behind such speculation questionable, but the notion of God undergirding it is deeply inadequate, in the measure that it posits God as a cause among many, fussily intervening in natural processes. Nor would I enthusiastically recommend taking up arguments from the supposed fine-tuning of the universe in the direction of the emergence first of life and then of consciousness. I say this not because I think there is no merit whatsoever to these arguments; but I fear, once again, that the God that they present is somewhat misleading. The Creator of the entire universe is not one cause, however intelligent and powerful, who intervenes occasionally or in one particular manner in the functioning of the world. Both the intelligent design and fine-tuning arguments, in a word, betray too much of their provenance in the deism of the Enlightenment.

However, there is a path that emerges from the world of science and that I would indeed recommend. This is the argument that commences from the mystical fact of the universe's radical intelligibility. Every science is predicated finally on the supposition that the world that the scientist goes out to meet through her senses and her curious, critical intelligence is marked by form, pattern, and understandability. Whether we are talking about the practitioners of psychology, biology, chemistry, astrophysics, or geology, every scientist must assume objective intelligibility. The medieval philosophers expressed this idea with typical pith: *ens est scibile* (being is knowable). They also held that there exists so deep a correlation between the searching mind and the intelligible object that, when they meet, each, as it were, actualizes the other. Each finds its purpose in the other, something like the two halves of the mythic figures from Plato's story of human origins in the *Symposium*.[13]

Of course, the philosophers of the classical period knew this truth as well. Pythagoras opined that everything is number, by which he meant marked by order, harmony, and measurable proportion. Plato took this truth to be so basic that he required its acceptance by any prospective student in his Academy. And contemporary scientists implicitly affirm it at every turn, as they use the most sophisticated mathematics to describe dynamics of reality at all levels. They speak indeed of the "laws" or at least the statistical probabilities that govern the biological and astronomical orders, but they also assume that even the most basic levels of being, invisible to the naked eye and accessible only through indirect indications, are governed by something like mathematical principles. In the words of Cambridge particle physicist and Anglican priest John Polkinghorne, "It is an actual technique of discovery in fundamental physics to seek theories which are expressed in terms of what mathematicians can recognize and agree to be beautiful equations."[14]

But why should this be the case? Though we take this principle (again, unprovable through the method that thoroughly presupposes it) utterly for granted, the more we stare at it, the stranger it seems. Why should the world, in every nook and cranny and as a totality, be marked by intelligibility? Why should the scientific enterprise be undertaken with such confidence? Furthermore, why should its findings inform such remarkably successful practical projects? I have continually been amazed at the number of atheist and agnostic commentators who are content simply to accept this astonishing state of affairs as dumbly given, just the way things are. But Paul Davies challenged his scientific peers with the simple but penetrating question: Where do the

13. Plato, *Symposium*, 189D–194E, trans. Alexander Nehama and Paul Woodruff (Indianapolis, IN: Hackett, 1989), 25–31.

14. John Polkinghorne, "The Trinity and Scientific Reality," in *The Blackwell Companion to Science and Christianity*, ed. J.B. Stump and Alan G. Padgett (Oxford: Blackwell, 2012), 524.

laws of nature come from?[15] And Einstein himself once quipped, "The most incomprehensible thing about the universe is that it is comprehensible."[16]

In his indispensable *Introduction to Christianity*, Joseph Ratzinger (Pope Benedict XVI) argued that the only finally satisfying explanation for objective intelligibility is something like a great intelligence that embedded these sophisticated patterns into the structure of the universe.[17] Ratzinger observes how our language reflects this intuition: we speak of *recognition* of truths—which is to say, re-cognition, thinking again what has already been thought. And here we can make appeal to the Bible. One of the most important and fundamental claims of the opening chapter of the book of Genesis is that God made the universe through great acts of speech: "Then God said, 'Let there be light'; and there was light" (Gen. 1:3). "And God said, 'Let the waters under the sky be gathered together into one, and let the dry land appear.' And so it was" (Gen. 1:9). We must not, of course, take these as literal descriptions, but rather as symbolic gestures in the direction of the intelligence that informs the act of creation. In the prologue to St. John's Gospel, which consciously hearkens back to the commencement of Genesis, we hear "In the beginning was the Word. . . . He was in the beginning with God. All things came into being through him, and without him not one thing came into being" (John 1:1–3). If everything came into existence through a word, everything is, necessarily, stamped by an intelligible form and intelligent purpose. And this is why, according to Ratzinger and a number of other commentators, it is not surprising that the modern physical sciences emerged precisely out of a culture shaped by this biblical imagination. If one believes in creation, one will readily make two assumptions necessary for the development of the sciences—namely, that the world is not God (and hence can be analyzed and experimented upon) and that the world is intelligible (and hence likely to

15. See Paul Davies, "The Nature of the Laws of Physics and Their Mysterious Bio-Friendliness," in *Science and Religion in Dialogue*, vol. 2, ed. Melville Y. Stewart (Oxford: Blackwell, 2010), 769–788.

16. Albert Einstein, "Physics and Reality," *Journal of the Franklin Institute* 221, no. 3 (March 1936): 351.

17. Joseph Ratzinger, *Introduction to Christianity*, 2nd ed., trans. J.R. Foster (San Francisco: Ignatius Press, 2004), 151–158.

yield results to those who examine it intelligently). What I find particularly illuminating about this observation is how it makes clear that religion is not only not the enemy of science but in fact the condition for its possibility.

A second rational approach to God, a second *manuductio*, commences with the radical contingency of the world. By this technical philosophical term, I simply mean the ontologically evanescent quality of everything in our immediate experience. The objects, animals, and people that surround us, the states of affairs that obtain, the weather, the stars and the planets—all of these exist but do not *have* to exist. One indication of this is the simple fact that all of them came into being and sooner or later will pass out of being. But an even simpler determination can be made by observing that all of these things and states of affairs *could be otherwise.* It is sunny now, but under different conditions, it would be cloudy; a car is racing past me on the road, but it could just as well be in the garage, or it is quite conceivable that it would not exist at all; I am currently typing these words on a keyboard, but I could just as well have chosen to be doing a thousand other things. What this simple thought experiment reveals is that all the matters under consideration do not contain within themselves the reason for their own existence, for if they did, they could not be otherwise than they are. And this is precisely why, by an altogether valid instinct, we look for their causes, for the conditions for their possibility, for the sufficient explanation of why they exist as they do. David Hume imagined that the idea of causality is illusory, since the causal relationship, as such, cannot be empirically observed.[18] Say what you will about Hume's analysis of the empirical verification of causality; he is certainly wrong to say that we have no rational warrant for accepting the metaphysical reality of causality, for such acceptance is a necessary correlate of contingency perceived as such.

And so such states of affairs are contingent—which is to say, they touch upon something else (*con-tingere*), they require an explanation extrinsic to themselves. But then we are naturally led to ask, in regard to those causes or

18. David Hume, *An Enquiry Concerning Human Understanding*, 2nd ed., ed. Eric Steinberg (Indianapolis, IN: Hackett, 1993), 15ff.

sets of causes, whether *they themselves* are self-explanatory or contingent. To return to one of our earlier examples, my typing of these words on a keyboard is contingent upon my at least relatively good health, the temperature of the room (which is poised sufficiently between extreme heat and extreme cold so as to render my activity possible), the stability of the desk upon which the keyboard rests, etc. But the curious mind continues to inquire: Are those causes self-sufficient or contingent? Immediately we perceive that they are the latter, for my good health depends upon the functioning of a number of bodily systems, upon the oxygen that I am breathing, my genetics, etc.; the temperature of the room is determined through the heating system in the room where I am situated, upon the structure of the house in which that room is found, upon the current state of the weather, etc.; and the stability of the desk depends upon the stability of the floor on which it rests, which depends upon the stability of the earth, etc.

So far, so obvious. But the restless intellect still has not found a sufficient justification for the existence of the contingent state of affairs under consideration. Our analysis of causes that are themselves contingent simply postpones any definitive answer. Can this type of causal regress be infinite or indefinite? The response must be in the negative, since an infinite postponement of the matter never adequately explains how something that does not have to exist actually exists. Therefore, we must conclude to the existence of some reality that ultimately explains contingent being and is not itself contingent. Thomas Aquinas referred to this reality as the *uncaused cause* or the *necessary being*. And this, he affirmed, is what reasonable people are referring to when they use the word "God."[19]

In order more fully to understand this argument, it might be wise to respond to one of the principal objections to this type of demonstration. Some say that the impossibility of an infinite regress of contingent causes cannot be excluded—in other words, that the chain of caused causes might simply go back indefinitely. Even Thomas Aquinas admitted that this objection would

19. Thomas Aquinas, *Summa theologiae* 1.2.3.

hold in regard to historical series of causes—that is to say, causes going back in time: I was caused by my father, he by his father, he by his, etc. In that sort of causal chain, the present causal activity of each member is not here and now dependent upon the causal influence of the immediately antecedent cause. Though my coming into being was dependent upon my father, I can act and influence other things even though he is no longer alive. And thus, one could not rule out an infinite regress in that context. It is instructive that typically when this sort of proof is attacked, the critic is assuming a causal series, to use the technical terms, subordinated *per accidens* (incidentally) and not *per se* (in itself).[20] What Thomas Aquinas denies is precisely that latter type of infinite causal series, in which each element is here and now dependent upon the influence of the cause immediately preceding it. In that kind of causal chain, the suppression of the first instance would indeed entail the suppression of all subsequent causality.

If the first kind of proof we looked at gives us a great Intelligence that stands behind the intelligibility of the world, this one gives us something even more fundamental—namely, a great source of being and actualization that stands behind the passing and ephemeral world of our experience. One of the prefaces to the Eucharistic Prayer in the Catholic tradition expresses the implications of this notion as follows: "In you [God] we live and move and have our being."[21] And this last quotation reflects, to be sure, one of the most basic intuitions of the biblical authors—namely, that God is the Creator of all things. This idea, spoken in supreme poetry in both the book of Genesis and in the middle chapters of the prophet Isaiah, is perfectly correlated to the notion of God as the noncontingent ground of all contingent existence. If God is the sheer act of to-be itself, in and through which all finite things subsist, then God can only be described as Creator.

A third path is more mystical and intuitive, less rationalistic. Though the arguments for God's existence offered by Thomas Aquinas are perhaps the best known, few realize that Thomas' insistence that we can and should

20. Thomas Aquinas, 1.46.2 ad 7 (Leon. 4.482).
21. "Preface VI of the Sundays in Ordinary Time," in *Roman Missal* (ICEL, 2010).

argue for God on the basis of what the senses deliver to us was, at the time, somewhat egregious. For most of the theological tradition that preceded and indeed surrounded him, the affirmation of the self-evidence of God's existence was far more common. St. Augustine is typical here. The great North African bishop maintained that God is not so much a true thing that the mind discovers, nor a good ideal that the will seeks. Instead, God is the light of truth itself by which the search for any particular truth is undertaken, the light of goodness itself that illumines the quest for any particular good or state of righteousness. This is why Augustine refers to God as the *prius* of all thought and action, the great undergirding condition for the possibility of these two fundamental moves of the soul.[22] Bernard Lonergan, though in a vein more Thomistic than Augustinian, caught this when he spoke of the hunger that drives the questing mind. The mind, he says, is empty, but not in the manner of a box but rather in the manner of a stomach, meaning it knows what it seeks.[23] Aquinas himself refers to the light of the agent intellect, designating the always already present energy that animates the intellect in its work of seeking the truth. In a word, there is some primordial sense of the Truth in its unconditioned form that drives the quest for particular truths. Apposite here is the Hindu adage that the atheist is like the man riding into town on the back of an ox saying, "I'm seeking an ox." Anyone sincerely looking for the truth has already been found by God.

Paul Tillich, operating here within a very Augustinian framework, speaks of revelation as the "breakthrough of the unconditioned."[24] Our ordinary experience is exclusively of conditioned things, and indeed the previous argument is predicated upon this fact. But in and through the conditioned beings of the world—and through the way in which we know those things—one can sense what Tillich calls "being itself" or the "truth itself." One of

22. See, for example, *De civitate Dei* 8.7; *De magistro* 11–12; *Soliloquia* 1.12–15; *De trinitate* 12.24–25.

23. Bernard Lonergan, "Metaphysics as Horizon," in *Collected Works of Bernard Lonergan: Volume 4 Collection*, 2nd ed., ed. Frederick E. Crowe and Robert M. Doran (Toronto: University of Toronto Press, 1988), 200.

24. Paul Tillich, *Dogmatik* (Düsseldorf: Patmos, 1986), 41.

the marks of the unconditioned is that it cannot be sequestered simply on one side or the other of the subject/object divide. It is both "in here" and "out there"; and it is neither "in here" nor "out there." It lies beyond the split between subjectivity and objectivity. And this is why those who describe the experience of receiving a breakthrough of the unconditioned will use language sometimes more subjective in tone and sometimes more objective. According to a number of contemporary theologians and philosophers of religion, the precipitating causes of this breakthrough are frequently "limit experiences," times when the finitude of the world and one's own finitude are *felt*. Thus, when we confront our own sin, our own physical weakness, our own mortality, our own practical incapacity, or when we feel the unresolvable tension between two competing ontological values, we come to a kind of edge beyond which we can sense a darkness both frightening and alluring. As Hegel put it, to know a limit as a limit is already to be beyond the limit.[25]

It is in light of this reflection on the nature of the unconditioned that we can properly understand one of the most famous and controversial of the arguments for God's existence—namely, the so-called ontological argument, first formulated by St. Anselm of Canterbury and commented upon, both positively and negatively, by some of the greatest figures in the philosophical and theological traditions. The demonstration itself is simple enough to lay out schematically. Step one: God is defined as that than which nothing greater can be thought; step two: it is greater to exist both inside and outside the mind than in the mind alone; conclusion: God exists. Now, detractors of this argument, from Thomas Aquinas to Immanuel Kant, have tended to see it as a kind of intellectual legerdemain, pulling the extra-mental out of the intra-mental. However, might we appreciate it as a sort of showing forth of the implications of an experience of the unconditioned? In the rarely read section of St. Anselm's *Proslogion*, which immediately precedes his articulation of the ontological argument, the saint tells us that he had been assiduously searching for a clinching proof of God's existence, and that only

25. Georg Wilhelm Friedrich Hegel, *The Science of Logic*, trans. A.V. Miller (New York: Humanity Books, 1969), 134.

when he let go of this quest did the argument come to him as a sort of gift. And it came, basically, in the form of a name, "that than which nothing greater can be thought."[26]

What is immediately clear is that this name corresponds to no being in the world, indeed to no possible being among beings. For to such a reality, something more could always be added: the conventional supreme being plus the world would be greater than the conventional supreme being alone. Nor could it simply correspond to an idea in St. Anselm's mind, for that idea plus any type of objectivity would be greater than that idea alone. Hence, what was given to Anselm through that name was an experience of unconditioned being. What the proof makes explicit is what is already implicit in the name, that the unconditioned is neither in the mind alone nor in the world alone, its perfection tantamount to a transcendence of those categories. Anselm was not moving, as his critics consistently maintain, from the intra-mental to the extra-mental; rather, he was witnessing to the existence of a reality that can be sequestered in neither of those categories. As I mentioned earlier, the view that God's existence is self-evident was the dominant one prior to Thomas Aquinas. Perhaps we might even see a link between this venerable tradition and the point of view, coming forth from John Calvin and enduring to the present day in Calvinist philosophical circles, that the knowledge of God's existence is "properly basic"—that is to say, known with the same kind of immediacy and indubitability as our knowledge of our own existence and that of the physical world.[27]

A fourth and final path is the moral. In his apologetic writings and in his more formal treatises on religious epistemology, John Henry Newman consistently took as his point of departure the experience of conscience. There are any number of psychological powers that enable us to evaluate dimensions of the world. For example, we have an aesthetic sensibility and an ability to read persons and their motives, but we also have the capacity to

26. Anselm, *Proslogion* 2–5, in *Anselm: Monologion and Proslogion*, trans. Thomas Williams (Indianapolis, IN: Hackett, 1996), 99–102.

27. See, for example, Alvin Plantinga, "Is Belief in God Properly Basic?," *Noûs* 15, no. 1 (1981): 41–51.

evaluate the goodness or evil of our moral acts. Yet, Newman argues, there is a qualitative difference between this last power and its analogues. For only in the case of moral evaluation do we feel ourselves in the presence of Someone whom we have either pleased or offended. If we make an erroneous aesthetic judgment, we might feel ignorant or foolish, but we do not, strictly speaking, feel ashamed. And this is precisely why we speak, only in the case of moral evaluation, of the "voice" of our conscience. *Someone,* we are convinced, is praising us or blaming us.

The German phenomenologist Max Scheler makes much the same point in his analysis of the act of repentance. "Repentance begins with an indictment! But before *whom* do we indict ourselves? Is it not then in the nature of an indictment that there should be a person who receives it and before whom the charge is laid? Repentance is furthermore an inward *confession* of our guilt. But to *whom* do we then confess. . . . Repentance ends with a clear consciousness of the removal . . . of guilt. But *who* has taken the guilt from us?"[28] What Scheler notices is that the feeling of real shame goes beyond a sense of responsibility toward another human being whom we have offended; it places us, painfully to be sure, in the presence of the source of moral obligation. And the feeling of being truly forgiven, similarly, passes beyond whatever psychological satisfaction we might derive from receiving the benediction of another human being whom we have hurt and introduces us into the presence of a grace coming from a transcendent place.

Scheler's phenomenological colleague Dietrich von Hildebrand drew a distinction between the "merely subjectively satisfying" and the "objectively valuable." The first is something that gives pleasure to the ego, that therefore takes its bearing entirely from the side of subjectivity. But this is to be sharply contrasted with a value that confronts the ego and demands a response, an acknowledgement. These values can appear in the aesthetic order—for example, Beethoven's Seventh Symphony or Van Gogh's *Starry Night* or Dante's *Commedia*. In the presence of such values, it would be comically inadequate

28. Max Scheler, *On the Eternal in Man*, trans. Bernard Noble (New Brunswick, NJ: Transaction, 2010), 61.

to say, "I just don't care for it." Their objective goodness is so overwhelming that the only proper response is surrender and appreciation. But these objective values also appear on the moral plane. Acts of kindness, forgiveness, self-sacrifice, self-forgetting love, etc. are not so much subjectively satisfying (they might be anything but); rather, they stand forth in their objective quality and demand what Hildebrand calls a "value response."[29] But these moral goods are seen as ultimately reflective of distinctively spiritual values, goods having to do with the *summum bonum*, the highest value, which is God. We might link this to an earlier path by drawing attention to the properly unconditioned nature of the moral demand. We are summoned, of course, to perform morally good acts, but underneath this demand is the pervasive and mysterious demand to be a good person, to do good and avoid evil, or to put it in more explicitly religious language, to follow the law of God. This is not a demand that can be legitimately put aside or compromised; rather, it presses upon us with unconditioned power. Paul Tillich speaks of what *uns unbedingt angeht*, of what ultimately concerns us in the moral sphere.[30]

Therefore, the intelligibility of the world, the contingency of ordinary states of affairs, immediate mystical experience, and the press of moral obligation all point in the direction of God. Is any one of these approaches airtight, beyond question, utterly convincing? Perhaps not. But we should keep Newman's epistemology in mind. Rarely, if ever, do we assent to a proposition on the basis of a single clinching argument. Typically, we do so under the influence of a congeries of arguments, intuitions, and experiences, all of which tend along the same trajectory, and this is eminently true of our assent to the proposition that God exists. I might make reference in this context to a final "argument": that from the *consensus gentium*—which is to say, the general agreement of people across time and space that God, or at the very least, some ultimate ground of reality, exists. As I mentioned above, our contemporary Western culture is anomalous in the extreme in the measure that it is the first ever widely to entertain God's nonexistence

29. See Dietrich von Hildebrand, *Christian Ethics* (New York: David McKay, 1953).
30. Paul Tillich, *Dogmatik* (Düsseldorf: Patmos, 1986), 41.

as a lively option. The arguments that I have sketched might be seen as the rational explications of fundamental intuitions that ordinary people have had from time immemorial. They represent the bringing into explicit consciousness of powerful and consistent perceptions about ultimate reality that have perdured and continue to perdure in the human heart.

CHAPTER 2

The Father

"The Father Almighty"

We have been discussing so far the object of the act of belief—namely, the transcendent source of the world's intelligibility, of its contingent existence, and of its moral values. God is not one more intelligible object among many, not a supreme existing thing among other existing things, not simply the highest value alongside other ethical goods. Rather, God is that which is intelligible in itself, that which exists through the power of its own essence, that which is good by its very nature. And this implies, the Creed insists, that the God in whom we believe is one. The unity of God is, of course, an elemental biblical claim: "Hear, O Israel: The LORD is our God, the LORD alone," says the great *shema* prayer in the sixth chapter of Deuteronomy, and monotheism, it is fair to say, is *the* distinctive mark of Jewish faith. The opening verses of the book of Genesis, the account of the creation of all things, mentions a whole series of finite things—sun, moon, planets, stars, animals, mountains, etc.—that in various cultures in the ancient world were worshiped as divinities. In insisting that they are creatures, the author of Genesis effectively dethrones them, placing all of them in a subordinate relation to the one God. Joseph Ratzinger has observed that the *shema* and this opening article of the Creed have in common a spiritual implication of enormous significance. To say that there is only one God or that one believes in *unum Deum* is to disempower any false claimant to ultimacy in one's life. To say that God is the only God is to say, necessarily, that no country, no political party, no human person, no movement, no ideology is of ultimate importance. It is, accordingly, to take a stand—both for and against.[1]

But this unicity of God can be shown in a more philosophical way as well. To say that God is the unconditioned source of finite existence is to say that God exists, not through any cause that actualizes a potential within him, but purely through the power of his own essence or nature. Hence, God is fully actual, utterly realized in being—*actus purus* in the language of Thomas Aquinas.[2] To put it in Lonergan's terms, God is strictly unconditioned.[3] And from this unique metaphysical manner of existing, God's unity necessarily follows, for difference is always a function of some potentiality, some form of nonexistence vis-à-vis that from which one thing is differentiated from another. A is not B in the measure that there is something in B that is not in A and vice versa.

Therefore, there cannot be two or more unconditioned realities, two or more uncaused causes of conditioned being. Now we might entertain the objection that, according to this logic, pantheism would have to obtain, since God could not be properly differentiated from the world. If we were to say, as we must, that God is not the world, then God would seem to have some potentiality vis-à-vis the world. But this is why we have to maintain that God's otherness is a noncontrastive or noncompetitive otherness—that is to say, that God, though certainly distinct from the world, is not lacking in any perfection that the world possesses. As Robert Sokolowski puts it, God plus the world is not greater than God alone, and "after creation there are more beings but not more perfection of *esse* [being]."[4] In point of fact, this unique manner of God's being is precisely what permits God to involve himself in the universe in a noninvasive and finally life-enhancing way. When the gods of ancient mythology enter the world, they always do so destructively,

1. Joseph Ratzinger, *Introduction to Christianity*, 2nd ed., trans. J.R. Foster (San Francisco: Ignatius Press, 2004), 110–115.

2. Thomas Aquinas, *Summa theologiae* 1.9.1 (Leon. 4.90–91).

3. Bernard Lonergan, *Method in Theology* (Toronto: University of Toronto Press, 2003), 101–103.

4. Robert Sokolowski, *The God of Faith and Reason: Foundations of Christian Theology* (Washington, DC: The Catholic University of America Press, 1995), 42.

something in the worldly order giving way in order for them to appear. But there is none of this in regard to the true God, whose relationship with creation is beautifully expressed in the biblical image of the burning bush. The closer God comes to a creature, the more that creature is enhanced and rendered splendid. We will pay very special attention to this dynamic when we turn to the creedal statements on the Incarnation of the Son of God.

Concomitant to the unity of God is what Thomas Aquinas calls the "simplicity" of God.[5] This is no way signals an imperfection or lack, as though God were not as developed or actualized as "complex" forms of existence—just the contrary. Fully in act, God is not a delimited or definable type of thing, not in this genus or that. In the technical language of the scholastics, God is marked by an identity between essence (what he is) and existence (that he is). A finite thing always exists in a determined way, but God's existence is unrestricted, infinite in scope and intensity. His act of being is not received, so to speak, in the receptacle of any essence that would define it, and hence God is properly described as infinite. In the classical philosophers, infinity, precisely as a type of measureless or formless existence, is deemed an imperfection; but the Christian philosophers appreciate it, on the contrary, as an implication of God's pure actuality.

This simplicity allows for the emergence of both highly kataphatic and highly apophatic theological speech—which is to say, language that is both positive and negative: the *via positiva* and the *via negativa*. Precisely because God is unlimited in actuality, any creaturely actuality or perfection can and should be attributed to him, though this should never be done in a straightforward way, as though God is, say, good just the way creatures are good or powerful just as creatures are powerful. Rather, our positive language should be attributed to God according to the discipline of the *via eminentiae* (the way of eminence). God is indeed good, but so surpassingly good that there is in fact a greater difference than similarity between his goodness and creaturely goodness. *In tanta similitudine maior dissimilitudo* (in however

5. Thomas Aquinas, *Summa theologiae* 1.3.

great a similarity, a greater dissimilarity) is how the Fourth Lateran Council expressed the dynamic.[6] By the same token, the divine simplicity dictates that the *via negativa* ought to govern our talk about God as well. This is because the simple one, who cannot be defined, delimited, or contrasted with any other existing thing, is *totaliter aliter* (totally other).[7] Hence, whatever ontological imperfection abides in creatures must be denied of God.

Guided by the first of these rules, theologians have said, for instance, that God is good. Thomas Aquinas articulates this as follows: the good is the desirable; all conscious agents desire some form of actuality or perfection; God is utterly actual; therefore, God is utterly good. What we mean by this exactly remains unclear, obscured, if you want, by the application of the *via eminentiae*. We can say, too, that God is personal—that is, in possession of the attributes of mind, will, and freedom. This follows quite naturally from God's full actuality. A reality void of these personal qualities would be highly conditioned and delimited in its mode of existing. Thus, we hold off those who might be willing to affirm the existence of an unconditioned ground of finitude but who would consider this to be an impersonal force or energy. And from these positive affirmations follows the claim that God is loving. To love is to will the good, and one cannot will what one does not know. But God possesses intellect, which allows him to grasp his own perfection, and hence will, which is tantamount to grasping the good as good and hence as desirable. Therefore, there are a number of positive things that we can and should say about God: he is one, simple, perfect, good, personal, intelligent, and loving.

At the same time, much of our descriptive language involving God is, perforce, negative in tone, the second rule applying. In the manner of a sculptor, the theologian does much of his work by removing from the idea

6. This maxim paraphrases the Latin text of the Fourth Lateran Council, which reads: "*Quia inter creatorem et creaturam non potest tanta similitudo notari, quin inter eos maior sit dissimilitudo notanda.*" (For between Creator and creature no similitude can be expressed without implying a greater dissimilitude.) Heinrich Denzinger et al., *Compendium of Creeds, Definitions, and Declarations on Matters of Faith and Morals*, 43rd ed. (San Francisco: Ignatius Press, 2012), no. 806, 269.

7. *Nicholas of Cusa on God as Not-Other: A Translation and Appraisal of* De Li Non Aliud, 2nd ed., trans. Jasper Hopkins (Minneapolis: Arthur J. Banning, 1983), 20–22, 49–53.

of God any creaturely imperfection that would be inappropriate to ascribe to the unconditioned reality. So, as we saw, we speak of God as infinite—which is to say, without any limit to his being. Every single reality that we confront in our experience is limited in some way. Hence, we do not really know what we are saying when we speak of the properly infinite. We know what it is not, but not what it is. Much the same protocol is in place when we speak of God as immaterial, as not marked by matter. Since matter by its very nature is malleable, capable of assuming a practically infinite variety of forms, it cannot mark the existence of what by its nature is utterly actual. But again, we do not entirely know what we mean when we use this term, since even the most abstract realities, such as mathematical and geometrical objects, are known to us only through the material things in which they are grounded.

Another standard attribution is that God is immutable or unchanging. In the second half of the twentieth century, under the influence of the so-called process theologians, this way of naming God came under heavy fire, since it seemed to indicate that God is unresponsive, unfeeling, coldly indifferent to the world that he made. In point of fact, the classical use of the term "immutable" in regard to God implies nothing of the kind. Change is the transition from potency to act, from potentiality to actuality. To state it a bit differently, it is the fulfilling of an unfulfilled condition: I was incapable of speaking French, and now I speak it fluently; I was here, now I am there. The unconditioned reality cannot, by definition, be marked by potentiality or unfulfilled conditions; otherwise, there would be some cause needed to actualize him. Therefore, we must say that God does not change in the creaturely mode; he does not get better or come to be a new way. None of this, of course, tells against his intimate connection to what he has made; on the contrary, that which grounds, actualizes, and fulfills the conditions of all finite things is indeed closer to them than they are to themselves. True, God does not "react" to events in the world, but this is not because he is coldly indifferent to them, but rather because he stands to them as ground and cause. Indeed, he "knows" finite states of affairs more intimately and completely than a "reactor" to those states of affairs ever could, since his knowledge is not passive and derivative but rather creative and antecedent.

Similarly, theologians say that God is eternal, which does not mean that God endures everlastingly, but rather that he subsists outside of time. Tillich characterized this as God's *Überzeitlichkeit*—that is to say, his standing "above time." This must be the case, since time, as Aristotle said, is the measure of change, and as unconditioned, God cannot change.[8] Precisely as "over" time, God can be present to any moment of time. Were he ensconced in time, he would be limited to a particular moment or series of moments. Now, what exactly it means to be a being outside of time is exceptionally difficult to tell. We can sound quite "positive" as we make this attribution of God, but we are in fact still very much operating out of the *via negativa.*

With respect to all of these attributes and appellations, I could revert to an older style of theologizing and simply line up scriptural citations that would support them. But this sort of proof-texting has long been discredited as unconvincing and finally disrespectful to the Bible. I would rather attend to what I would consider one of the central themes of the Scriptures and situate the names of God that we have been discussing within that framework. I am referring to a fundamental assumption, on display practically everywhere in the Bible, that the God of Israel can be neither grasped nor hidden from. In his transcendence, God escapes any of our feeble attempts to manipulate him with our wills or take him in with our minds. At the same time, in his radical immanence, God effortlessly confounds any of our attempts to avoid him, marginalize him, or run away from him.

In the poetic language of Genesis, Adam and Eve first attempt to grasp at God, seizing the prerogative that belongs to him alone—namely, the determination of good and evil—and when that effort fails, they try to hide from him, covering themselves in the underbrush of Eden. Neither strategy can possibly work, for Being itself is beyond any of the beings in the world, and, at the same time, Being itself is present to all forms of finite existence. "As the heavens are higher than the earth, so are my ways higher than your ways

8. Aristotle, *Physics* 4.10–14, trans. C.D.C. Reeve (Indianapolis, IN: Hackett, 2018), 74–86.

and my thoughts than your thoughts" (Isa. 55:9); and, just as truly, "I have inscribed you on the palms of my hands" (Isa. 49:16). From the beginning to the end of the Bible, idolatry in all of its forms is condemned—which simply means that all attempts to control or manipulate God are forbidden. At the same time, all efforts to avoid the press of God are confounded. "If I ascend to heaven, you are there. . . . If I take the wings of the morning and settle at the farthest limits of the sea, even there your hand shall lead me, and your right hand shall hold me fast" (Ps. 139:8–10). Jonah, fleeing from the demand of the Lord and being swallowed up by the fish operating under the direction of God, is a humorous presentation of this dynamic. Perhaps the clearest account of this both/and is the story of Moses and the burning bush. On the one hand, Moses is lured by the radiant immanence of God, the luminous presence of the God of Israel. Further, he is beguiled by this God's intimate knowledge of him and his people and by God's evident desire to liberate them from slavery. But when he draws close to the fire, he is told in no uncertain terms to take off his shoes, "for the place on which you are standing is holy ground" (Exod. 3:5). And when he inquires after the name of the God who speaks to him, he is told, enigmatically enough, "I Am Who I Am" (Exod. 3:14), a name that, in one sense, says nothing at all, thereby holding off the tendency to grasp. Of course, on closer examination, this name says everything and in fact provides the key to the spiritual dynamics on display. "I Am" is obviously unlike anything in the world, which exists only in a determined or conditioned way; but "I Am" is also closer to the world than the world is to itself, since it necessarily grounds whatever has being in the finite order. So this consistent biblical sense of the strangeness of God—his simultaneous ungraspability and unavoidability—is what lies behind the way in which the theological tradition names God.

So from the unity of God, we have derived a number of names that can legitimately be ascribed to God, though they are not laid out in the Creed itself. Now, the Creed does indeed refer to the one God as "Father almighty." Therefore, we are obliged to look at these two words with serious attention. When it comes to the name "Father," we immediately meet with an ambiguity, for on the one hand the term seems to be referring to God as such, especially in his capacity as Creator, but we will see, in very short order, when it is used in relation to the one the Creed calls his "Only Begotten Son," it means something else altogether. Let us simply divide these two meanings and consider the first one first.

"Maker of Heaven and Earth, of All Things Visible and Invisible"

In examining the unity, simplicity, intelligence, personhood, goodness, and perfection of God, we were looking at attributes that belong, if you will, *ad intra*—that is to say, to the inner reality of God. But when speaking of his Fatherhood in the first sense of the term, we are looking more *ad extra*, to the manner in which God relates to what stands outside of him. To be a father is to be one who generates or gives rise to something other. But that characterization, though true, is more than a little austere, especially in light of Jesus' own address to God as *Abba* (Father, in a very familiar sense). A father gives rise to another, but he also cherishes the other to whom he gives rise. One of the most compelling and puzzling questions regarding creation is why God would create at all. We have seen that God, in his simplicity and unity and unconditioned perfection, is utterly good. Nothing could possibly add to his glory or his joy. So then why does he bring about finite existence? The classical answer is that he does so not out of need but simply out of a desire to share his goodness and glory, in accord with the ancient principle *bonum diffusivum sui* (the good is diffusive of itself).[9] We recall that according to Plato, the form of the good lies beyond the realm of beings and its basic function is to give. This is why Plato compares the form of the good to the sun, that power in whose light everything else is seen. And from this follows something of tremendous moment—namely, that God creates purely

9. See, for example, Pseudo-Dionysius, *The Divine Names* 4, in *Pseudo-Dionysius: The Complete Works*, trans. Colm Luibheid (New York: Paulist, 1987), 71–96. For the phrase *bonum diffusivum sui*, see Thomas Aquinas' discussions of Dionysius' principle in *Summa theologiae* 1.5.4, 1.27.5, 1.73.3, 1–2.1.4, and elsewhere.

as an act of love. Love is not a sentiment, but a movement of the will. In the language of Thomas Aquinas, it is to will the good of the other.[10] Some contemporary commentators have intensified the meaning of the Thomistic definition by adding the phrase "as other" to the end of the line. To love is to break out of the gravitational pull of the ego, truly and sincerely wanting what is best for the other. This is why Jesus can say, "No one has greater love than this, to lay down one's life for one's friends" (John 15:13), implying that authentic love expects nothing in return. It is not the indirect egotism that often masquerades as love: I will be kind to you that you might be kind to me.

In giving rise to the world, God manifests the purest kind of love, since he cannot possibly benefit from the act. As one of the prefaces to the Eucharistic Prayer in the Roman rite has it, "Our praises add nothing to your greatness."[11] And as we saw when examining the ontological argument, God plus the world is not more perfect than God alone. Hence, the very existence of the universe is, necessarily, the consequence of an act of absolutely disinterested love. As we will see when considering the Trinity, this creative move is not surprising, since the innermost nature of God *is* love. Creation must be construed, indeed, as an icon or external manifestation of that primordial love. As many have pointed out, this is reflected in the German term for "there is," which is *es gibt* (it gives). This reflects the profound intuition that what appears before us *is*, but does not *have* to be, and that therefore some cause ultimately gave it to us, or better, is giving it to us. The proper response in the presence of a gift is gratitude, which is why we say "thank you" when some good is presented to us that need not be there. By a metaphysically correct instinct, we acknowledge the existence of a generous giver whenever we appreciate the gratuitous existence of the contingent world.

So, God creates; he gives rise to what is other than himself; he shares his being. It is most important to distinguish between the unique act of creation, which belongs to God alone, and the various forms of making. These latter

---

10. Thomas Aquinas, *Summa theologiae* 1–2.26.4 co.; *Summa contra Gentiles* 1.91.2–3, trans. Anton C. Pegis (New York: Hanover House, 1955). See also *Catechism of the Catholic Church* 1766.

11. "Common Preface IV," in *Roman Missal* (ICEL, 2010).

always involve the shaping of something already existing, the way that a carpenter makes a desk out of wood, or a painter makes a painting out of oils and canvas, or a river carves out a canyon. We speak casually in this context of creating, but we really mean making. But since God is one, and properly unconditioned in his being, nothing can stand apart from him for which he is not himself ontologically responsible. There can be no matter or energy or stuff with which God works, nor pre-existing context in which he operates, for otherwise this would condition and delimit him. Time, space, energy, and matter, accordingly, are all themselves creatures of God.

This is why the great tradition speaks of God's creation of the universe *ex nihilo* (from nothing). This is no violation of the causal principle *ex nihilo nihil fit* (from nothing comes nothing), since the world does indeed come from God as a first cause. What the adage implies is that God does not make the world out of anything, nor does he project it into anything pre-existing. In his disputed question *De potentia Dei*, Thomas Aquinas states this truth in a highly paradoxical way, reminiscent of a Zen koan: that which receives the act of creation is itself being created; and the creature is a kind of relation to God with newness of being (*creatio nihil est aliud realiter quam relatio quaedam ad Deum cum novitate essendi*).[12] Thomas carefully draws out some of the implications of this insight. First, creation cannot be construed as a type of motion or change, since there is no uncreated substrate that undergoes a reduction from potency to act. Further, it does not take place in time, since time itself, as we saw, is a creature. Hence, it is nonsensical to speak of what obtained "before" the world began or even to speak of the "moment" of creation, as though time were marching along and then creation happened at a given point in time. What furthermore follows is that creation is not a one-off event, something that happened long ago and now is simply in the past. Given the rapport between unconditioned being and conditioned being, creation is a continual state of affairs, obtaining moment to moment. God sustains the universe the way a singer sustains a song, in the words

12. Thomas Aquinas, *Quaestiones disputatae de potentia Dei* 3.3, in *Quaestiones disputatae*, vol. 2, ed. P. Bazzi (Turin: Marietti, 1949) (my translation).

of Herbert McCabe.[13] Thomas Merton showed the spiritual power of this teaching, commenting that contemplative prayer is finding the place in you where you are here and now being created by God.[14] Not only is this dynamic perpetual, but it is also unmediated, since there is quite literally nothing that stands between the creature and the Creator, no matter or energy or potentiality that mediates their relationship. Again, this is not pantheism, since finite being is radically other than unconditioned being, and the one can never be reduced to the other. However, creation metaphysics justifies Augustine's claim that, even as he remains higher than anything we can imagine, God is also closer to us than we are to ourselves.[15]

A further implication of the doctrine of creation is that all things in the universe are connected to one another as ontological siblings, since all are coming forth from moment to moment from the same ultimate source. Though they can appear simply as separate beings, the things that make up the world are joined, as it were, through a common center. As we shall see in greater detail below, the ethical teachings of Jesus, especially regarding the love even of our enemies, are grounded finally in this metaphysical perception. Even those who seem on the surface most alienated from us are, in point of fact, our brothers and sisters, and in a sense far deeper than the merely biological or sociological. If I might highlight a moral and spiritual feature of this teaching: God's capacity to create the world out of nothing is mirrored in God's recreation of the soul out of the nothingness of sin. As a corruption of the will, sin is, strictly speaking, a type of nonbeing. Without any initiative on our part, God can reach out and remake a lost soul, just as, without any cooperation from another, he causes the world to be.

We must also speak, in this context, of God's providence over creation. Conditioned as we are in the West by forms of deism, we tend to think of God as a distant cause, but this is entirely unbiblical. The God of biblical revelation is intensely involved in his world, presiding over it, worrying

13. Herbert McCabe, *God Still Matters*, ed. Brian Davies (New York: Continuum, 2005), 234.

14. See Thomas Merton, *New Seeds of Contemplation* (New York: New Directions, 1961), 1–5.

15. See Augustine, *Confessions*, trans. F.J. Sheed, ed. Michael P. Foley (Park Ridge, IL: Word on Fire Classics, 2017), 50.

about it, directing it toward an end. And this is confirmed philosophically as well, for the infinitely intelligent and personal God can never be other than personally present to the world that he constantly maintains. God is necessarily in the world in a deeply intentional manner. All finite reality comes forth from him, and since God always acts for a purpose, all finite reality will, in one way or another, come back to him as to an end. This is the *exitus-reditus* (going out and coming back) notion so dear to the medieval theologians and so central to the spiritual tradition. Now, some have maintained that God's providence takes place at higher levels of the created order but is not operative in all things. However, this is repugnant to the range of God's causal influence. Aquinas says that the divine providence extends to particulars, since God, as universal cause of being, is necessarily in all things "by essence, presence, and power."[16] The book of Wisdom confirms this in its lyrical statement: the wisdom of God "reaches from end to end mightily, and orders all things sweetly" (see Wis. 8:1 D-R). It is worth meditating on that term "sweetly." Once again, in accord with the metaphysics of the burning bush, God's causal influence is not manipulative, interventionary, or extrinsic to the effect, for God, as we saw, cannot be construed as one competing cause among many. God draws creation to himself nonviolently, allowing the creature under the divine influence to become itself most fully. In regard to nonrational creation, this is exercised through the intelligibility that God places within the world, which permits things to unfold according to their intrinsic meaning.

Nowhere is the noncoercive nature of providence clearer than in regard to the direction that God gives to his rational creatures. God moves us by luring our wills in a particular direction, and this never amounts to a violation of freedom. To understand how this can be true, we have to make a distinction between two understandings of freedom. On a more modern construal, which predominates in our Western culture, liberty is the capacity to choose among a variety of options without any extrinsic compulsion. It is sovereign choice

16. Thomas Aquinas, *Summa theologiae* 1.8.3, trans. Fathers of the English Dominican Province (New York: Benzinger, 1947).

and self-determination. But on a more classical and biblical reading, liberty is not so much free choice—though it involves this—as it is the disciplining of desire so as to make the achievement of the good first possible and then effortless. Thus, we speak of a person coming to play the piano freely or to speak a language freely. Such liberty has not a thing to do with radical self-determination, but rather is a function of internalizing the rules of the relevant discipline to such a degree that they become second nature. As John Paul II said, "Freedom consists not in doing what we like, but in having the right to do what we ought."[17] So God, the supreme good, nonviolently draws his rational creatures to his own purposes by proposing modes of the good to them, and prompting those creatures to internalize them. In this process, he makes them more—not less—free. To grasp this principle of God's noncoercive providence is to understand the heart of Christian moral theology and spirituality.

Perhaps the most vexing theological issue of all—indeed what some consider the neuralgic point from which all of theology develops—is the question of evil, of why wickedness and suffering exist in a universe that the infinitely good God has made and that he continually directs. In one of the objections to the claim that God exists, articulated in the famous second question of the *Summa theologiae*, Aquinas writes, "If one of two contraries be infinite, the other would be altogether destroyed. But the word 'God' means that he is infinite goodness. If therefore, God existed, there would be no evil discoverable; but there is evil in the world. Therefore God does not exist."[18] In its very laconicism and concision, it is a very powerful argument indeed, and it gives precise expression to what many, many people today feel but cannot quite articulate.

In providing a response to this objection, the great tradition has made a few indispensable moves. The first—which constituted a major discovery for the young Augustine—is that evil is not a positive force opposing the good, but rather a sheer negativity, a privation of being, the lack of a good that

17. John Paul II, "Homily of His Holiness John Paul II, Oriole Park at Camden Yards, Baltimore," Vatican website, October 8, 1995, http://www.vatican.va/content/john-paul-ii/en/homilies/1995/documents/hf_jp-ii_hom_19951008_baltimore.html.

18. Thomas Aquinas, *Summa theologiae* 1.2.3.

ought to be present.[19] It is crucial to grasp that one can think of good apart from evil, but not vice versa, for to consider evil is, necessarily, to consider the good which it corrupts or compromises. Given this definition, a cavity in a tooth or a cancer in an organ are both evil, but my lack of wings should not be so conceived, because there is nothing in my humanity that requires the presence of wings. And this implies that God never "creates" or "produces" evil; it cannot be ascribed to him as to a cause and it, in no sense, stands against God as an ontological rival. Since evil is always parasitic upon the good, all forms of Manichaeism and other metaphysical dualisms that posit coequal forces of good and evil are ruled out. We therefore should speak not of God causing evil but of God's permission of evil within the confines of his creation. One might see the presence of the serpent in the Garden in the book of Genesis as a poetic expression of this principle.

But still the question remains, why would God do such a thing? Why would God permit the evil that assuredly plagues the world on a massive scale? The standard answer is that God does so in order to bring about some greater good, which could not have been accomplished otherwise. Even a superficial examination of our own experience reveals that there is something to this way of thinking. Without the painful and invasive surgery, the health of a person's body would never have been restored; without failing in one area of life, success in another might never have occurred; without the excoriating speech from a coach or teacher, one might never have realized his full potential; etc. And thus Thomas Aquinas argues that the flourishing of the lion would never have occurred without the bloody death of the antelope or even that there would be no patience of the martyr without the cruelty of the tyrant.[20]

Still, many people, though they might accept this explanation in principle, have a difficult time seeing its application in every case on the ground.

---

19. Augustine, *Confessions*, 139–167.

20. Thomas Aquinas, *Summa theologiae* 1.48.2 ad 3; *Quaestiones disputatae de potentia Dei* 3.6 ad 4. For a recent translation of this work based on the forthcoming Leonine Latin edition, see *On Creation [Quaestiones Disputatae de Potentia Dei, Q. 3]*, trans. Susan C. Selner-Wright (Washington, DC: The Catholic University of America Press, 2011).

How could we ever "justify" the horrific suffering of the innocent through appeal to some ultimate end? We might think of the terrible stories told by Ivan in *The Brothers Karamazov* of the intentionally cruel treatment of children, which were designed to disabuse his mystical brother Alyosha of his religious faith.[21] Many of the atheists of the present day will present a version of this argument and are even more willing than Ivan Karamazov to introduce cases of seemingly inexplicable suffering on the part of innocents, especially children. Anyone with a modicum of human feeling senses the brutal power of this great counter-argument to the existence of God. David Hume offered a somewhat more elaborated version of the pithy syllogism of Aquinas. The eighteenth-century Scottish philosopher said that, if evil exists, God cannot be, simultaneously, all-knowing, all-powerful, and all-good. For if he knew about evil, could do something to stop it, and would want to stop it, it would not exist.[22] Anyone who, in the face of terrible suffering, has looked imploringly to God and wondered why he is not acting is feeling the press of this demonstration.

Even granting all of this—and I do so not only as a theologian but also as a pastor who has dealt with many people experiencing acute suffering—I must observe that this sort of argument appeals much more to our emotions than to our reason. For in order for this line of thought to be successful—again, as a strict logical demonstration—one would have to assume a godlike grasp of practically all of space and all of time. The major premise of the proof is that there are types of evil and suffering that can never in principle be justified through appeal to a good that might come as a result. But in order definitively to say that a given state of affairs has no possible justification, one would have to see every conceivable implication and consequence and circumstance, stretching out indefinitely into the future. But no finite subject could ever claim such all-embracing consciousness. Demonstrating this was, of course, the principal burden of

21. Fyodor Dostoevsky, *The Brothers Karamazov*, trans. Richard Pevear and Larissa Volokhonsky (New York: Farrar, Straus & Giroux, 1990), 236–246.

22. See David Hume, *Dialogues Concerning Natural Religion*, 2nd ed. (London, 1779), 186.

the book of Job. That God speaks to Job out of the whirlwind signals that the divine purposes are always, for the most part, obscure to us (Job 38:1). How could it be otherwise? When speaking of the divine cause, we are referencing the unconditioned reality, whose mind is without limit and whose providential scope is unrestricted. Claiming that we can prove a negative in regard to the ultimate meaningfulness of a conditioned state of affairs is as ludicrous as a child of four confidently asserting that his parents' decisions are baseless or a neophyte in mathematics declaring that a page of trigonometric calculations is nothing but gibberish. Hence, God reduces Job to silence by reminding him of how much he cannot even in principle understand of the world that God has made and over which God presides (Job 40:3–5, 42:1–6).

At the close of God's speech in the book of Job, by far the longest oration of God in the Bible, the Lord invokes two of his greatest and most hidden of creatures: Behemoth and Leviathan (Job 40–41). Hebrew experts tell us that the meaning of the underlying terms are ambiguous, but they probably refer to a hippopotamus or rhinoceros in the first case and a whale in the second, or perhaps some mythic combination of these. But despite their wonderful ferocity, they are utterly under God's control, for one is on a leash and the other has a ring through its nose. The point is this: everything in God's creation, even those powerful creatures that are largely hidden to us, operate according to God's providence; and furthermore, the Lord loves these bizarre and frightening creatures just as he loves us human beings: "Look at Behemoth, which I made just as I made you" (Job 40:15). Teilhard de Chardin added some texture to this discussion by observing that, to a degree, "good" and "evil" can be relative terms. Thus, as cancer cells are ravaging an organ, those cells are flourishing; and as a virus sickens millions of human beings, the virus itself is successfully surviving. Or to return to Aquinas' example cited above, the antelope, as it is being devoured by the lion, experiences supreme evil, but the lion, as it does the devouring, is enjoying a supreme good. And God, strangely, loves them all: cancer cells, viruses, antelopes, and lions.

So why does God permit evil? We can answer the question correctly and adequately only at the most abstract level. "To bring about a greater good" is a legitimate response, but as to the details of that relationship, how precisely this particular evil conduces to a particular good or set of goods, we cannot possibly say. However, our incapacity to respond to that more exacting question should not tell against the divine providence; it should awaken in us a certain humility before the purposes of God.

If I might provide just one more clarification regarding this famously complex matter of God's providence: God seems to delight in the process of growth. This principle appears to govern most aspects of God's creation that we can immediately take in: the vegetative, the animal, the human, the cosmic. There is a seminal quality to things—that is to say, they are like seeds that develop, burst forth, and emerge over time into what they are meant finally to be. God's creation is good, but it is not perfect; it might be better to say that it is perfecting, reaching out, seeking to attain its end. Now, development, as John Henry Newman saw in regard to the evolution of ideas, contains almost inevitably the possibility of corruption or misdirection. Therefore, the very process by which organisms evolve—random mutation and natural selection—is at the same time the process by which cancers develop. And the very process by which saints are made—the expression of the free will—is at the same time the process by which wicked people are made.

And this allows us to circle back to the problem of evil with renewed insight. John Polkinghorne has suggested that just as we invoke a "free-will defense" when speaking of God's permission of moral evil, we might speak of a "free-process" defense when attempting to explain physical evil.[23] God permits human freedom to express itself, and God typically permits natural processes to unfold according to their own rhythm. A God intervening at every turn to prevent evil or suffering would result in a creation utterly lacking in integrity or independence. Moreover, in a finite, conflictual universe, no amount of divine intervention could ever completely eliminate suffering,

23. See, for example, John Polkinghorne, *Serious Talk: Science and Religion in Dialogue* (Harrisburg, PA: Trinity International, 1995), 13, 53, 57, 74.

for the flourishing of one part of that creation, as we saw, almost inevitably involves the languishing of another. That this will not be the case in heaven is a function of the graced and elevated finitude that will obtain there.

The Creed specifies that God is the Creator of both "heaven and earth." On the one hand, this is simply ancient code for "everything"—that is to say, all finite existence. Both what is above and what is below is a creature of God. To state this in more precise metaphysical language: whatever is finite and contingent in its manner of being must be traced to the unconditioned as to a first cause. This principle obtains whether we are talking about the things and people in our ordinary experience (the earth) or the highest and most rarified elements within the universe (heaven). Sometimes atheists suggest that the multiverse theory, the proposal that there are, in fact, a variety of separate universes, somehow militates against belief in God, but this is silly. Let us suppose there is an infinite number of "universes." If they are finite and contingent, then they depend, ultimately, upon the one reality that is not finite and contingent.

In the Bible, "heaven" refers sometimes to the literal sky and those things in the sky, but it also designates a realm that belongs in a unique way to God and is hence to be differentiated from "earth," which belongs more peculiarly to us. In later theology, "heaven" in this sense is appreciated as the place where the angels and saints dwell. The next phrase in the Creed might help us understand this better: "of all things visible and invisible." Heidegger recovered the primordial understanding of truth as visibility or coming into the light.[24] Undoubtedly, the rational faculty is ordered, first, to what is at hand, to what visibly shows up: the phenomenal world of practical activity, nature, and human interaction. Following Aristotle, Thomas Aquinas states that all knowledge begins in the senses—and makes thereby much the same point.[25] God creates this visible, more immediately obvious, realm. But as Plato and his numberless disciples over the centuries have reminded us, there

24. Martin Heidegger, ***Being and Truth***, trans. Gregory Fried and Richard Polt (Bloomington, IN: Indiana University Press, 2010), 110–152.

25. See, for example, Thomas Aquinas, *Questiones disputatae de veritate* 1.11, trans. Robert W. Mulligan, SJ (Chicago: Henry Regnery, 1952).

is a dimension of being that is not visible but yet eminently real, indeed, more real than the visible dimension. The purpose of Plato's parable of the cave is to show how the philosopher escapes from the realm of mere fleeting appearance and comes to a more substantial, though invisible, world of pure forms.[26] One might think, also along Platonic lines, of mathematical objects and pure numbers, which are undoubtedly real but invisible, though visible representations of them can be contrived. The point that the Creed insists upon is that these realities, too, are creatures of God, despite their more elevated, less ephemeral, ontological status. We might say that they participate in the divine being in a more intense way, or perhaps, that they share in and mirror certain aspects of God's existence that material creatures do not.

Under this rubric of the invisible created realm, we must speak also of angels. The existence of angels is consistently affirmed by Sacred Scripture, both Old Testament and New, most notably by Jesus himself—and the reality of spiritual powers is confirmed across the centuries and across the cultures. Giving full weight to a legitimate skepticism regarding these claims, it still seems that only an exaggerated and ideological materialism would dismiss them simply out of hand. And following the prompts of certain theologians, both classical and contemporary, we might offer some justification for this belief. Both Thomas Aquinas in the Middle Ages and Teilhard de Chardin in the twentieth century made the observation that it would be anomalous were there simply to yawn a great ontological abyss between the wildly diverse world of physical reality—from quarks to galaxies—and the being of God. Would it not make more sense, both theologians suggest, that in between the realm of pure matter and pure actuality there would be a dimension of reality, perhaps as richly diverse as the material world, but made up of spiritual creatures? Here one might reconsider Pseudo-Dionysius the Areopagite's speculations concerning the nine choirs of angels as something more than merely fantastic.[27] And would not it make sense, as the Bible clearly indicates,

---

26. Plato, *Republic* 514a–520a, trans. C.D.C. Reeve (Indianapolis, IN: Hackett, 2004), 208–214.

27. Pseudo-Dionysius, *The Celestial Hierarchy*, in *Pseudo-Dionysius: The Complete Works*, trans. Colm Luibheid (Mahwah, NJ: Paulist, 1987), 143–191.

that this collection of spiritual creatures would serve a properly mediating function, acting as messengers (*angeloi*) between heaven and earth? With this last point in mind, permit me to say something about the possibility of spiritual creatures interacting with the material world. We ought not to think of the immaterial realm as simply other than the material, a ghostly order running, as it were, parallel to a physical order. What we refer to as the "spiritual" is a mode of existence more metaphysically simple and hence more elevated than the material. Thomas Aquinas occasionally uses the metaphor of heat to suggest the varying degrees of ontological intensity: material realities are "cooler" and spiritual realities are "warmer," for the latter stand closer to the pure fire of God's manner of existence.[28] Therefore, an angel can, so to speak, condescend to interact with the physical world, almost in the way that an adult can enter into the language and consciousness of a child—though in neither case can the interaction move in the opposite direction. No child can, even in principle, understand an adult conversation; and no physical entity can, through its own power, move into the spiritual realm. Rather, the latter has to stoop down and lift up the former.

And perhaps just a brief word on a complex subject—namely, the presence of evil or fallen angels. Once we grant that pure spiritual subjects exist—what Aquinas called "separated intelligences"[29]—it makes perfect sense that some of these maintained their moral integrity and connection to God and that others did not. Those who opted to turn from God retained their intelligence and power to will, but their intelligence was darkened and their will was twisted, resulting in the compromising of their being. They became, therefore, powerful enemies of God, but it is essential to note that they never became (because they *cannot* become) rivals to God, as though they were, in a Manichean sense, equal opponents of God. Whatever being and capacity for action they have comes as a direct gift of the Creator, and therefore whatever havoc they wreak is permitted as part of God's providential

28. See, for example, Thomas Aquinas, *Summa theologiae* 1.2.3.

29. See, for example, Thomas Aquinas, *Commentary on the Book of Causes*, trans. V.A. Guagliardo, C.R. Hess, and R.C. Taylor (Washington, DC: The Catholic University of America Press, 1996), 41.

guidance of his creation. Why God should permit this sort of deep corruption would have to be considered as a special case under the rubric of theodicy explored above. We can confidently say that some good comes even from the rebellion of the wicked angels, though, as is typically the case, we can barely glimpse what that might be.

And this brings us to a final observation—namely, that creation, in its staggering diversity, both material and nonmaterial, serves as an iconic representation of God's existence. In his simplicity, God contains the fullness of the power of existence, and he requires the multiplicity of creation to represent that fullness, creatures emerging, we might say, as the variety of colors emerge from a prism upon which pure white light is shining. The astonishing variety on display in every corner of the created world is God's attempt to manifest the intensity of his perfection in a finite mode. Though God does not exist in a creaturely way, every conditioned thing tells of God in its own absolutely distinctive manner. Plato famously wrestled with a troubling implication of his theory of forms—namely, whether there are forms of ordinary and crass things, such as mud and hair?[30] A Christian theology of creation would have no problem seeing even the most ordinary creaturely realities as bodying forth an aspect of the divine perfection.

30. Plato, *Parmenides*, 130b–c, trans. Mary Louise Gill and Paul Ryan (Indianapolis, IN: Hackett, 1996), 130–131.

CHAPTER 3

The Son

I. The Son of God

"One Lord Jesus Christ"

With this assertion of the Creed, we come to the heart of the matter, for all of distinctively Christian faith begins and ends with a particular person, Jesus from Nazareth, recognized to be the Son of God. One might argue that practically everything I have said to this point, including the reflections on the nature of belief, the existence of God, creation, and providence could be affirmed by devout Jews and Muslims, and perhaps even by many religiously unaffiliated. But when we come to Jesus, we arrive at a watershed, a point of demarcation. The Nicene Creed implicitly acknowledges this distinctiveness, since the section regarding Jesus is, by far, the longest in this ancient statement of faith.

The name "Jesus" (in Hebrew, *Ieshuah*), common enough in first-century Jewish culture, means "Yahweh saves." And therefore the name at the heart of Christian faith compels us to acknowledge both that God is incomparably good (for he is in the business of saving) and that something has gone wrong with God's good creation (for it *needs* saving). As we saw, God does not create the world through violence or by opposing rival gods. Original blessing, accordingly, comes first, both chronologically and ontologically. Nevertheless, something has gone so dramatically wrong with God's creation that the intervention of God himself is required to set it right. The book of Genesis tells us what this dysfunction is. In the compelling poetry of the opening verses of the first book of the Bible, we find a dual assertion being made. As God speaks the world into being, as light, sky, stars and planets, dry land, water, and animals come forth from the Creator in an orderly way, day following upon day, we are meant to see something like a liturgical procession. At the end of that sacred parade comes the human being, and the figure at the end of such a procession is always the one who will lead the praise. Hence, we understand the role of creatures in relation to the human creature: the latter is to lead the former in a chorus of praise of the Creator.

When God is given highest praise (when he is worshiped properly), then right order obtains both within the worshiper and around her. "Glory to God in the highest and on earth peace to people of good will." Concomitantly, when something or someone less than God is adored, disintegration follows. This is the second great move being made in these opening verses, for everything mentioned in the litany of creation—moon, sun, planets, animals, etc.—were, as we saw, worshiped in certain cultures in the ancient world. By naming them as creatures, the author of Genesis is deposing them, disqualifying them as objects of worship. Hence the basic formula, articulated by St. Augustine: sin is turning from God to creatures.[1] It is engaging in wrong praise; it is a suspension of orthodoxy (*ortho doxa*, "right praise"). In making themselves the criterion of good and evil, Adam and Eve turn to themselves rather than to God, and the result—in the evocative rendering of the author of Genesis—is an animosity among themselves, and between them and nature. This is the fallen condition, the depth-level dysfunction, from which it is, in principle, impossible to extricate themselves. Since the compromised will is the problem, more human willing will not be the solution; since the fallen mind is the problem, more human thinking will not ultimately solve anything.

Rather, some power has to come radically from without the fallen situation, but at the same time it has to enter fully into it. Though I am anticipating the fuller argument a bit, Jesus (Yahweh saves) is precisely that figure. Savior, derived from the Latin *Salvator*, the bearer of the *salus* or health, is related to the English word "salve." Jesus is, in his very person,

1. Augustine, *Confessions*, trans. F.J. Sheed, ed. Michael P. Foley (Park Ridge, IL: Word on Fire Classics, 2017), 24–25.

the salving of the wound caused by false praise. The common name *Ieshuah* (Joshua in its most direct English rendering) called to mind for first-century Jews the figure of Joshua from the Old Testament, the loyal lieutenant of Moses who led the conquest of the Promised Land after the death of Moses. And this suggests another powerfully symbolic way to consider the life and work of Jesus of Nazareth. He was a warrior, who set out to fight not the worldly enemies of Israel but the spiritual enemies of the human race. From the beginning of his life—even as an infant—he was violently opposed, precisely because a fallen world resists its own correction. His battle comes to a climax on the cross, and we will look in great detail at this struggle below.

The second name that the Creed gives for this Jesus is "Christ." From the Greek *Christos,* the term renders the Hebrew *Mashiach*, which means "the anointed one." Though priests and kings were anointed in the ancient Hebrew tradition, the term is used most often and with greatest resonance of David, the greatest of Israel's kings. We find in 1 Samuel the moving account of the young David being anointed by the prophet Samuel: "And the spirit of the Lord came mightily upon David" (1 Sam. 16:13). David does indeed become a priest, since he brings the ark of the covenant into his new capital Jerusalem, leading a dance while wearing the distinctive garment of a priest. He also commences the preparations for the building of the temple, which will be completed by Solomon his son. The point is that David sees the re-establishment of right praise as essential to the success of his kingdom: all the tribes of the Lord united around the worship of the one God. And David is assuredly king, indeed the greatest of Israel's leaders. His triumph was to have held off the enemies of the nation and to have expanded its borders so as to establish a kind of empire. This was, in the estimation of the ancient teachers of Israel, the mission given originally to Adam. Our first parent was meant not to remain self-satisfied in Eden, but rather to expand the borders of that paradise outward. One of the effects of the original sin is precisely a suspension, or at least compromising, of that mission. The various kings of Israel, to varying degrees, took up the Adamic task, but none realized it as fully as David.

However, what becomes eminently clear in the biblical account of King David is that, though he was to be sure a morally and spiritually imposing figure, he did not utterly fulfill his destiny. His priesthood is undermined by his frequent moral failures, most notably in connection with Uriah and Bathsheba; and his kingship is undermined by the rebellion of his son Absalom and by David's own laziness and inattention. And therefore Israel began to dream of a perfect or definitive David who would deal finally with the enemies of the nations, who would gather the scattered tribes of Israel, and who would restore right praise to the nation, and through the nation, to the world. This is the *Mashiach* whose coming the prophets predict and whose reign the Psalms celebrate in anticipation.

There is probably no greater anticipation of the coming of the definitive David than in the words spoken by the prophet Nathan to David himself (2 Sam. 7:12–17). The Lord has promised, the prophet tells the king, that the Lord will put a descendent of yours on the throne forever and that his reign will last for all time. Israel noticed soon enough that this did not have to do with the endurance of the Davidic line in history—since that line was broken at the Babylonian exile—but they preserved the hope nevertheless. In the opening chapter of the Gospel of Luke, we find the account of the Annunciation. The angel Gabriel tells the Virgin Mary that, through the power of the Holy Spirit, she will give birth to a son and that "he will be great, and will be called the Son of the Most High, and the Lord God will give to him the throne of his ancestor David. He will reign over the house of Jacob forever, and of his kingdom there will be no end" (Luke 1:32–33). This is nothing other than the announcement of the fulfillment of Nathan's prophecy that a definitive son of David would come, a *Mashiach par excellence*, the warrior and the priest, the Christ.

When we consult the Old Testament texts in reference to the Messiah, we encounter a fact both fascinating and more than a little puzzling. When the Psalms and prophets speak of the deliverer, they are referring to a human figure, an earthly king like David, a conventional monarch. On the other hand, they frequently refer to God himself as the Savior of his people. Think for example of Ezekiel's observation that, after the failure of so many earthly shepherds (kings), God would come in person to shepherd his people Israel. Or of Isaiah's suggestions along the very same line: "[God] will gather the lambs in his arms, and carry them in his bosom, and gently lead the mother sheep" (Isa. 40:11). And then, in the remarkable text from Daniel chapter 7, we see practically conflated the figure of the Ancient of Days and a human figure, "one like a son of Man," both ruling over the world. For to this Son of Man is given "dominion and glory and kingship, that all peoples, nations, and languages should serve him" (Dan. 7:13–14). Perhaps the best way to understand this juxtaposition is to assert that somehow Yahweh, the God of Israel, would indeed come to set things right and that he would do so through the instrumentality of a human being, the act of salvation involving both divine and human agency. What we notice in the Creed—and it can be a bit wrenching—is precisely this oscillating back and forth between language describing the inner life of the unconditioned source of existence and language describing a very particular first-century Jew. The "one Lord Jesus Christ" is this figure in his complexity. Whenever the Church wrestles with the issue of the "two natures" in Jesus—and we will consider this matter shortly—it is not engaging in purely philosophical speculation. On the contrary, it is trying to express, with at least relative adequacy, that the strange Savior, both divine and human, long anticipated throughout the Old Testament, had indeed come in the person of Jesus.

"The Only Begotten Son of God"

The title "Son of God" can be found in many places in the Old Testament. For example, in the book of Job, angels are referred to as "sons of God" (Job 1:6). In 2 Samuel, God says that King Solomon will be called his "son." In the book of Exodus, the entire people Israel is referred to as God's child: "Israel is my firstborn son" (Exod. 4:22). Moreover, the Psalms make reference to the king of Israel as a "son," "begotten" of God (Ps. 2:7). Even in the New Testament, we find references to divine sonship regarding people other than

Jesus himself. Thus, in 1 John we have a description of those who have the right to be "called children of God" (1 John 3:1). So it appears as though "son of God" carries the sense of close rapport with God, or deep friendship with God, or familial belonging to him. Another term that is used throughout the Bible to designate those who have been entrusted with a mission is "sent." In point of fact, no one in the Scriptures is ever given an experience of God without being, at the same time, sent forth. This is true of Abram, Jacob, Joseph, Moses, Joshua, Samuel, David, Isaiah, Jeremiah, Peter, James, John, Paul, etc.

And so Jesus is referred to clearly as the Son of God and, particularly in the Gospel of John, as the one who has been sent by the Father. For example, at his baptism, a voice is heard from heaven: "This is my Son, the Beloved, with whom I am well pleased" (Matt. 3:17). And at his trial before the Sanhedrin, Jesus is asked whether he is the Son of God, and he answers in the affirmative. Most strikingly perhaps, in Caesarea Philippi, when Jesus asks his disciples who they say that he is, Peter responds, "You are the Christ, the Son of the living God" (Matt. 16:16). When people inquire of Jesus what they must do to be saved, he responds, "This is the work of God, that you believe in him whom he has sent" (John 6:29). At first glance, therefore, the Bible seems to be indicating that Jesus is the latest in a long line of prophets, patriarchs, messengers, and friends of God who have been entrusted with a special task on behalf of God.

But we must dig deeper. Even the most superficial analysis of the relevant New Testament texts reveals that the manner of Jesus' sonship is qualitatively different from that of anyone else named son or child of God in the Bible. For Jesus consistently speaks and acts in the very person of the God of Israel—and examples of this abound in the Gospels. Some years ago, it was a commonly accepted view that the divinity of Jesus was stressed particularly, even exclusively, in the Gospel of John and that the synoptic Gospels presented a more straightforwardly human Jesus. The "high" Christology of John was contrasted with the "low" Christology of Matthew, Mark, and Luke. But this simply is untenable. While John expresses the teaching regarding Jesus' divinity in relatively clear conceptual language—"In the beginning was the Word, and the Word was with God, and the Word was God" (John 1:1)—the synoptics equally insist on the full divinity of Jesus, though using a different kind of language and symbol system, one deeply rooted in the more poetic and allusive manner of the Old Testament. Thus, for example, in the account of the healing of the paralyzed man in the Gospel of Mark, we hear Jesus say, "Son, your sins are forgiven" (Mark 2:5). Understandably, the bystanders wonder, "Why does this fellow speak in this way? Who can forgive sins but God alone?" (Mark 2:7). The point is that Jesus had unambiguously seized the prerogative of the God of Israel. Similarly, at the commencement of the Sermon on the Mount in the Gospel of Matthew, Jesus blithely remarks, "You have heard it said, but I say . . ." (see Matt. 5:21–48). What he is referencing is the Torah, the supreme authority within Judaism, given directly by God to Moses on Mt. Sinai, that to which every teacher in Israel finally appealed. By placing his own teaching above that of the Torah, Jesus is assuming the authority of God himself.

It would be very difficult to imagine a prophet or mere teacher in Israel saying, "Heaven and earth will pass away, but my words will not pass away" (Matt. 24:35), as Jesus does in the Gospel of Matthew. Nor could we envision an ordinary prophet asserting, as Jesus does, "Whoever comes to me and does not hate father and mother, wife and children, brothers and sisters, yes, and even life itself, cannot be my disciple" (Luke 14:26), implying that he himself, in person, is the highest good. Jeremiah or Ezekiel might have said, "You must love the Lord God of Israel more than your very life," but neither great Israelite prophet would ever have encouraged people to direct their unconditioned love toward himself.

In all four Gospels, we find accounts of Jesus walking on the water and calming a storm at sea. Though contemporary interpreters might be tempted to see here only a miraculous display of power, no first-century Jew would have missed the reference to the Spirit of Yahweh hovering over the primal watery chaos at the beginning of time or of the claim of the Psalmist that "he [Yahweh] made the storm be still, and waves of the sea were hushed" (Ps. 107:29). In fact, an extremely subtle reference to the divinity of Jesus can be found in Mark's account of the calming of the sea in the sixth chapter of his Gospel. Jesus comes walking on the water toward the disciples in the boat, but then, we are told, "he intended to pass them by" (Mark 6:48). In terms of the narrative, this little detail is puzzling indeed. Why would he have walked on the water out to their boat if he had no intention of engaging them? But an attentive student of Scripture would not have missed the intriguing reference to a passage in the ninth chapter of the book of Job: "[He] who alone stretched out the heavens and trampled the waves of the Sea; who made the Bear and Orion . . . who does great things beyond understanding, and marvelous things without number. Look, he passes by me, and I do not see him; he moves on, but I do not perceive him" (Job 9:8–11).

What would have struck his first-century Jewish audience as blasphemous in the extreme was Jesus' declaration of superiority to the temple, which he did both through action and through speech. Under the first rubric, Jesus encourages people to come to him to find what they customarily sought in the temple—namely, the forgiveness of sins, the teaching of the Torah, and the healing of their bodies. Under the second rubric, it is instructive to consult one of the single most remarkable of Jesus' statements regarding himself: "Something greater than the temple is here" (Matt. 12:6). The Jerusalem temple was, in a practically literal sense, the dwelling-place of God on earth, the most sacred site imaginable for a Jew of Jesus' time. To claim supremacy to the temple, therefore, could only be interpreted as claiming the prerogative of God himself.

I have brought forward these examples from the synoptic Gospels—and there are many more besides—to show that the view of the synoptics as one-sidedly emphasizing the humanity of Jesus is simply preposterous. Once we read those Gospels correctly, we see that their Christology—at least the "height" of it—is perfectly congruent with the "height" of John's Christology. It is furthermore worth noting that though John's Gospel, as I said, contains numerous explicit and philosophically precise designations of the divinity of

Christ, it also includes some remarkably "Jewish" affirmations of this same truth. Perhaps the most striking are the frequent *ego eimi* (I am) statements that he attributes to Jesus: I am the Good Shepherd; I am the bread of life; I am the gate; I am the vine; before Abraham was, I am; etc. These, of course, call to mind the divine self-designation of Yahweh in the third chapter of Exodus. When Moses asks the one who speaks from the burning bush his name, the answer comes: "I AM WHO I AM" (Exod. 3:14), which appears as *ego eimi ho ōn* in the Septuagint, the Greek version of the Old Testament that the author of John was most likely using.

All of this proves unequivocally that Jesus' sonship and his status as the One Sent are qualitatively different than those of any other figure in the biblical tradition. Moses, Isaiah, Ezekiel, David, and Abraham might have seen themselves as servants of the God of Israel, bearers of his message, doers of his will; but none of them ever saw himself as operating in the very person of the God of Israel, doing and saying what only God could legitimately say and do. Now, as C.S. Lewis and many of his followers have pointed out, these outrageous claims on his own behalf might be construed as signs of either lunacy or moral turpitude, but Jesus' bearing and overall manner of life make these explanations completely unconvincing.[2] However, the most powerful affirmation of Jesus' claims regarding his own person come—and we will consider this phenomenon in much more detail later—from his Resurrection from the dead, by which the one he called "Father" ratified in the most dramatic way possible Jesus' self-identification.

Therefore, when the Creed, reflecting this biblical consensus, refers to Jesus as the "Only Begotten Son of God," it is signaling this qualitative difference. It is insisting that Jesus the Son shares divinity with the Father who sent him, "Son" and "sent" in no way implying ontological inferiority to the Father and Sender.

---

2. C.S. Lewis, *Mere Christianity* (New York: HarperOne, 2009), 47–52. See also Peter Kreeft and Ronald Tacelli, *Handbook of Catholic Apologetics: Reasoned Answers to Questions of Faith* (San Francisco: Ignatius Press, 2009), 166–183.

"God from God, Light from Light, True God from True God"

The Creed that we are considering is called the "Nicene" Creed, since it came out of the deliberations and determinations of the Council of Nicaea in 325. Therefore, at the time of the Creed's formulation, Christians had been teaching, preaching, and theologizing about the biblical witness concerning Jesus for almost three centuries. In many ways, the Nicene declaration represents a summary and distillation of that long process of reflection. Prompted by a particular challenge and operating within the conceptual framework of the time, the Nicene Creed was the Christian community's way of saying, "If you want to tell the Christian story correctly, you must follow this template." A full analysis of the historical and theological context for the seminal Council of Nicaea would take us way too far afield, but suffice it to say that it was summoned as a response to the Christology proposed by Arius, a priest of Alexandria. Under the influence of both Greek mythological patterns of thought and the regnant Neoplatonism of his time, Arius opined that Jesus is a hybrid of a semi-human and a semi-divine nature. The "divinity" that was incarnate in him was the highest of creatures, the first emanation from the Creator, a purely spiritual Logos or Word of God, but not true God. In the famous formula that Arius and his followers propagated, "There was a time when he was not," meaning that this Logos does not possess the eternity that is the unique prerogative of the high God.[3] Furthermore, the "humanity" in which this quasi-divine Logos resided was not a complete human nature, but rather a body, controlled by the Logos which had, as it were, supplanted the properly human soul. This is why I spoke of a mythological framework for Arius' thinking, for the hybrid of divinity and humanity that he proposes is not entirely unlike that which obtained in Achilles or Hercules, both semi-divine/semi-human figures.

Supported by Arius' own persuasive preaching, as well as, it is said, the popular songs that he composed in its defense, this point of view gained

3. Quoted in Alexander of Alexandria, *Deposition of Arius* 2.2 (*NPNF*² 4:70).

traction, first in Arius' native Alexandria and then, in time, throughout the eastern Mediterranean territories. But it also excited vigorous opposition. Various local councils were summoned to address the controversy, and finally, in 325, the Ecumenical Council of Nicaea was called by the Emperor Constantine himself, eager to assure that his newly won political unity would not be undermined by theological squabbling.

After much debate—some of it quite rancorous—the Fathers of Nicaea decided to condemn the Christology of Arius and to adopt, in consequence, a strongly anti-Arian statement. The familiar lines of the Nicene Creed, descriptive of the Son of God—"born of the Father before all ages," "God from God, Light from Light, true God from true God"—are all explicit refutations of the Arian view that the Logos incarnate in Jesus was less than the Creator God. "Born of the Father before all ages" was designed specifically to counter the rallying cry "There was a time when he was not." The peculiar phrases "God from God, Light from Light, true God from true God" were all crafted for the purpose of indicating that though this Son of God proceeds from a source (he is "from" another), that procession implies in no way an ontological inferiority vis-à-vis the source from which he comes. And these precisions are not, as some critics suggest, the result of the imposition of an alien philosophical framework on the biblical witness. Rather, they are attempts to preserve the scriptural testimony concerning the uniqueness of Jesus' sonship, using the most refined intellectual tools available at the time.

Following these evocative phrases comes a philosophical distinction of crucial importance. The Fathers of Nicaea tell us that the Son of God, incarnate in Jesus, is "begotten, not made" (in Greek, *gennetos* rather than *genetos*). In attendance at the Council of Nicaea, serving his bishop Alexander of Alexandria, was a young deacon called Athanasius. Upon the death of Alexander, not long after the conclusion of the council, Athanasius became bishop of his native city. Throughout the rest of his long life, he ardently defended the formulas of the Council of Nicaea, convinced that they constituted a standing or falling point for the Christian faith. Enduring almost constant harassment, threats of violence, and several exiles at the hands of his intellectual and political opponents, Athanasius insisted on the full divinity of Jesus. And he knew that crucial to that defense is the demarcation between *gennetos* and *genetos.*

In his masterpiece, entitled *Four Discourses Against the Arians,* the bishop of Alexandria clarified the subtle distinction between begetting and making.[4] Both, he argued, imply the coming forth of one reality from another. But what is begotten entirely participates in that from which it comes, whereas what is made only imperfectly participates in its source. Finally, what is begotten issues, as it were, automatically from its source, while what is made comes forth through an act of the free will. Hence, the Son of God, eternally begotten of the Father, does indeed come forth from the Father, but he comes forth precisely as one who shares utterly in the being of the one from whom he comes. And he proceeds not as the product of the free choice of the Father but as a necessary accompaniment, as light comes from the sun or as wetness follows from the nature of a fountain. This is in sharp contrast to what is made by God—namely, creatures. None of these, even the highest, shares completely in the Creator's manner of being, and all of these have come not of necessity but through the choice of the Creator who was not obliged to make them. If Arius were right, the Logos incarnate in Jesus would have been, like any other creature, made. Now, lest all of this remain at the level of desperately abstract metaphysics, Athanasius shows us, in that same text, the soteriological implications of this distinction. Since God alone can save, were Jesus simply a creature, he would not be savior. If he were made, he would require, like any other creature, the grace of God to be saved. But the consistent claim of the Church is that Jesus is not in need of salvation but is instead the source of salvation.

It is, by the way, fascinating to see how Athanasius' stance in the fourth century has been appreciated by some of the greatest spirits of the Christian tradition as indeed of decisive significance. In the nineteenth century, the Catholic theologian Johann Adam Möhler, after a dalliance with liberal

4. Athanasius, *Four Discourses Against the Arians* (*NPNF*[2] 4:306–447).

Protestant thought, recovered his equilibrium and composed a text entitled *Athanasius der Grosse* (Athanasius the Great), in which he revisited and reiterated the Christology of the Alexandrian.[5] And at almost the same time in England, the young John Henry Newman, struggling against what he took to be liberalizing elements within his Anglican Church, said that what was needed was a new Athanasius.[6] Even Paul Tillich, in the twentieth century, appreciated that Athanasius' resistance was like the Battle of Gettysburg, the fight upon which the success of the war ultimately depended. It is therefore not surprising that the Church compels us, every Sunday, to rehearse Nicaea's victory over Arius. Were Arius right, Christianity would lose its soul, devolving into one more mythic or vaguely philosophical system.

Serving as a sort of orchestral crescendo to this line of argumentation comes perhaps the most famous and controversial word in the Nicene Creed: "consubstantial" (in Greek, *homoousios*). The Son of God, we are told, is "consubstantial with the Father." The term itself, derived from *homo* (same) and *ousia* (substance, essence, or being), was coined by the Emperor Constantine's theological advisor, Hosius, who was present at the Nicene deliberations. An older English translation of the Creed rendered the word, legitimately enough, as "one in being." The most recent rendering carries the same sense: one in substance or essential, underlying reality. The obvious objection, raised by some of the Nicene Fathers themselves and reiterated by theologians and philosophers in the immediate wake of the council, is that this term effectively eliminates *any* distinction between the Father and the Son, turning those designations into names of different modes of God's appearance in history. Much of the theological debate in the centuries following Nicaea circled around this eloquently ambiguous word.

This entire discussion places the Christian tradition squarely on the horns of a dilemma. On the one hand, it seems incoherent, given the unity and simplicity of God, even to speak of begettings and proceedings within the divine being; on the other hand, to speak of the Son of God as "one

5. Johann Adam Möhler, *Athanasius der Grosse*, 2 vols. (Mainz: Florian Kupferberg, 1827).
6. John Henry Newman, *The Arians of the Fourth Century* (London: Rivington, 1833), 421–422.

in being" with the Father, hence honoring the divine simplicity, seems to render impossible any sort of real play between Father and Son. One way to characterize the Christological debates that preceded and followed upon Nicaea is to appreciate them as an oscillation between the extreme poles of tri-theism (belief in three gods) on the one hand and modalism or Monarchianism (a rejection of the objective reality of the Trinitarian persons) on the other. When one overstresses the differentiation of the Trinitarian persons, one ends up affirming that there are three separate beings, each bearing the designation of "God." When one under-stresses the differentiation of the persons, one ends up affirming that God is one *tout court*, a "monarch" who simply displays himself according to varying "modes" of appearance.

Nicaea plays a deft both/and game, insisting that the Son of God is fully divine, "consubstantial" with the Father from whom he proceeds and, at the same time, really other than the Father, since he is "from" the Father, begotten by him. Even as the divine unity is never compromised, a real play of otherness obtains within the divine essence. Now, in the immediate wake of the Council of Nicaea, many theologians continued to struggle with the implications of its teachings. Though Arius himself died shortly after the council concluded, his point of view did not fade away; in fact, it intensified in many parts of the Christian world, both East and West, throughout the fourth century. Moreover, a compromise position also emerged, one that stood, it seemed, midway between Arianism and Nicene orthodoxy—namely, the *homoiousian* point of view. The addition of the Greek letter *iota* to *homoousios* indicated that the Logos that became incarnate in Jesus was not of the *same* substance as the Father, since this would seem to imply modalism, nor was he of a totally different substance, since that would seem to imply Arianism. Instead, he was of *similar* (*homoi*) substance to the Father. As one might expect, this compromise ultimately pleased no one, the Arians seeing it as crypto-monarchianism and the Nicene orthodox seeing it as surreptitious Arianism.

Very much in accord with John Henry Newman's speculations about the way in which doctrine develops through the play of lively minds, the

Church's understanding of the Nicene teaching deepened and broadened during these controversies. In the crucible of the battle between tri-theism and modalism, a new set of terms and concepts emerged. Playing a key role in this evolution were the so-called Cappadocian Fathers: Gregory of Nyssa, Gregory of Nazianzus, and Basil the Great. These bishop-theologians from the eastern provinces of Asia Minor began to develop the linguistic tools that would enable Christians to affirm the *homoousios* doctrine without falling into either problematic extreme. Their efforts came to full fruition in the speculative theology of St. Augustine of Hippo. In his seminal *De trinitate* (*On the Trinity*), composed roughly a century after Nicaea, Augustine proposed an analogy for the Trinity that went a long way toward resolving the dilemma bequeathed to the Church by the Nicene Creed and that, sixteen centuries later, still beguiles and illumines.[7]

Augustine commences with the affirmation, clearly articulated in the book of Genesis, that we human beings were made in the image and likeness of God. Since this similarity cannot be a physical one, God having no body, it must obtain at the spiritual level. Therefore, it has to do, Augustine concludes, with our spiritual faculties of mind and will. Somehow in their dynamics something of the unity and diversity within God will be on display. So we turn to the mind, *mens* in Augustine's Latin. It is most important to note that this term signifies much more than the purely calculating, ratiocinative power designated by our word "mind." *Mens* is much closer to *esprit* in French or *Geist* in German, both of which carry the connotation of intellect, to be sure, but also of "spirit," "wit," even "soul." *Mens* is the aboriginal, chthonic ground of all of the spiritual activity of which a human being is capable. Now, this elemental mind, Augustine says, has the capacity to know itself, to pose itself as an "other" for its own contemplation. Though this sounds rather peculiar, we experience it regularly and it is reflected in our ordinary parlance. "What was I thinking?" we say, or "I wonder what I will do today?" Such language presupposes our capacity to split the self into an

7. Augustine, *De trinitate* 9. For a recent English translation of this work, see *The Trinity*, trans. Edmund Hill, ed. John E. Rotelle, in *The Works of Saint Augustine: A Translation for the 21st Century*, vol. 5 (New York: New City, 1919).

interrogator and an interrogated, into a looker and a looked-at. The French term for "I wonder" (*Je me demande*, literally, "I ask myself") and the Spanish expression for the same (*Yo me pregunto*) are both intelligible only in light of this distinction. This process of interior duplication finds more complex expression when, under the guidance of a good therapist or spiritual director, we come to see dimensions of ourselves that we had never before appreciated. Any journey of conscious self-discovery presupposes the distinction under consideration. The act by which this othering takes place Augustine calls *notitia sui* (knowledge of self).

Now, no one thinks that the person engaging in this sort of self-examination has split in two. No one who says *Je me demande* has become utterly other to himself. Yet the play between *je* and *me* is not illusory; it is grounded in a metaphysical and psychological truth. Finally, Augustine argues, when *mens* understands itself through the othering act of *notitia sui*, it falls in love; it wills itself as something good. This act of self-possession through the will he terms *amor sui* (love of self). Similarly, this primal awakening of the desire involves no bifurcation or trifurcation of the person. It is still the self-same individual who loves himself, though there is a distinction between the loving and being loved, between the lover and the beloved. As should be clear enough, Augustine sees this spiritual dynamism as a strikingly good analogy for the Trinitarian relations within God. The "Father" is the divine *mens*, the elemental ground of God's life. The "Son" is God's *notitia sui*, his great act of self-knowledge, appropriately designated as Logos or interior Word. And the Holy Spirit (to whom we will return in much greater detail later in this book) is God's *amor sui*, the love shared by the Father and the Son. As is the case in regard to human psychology, the distinctions are real, but none of them involves a compromising of the unity and simplicity of the divine nature. We can at least begin to see how the Son could be "from" the Father and still be "true God from true God," how he is indeed begotten but not made.

Though this language can seem hopelessly abstract and thin, in point of fact, it puts us very concretely on holy ground. When we speak of God, we are speaking of the source and ground of all finite reality, that which is most real, the fullness of being. To remark, therefore, a play of relationality in the very heart of God is to make a metaphysical claim of extraordinary reach and power. Whereas the classical philosophers tended to make self-subsistence the quality of ultimate reality, and relationality a quality of created or dependent being, the doctrine of the Trinity compels us to say that ultimate reality is itself characterized by relationship. To be sure, this is not to imply that God has the properly creaturely quality of ontological dependence, but it is indeed to say that something like "being toward another" belongs to the very essence of God. And since God is the ground of finite being, this ordering to another is, somehow, ingredient in every aspect of the universe. Though our language and typical manner of thinking compels us in this direction, the world is not, most basically, a collection of individual beings or discrete states of affairs. On the contrary, co-inherence is ontologically fundamental.

Moreover, whereas classical philosophy consistently associated unity with ultimate reality, and plurality with the lower realm of creatures, the doctrine under consideration demands that we rethink this bifurcation. The unity and simplicity of God do indeed dictate that God cannot be marked by ordinary creaturely plurality, as though he were somehow made up of a variety of separate "beings." Nevertheless, something like plurality obtains within absolute being. The creative ground of all existence is, in its innermost nature, a looking toward, a being toward another. Indeed, the term used typically to designate the ontological status of the Father, Son, and Holy Spirit is "person," from the Latin *persona*, derived, in turn, from *per-sonare*, to sound through. In its original sense, *persona* indicates the mask worn by a theatrical actor, which had within it a device for the amplification of the performer's voice, so that he could "sound through" to another actor or to the audience. Something like speaking to, communicating with, belongs to the ground of reality, even before the act of creation established other beings with which or with whom God could communicate. And this implies, once again, that communication and communicability belong to the existential structure of the world.

In light of these metaphysical clarifications, we can begin to understand the ethical teaching of Jesus more profoundly. When Jesus urges his followers to love (to will the good of the other) in the most radical way, loving even those who hate us, even those who are our enemies, turning the other cheek when we are struck, refusing to answer evil for evil, he is moving far outside the ambit of standard ethics, either ancient or modern. He is proposing something far beyond the goodness of the ethically upright person imagined either by Aristotle, Kant, or Wittgenstein. The radicality of his program of love is grounded in his Father's manner of being—which is to say, God's indiscriminate pouring forth of love, "[making] his sun rise on the evil and on the good . . . and [sending] rain on the righteous and the unrighteous" (Matt. 5:45). Many other religions and philosophies speak of God having the quality or attribute of love, but only Christianity makes the astonishing claim that "God *is* love." And this can be true if and only if a being toward the other marks the ownmost nature of God, even prior to creation. Therefore, G.K. Chesterton was right when he observed that the doctrine of the Trinity is simply the conceptually precise manner of saying that God is love, that there is, in the divine reality, a play of lover (the Father), beloved (the Son), and shared love (the Holy Spirit).

It is most important never to forget that, even as we climb the heights of metaphysical speculation in regard to the Trinity, the roots of this doctrine are in the very particular Jew, Jesus of Nazareth. Prophets and patriarchs spoke to God and even, in some sense, heard the voice of God. But when Jesus speaks to his Father, or when the Holy Spirit intervenes in the life of Jesus, we are not witnessing just one more human being in dialogue with his Creator; rather, we are overhearing, as it were, a conversation taking place within the inner life of God. We know that God *is* love not through abstract musing on the nature of ultimate reality but from the awful dialogue between Jesus and his Father on the cross. The Son was sent, precisely in the Holy Spirit, to the limits of our sinful condition in order to gather all of us sinners into the divine life. This was the iconic manifestation in time and space of the love that obtains within God from all eternity. The Son, crucified, killed, and buried out of love for sinful humanity, is "God from God, Light from Light, true God from true God."

II. The Son of Man

"For Us Men and for Our Salvation He Came Down from Heaven"

The "why" of the Incarnation is one of the most contested questions in the history of Christian theology. The first point of contention is this: Does the Son of God come exclusively to save the human race or does his salvific enterprise have a wider scope? The Creed clearly says "for us men," and so it seems as though solving some purely human problem is the *raison d'être* for God becoming human. But this seems, on the face of it, to be narrow, even arrogant. The almighty source of all things visible and invisible, the simple, absolute act of Being itself, is only concerned with "us men"? But we must remember that the Bible, as we saw, always places human salvation within the framework of God's grander intentions vis-à-vis the entire created order. Since human beings are the stewards of finite creation, the priests who lead the totality of creatures in praise of God, whatever goes wrong with us will have deleterious implications for the entirety of the cosmos. When the high priest fails in his essential duty, the song of praise that all of matter, space, and time are supposed to sing becomes cacophonous. And this is why St. Paul, for instance, can speak of the "groaning" of all of creation for redemption (Rom. 8:22) and of Christ as the "recapitulation" of all things (Eph. 1:10). He came indeed for us men, but we can never be understood in isolation from the totality of what God has made.

A second and related point of contention is whether he came primarily to save us from sin or to bring humanity and all created reality to fulfillment. One way to frame the question is this: Would the Son of God have become incarnate had we never sinned? One school of thought, customarily associated with St. Thomas Aquinas (though this is not really fair to the complexity of Thomas' thinking on the matter), would hold that the Incarnation was a response to sin. Hence, as the great Exsultet Easter hymn has it, "O happy fault that earned so great, so glorious a Redeemer!"[8] Another approach, usually associated with the Franciscan school of Duns Scotus, maintains that even if we had never sinned, the Incarnation would have occurred so that God might crown his creation and bring it to divinization. The roots of this second position are in St. Irenaeus of Lyons and in a wide variety of scriptural texts, mostly drawn from the Pauline corpus.

A fairly simple way to resolve the dilemma is to acknowledge that the "Scotist" solution should be taken as the default position, since it can "contain" the Thomist position, though the reverse is not true. We have, in point of fact, sinned, and therefore in order to bring his creation to its perfection, God has to deal with the distortions produced by sin, but his ultimate purpose far surpasses this curative move. Another way to handle the tension between the two points of view is to allow the word "salvation"—*soteria* in the original Greek of the Creed—to find its full amplitude, so that it means not just the "healing" of the wound of sin but the full elevation, perfection, and divinization of the human person.

What we find in the New Testament, in marvelous variety, is an array of metaphors and images, each one expressing, in a unique way, the *experience* of coming into contact with Jesus, either directly or indirectly through the mediation of the Church. Though each of these symbols gave rise in time to doctrinal positions, it is a useful exercise to sense the feeling-tone that they were originally trying to convey. Jesus' death and Resurrection were like a liberation. So Paul can say, "For freedom Christ has set us free" (Gal. 5:1). It was like being ransomed from slavery—and thus Paul can speak of Christians being delivered from powers and principalities. It brought peace and joy, what biblical Jews would have called *shalom*—and therefore the word "peace" rings like a bell throughout the New Testament. It was like being set right, straightened out—and so St. Paul, again and again, could speak of the "justification" that comes from participating in the life of Jesus. And it was like receiving a completely unmerited gift—and

8. "Easter Proclamation," in *Roman Missal* (ICEL, 2010).

thus almost all of the authors of the New Testament speak of "grace" in connection with the Lord.

Now, the biblical authors were not choosing their images and metaphors at random. Rather, they reached, as we would expect, to their Scriptures, which had schooled them to expect certain favors from the God of Israel. The entire Exodus narrative, which haunted the minds of practically every New Testament author, taught them to look for God's liberation and deliverance from oppression. The prophets—especially Isaiah and Jeremiah—predisposed them to expect that God would act to set things right and to establish a lasting peace. They knew from the entire drama of Israel's history that God had chosen Israel not because of its accomplishments and merits, but simply as an act of gracious love. And thus they saw all of this brought to complete and unexpected fulfillment in the life, death, and Resurrection of Jesus of Nazareth. I believe that all of the above is implied in the creedal phrase "for us men and for our salvation . . ."

If anyone is ever tempted to see the Nicene Creed as simply an abstract doctrinal catalogue, this very line should disabuse him of the notion. What is at stake in this series of propositions is *salvation*, not just the clarification of concepts. How wonderful that the language of the Creed turns subjective at this juncture. To this point, it has directed us outward to the truths that we believe, but here we are directly and existentially involved: "*for us men and for our salvation.*" In a word, what we are dealing with in this Creed is the be-all and the end-all of the human endeavor. It treats of what matters most, or to use Paul Tillich's phrase, "ultimate concern."[9]

The Creed then tells us, a bit quaintly, that the Son of God "came down from heaven." We are obviously not meant to take this language literally, as though God dwells up in the sky and has to make a physical transit to the earth. As we saw earlier, the unconditioned source of all creaturely existence cannot be located in space, since such a location would render him conditioned. Further, as purely actual, the Creator God is not a thing that can move from

9. Paul Tillich, *Systematic Theology* (Chicago: University of Chicago Press, 1967), 8–12, 211–213.

place to place. "Heaven" is being used here as a symbol for the transcendence of God, for his otherness to the world of conditioned objects and events. It is also evocative of God's moral manner of being, which is radically different from the world of fallen moral agents with which we are accustomed. And thus we see the importance of saying that the Son of God "descended" from the realm of divine transcendence. If sin is a kind of dysfunction that has infected the whole of the human family—and this is indeed the best way to understand the doctrine of original sin—then the solution has to come from outside of the dysfunction. Just as someone fully in the grip of an addiction cannot lead another addict out of his misery, so someone who is completely conditioned by sin cannot save another sinner. Rather, as we saw, the Savior from sin must indeed enter into the world of sinners, but he cannot be himself a sinner. Instead, as Athanasius clearly saw, he had to "descend" from a realm not marked by cruelty, hatred, violence, and fear.

"And by the Holy Spirit Was Incarnate of the Virgin Mary"

It is a peculiarity of the Nicene Creed that the Holy Spirit is mentioned, almost in passing, before belief in him is formally professed. I will have much more to say about the third person of the Trinity in due course, but it is worth sharing at least a word about the Spirit here, particularly as he is mentioned in connection with enfleshment or incarnation.

The Holy Spirit is referenced in the very opening lines of Sacred Scripture. The author of Genesis tells us, "In the beginning when God created the heavens and the earth, the earth was a formless void and darkness covered the face of the deep, while a wind from God swept over the face of the waters" (Gen. 1:1–2). The "wind from God" is the *ruach Yahweh*, often rendered as the "spirit" of God, and his "sweeping" or "hovering" over the surface of the deep carries in the Hebrew the sense of a mother bird beating her wings over her young, encouraging them to fly. The *ruach Yahweh* is, accordingly, the creative power that will give rise to the universe in all of its complexity and its variegated physicality: waters, sky, earth, plants, trees, animals, and humans. Throughout the history of salvation, the spirit of God is what stirs the prophets to speak and empowers kings—think of the *ruach* that "came mightily upon" David when he was anointed by Samuel the prophet. Moreover, the Spirit of the Lord came down upon Jesus himself at his baptism and then "drove him out into the wilderness" (Mark 1:12). He is an active, creative force who makes things happen and compels people to move. Therefore, it is hardly surprising that the *ruach Yahweh* is intimately involved in the enfleshment of the Son of God, an event that will result in a renewal of creation.

The clear implication of the Creed is that the two principal agents in the bringing about of Jesus Christ were the Holy Spirit and the Virgin Mary, grounding the doctrinal conviction that in him two natures—divine and human—came together. And so we turn to a consideration of the Virgin Mary. The Creed's unabashed affirmation of the virginity of Mary the mother of Jesus is grounded in the biblical claim, on clear evidence in both the Gospel of Matthew and the Gospel of Luke, that Mary became pregnant without the intervention of a human father. When, in Luke's account, the angel tells Mary that she will become the mother of the "Most High," the young girl responds, "How can this be, since I am a virgin?" And Gabriel assures her, "The Holy Spirit will come upon you and the power of the Most High will overshadow you; therefore, the child to be born . . . will be called Son of God" (Luke 1:34–35). In Matthew's telling, an angel appears in a dream to Joseph, Mary's betrothed, and explains how her pregnancy came about: "Joseph, son of David, do not be afraid to take Mary as your wife, for the child conceived in her is from the Holy Spirit" (Matt. 1:20).

The virginity of Mary seems fitting for a number of reasons. First, it indicates, as clearly as possible, that God is involved in the coming to be of Jesus. Though human cooperation, at both the physical and moral level, is required, the Incarnation would not have happened without a gracious divine initiative. Further, it signals that the Incarnation involves not simply a revolution in the moral and spiritual order but an entirely new creation. Just as Adam, on the biblical telling, is made through the direct causality of God, so the New Adam is made *de novo,* and not in the ordinary course. Finally, the virginity of Mary is a sign of the purity and completeness of her devotion to God, making her a fit vessel for the divine Messiah. She becomes mother in the physical order, though she is given utterly over to God; she is, as classical Christian piety would have it, spouse of the Holy Spirit. All of this, one might argue, is summed up in the greeting that the angel gives Mary at the Annunciation, the most sublime offered to any human being in the biblical tradition: *kecharitomene,* "full of grace."

Many skeptics across the ages have put the doctrine of the Virgin Birth of Jesus forward as an indisputable sign that the Church is retrograde, stuck in a prescientific, superstitious mindset. Is not the birth of Jesus from a virgin, they wonder, just another iteration of a mythic trope found in cultures around the world? First, as Hans Urs von Balthasar has argued, the story of the birth of Jesus from a virgin and those similar narratives from mythic traditions are only superficially similar.[10] The more intently one studies the Gospel stories, the more unique and distinctive they appear. One clear indication: in almost all of the tales of the birth of divine children from virgin mothers, the pregnancy happens through the violent rape of the human mother by a divine father. There is none of this in the Gospel narratives. Indeed, in the courtly play between the angel of the Annunciation and the Virgin Mary, practically the opposite of rape is on display. But the most striking difference is that the myths give themselves away by their very genre: they are, quite obviously, symbolic literature, intended to indicate natural processes or general truths about the rhythms of the seasons. But the Gospel narratives concerning the birth of Jesus are placed very purposely within a recognizable historical and geographical context, grounding them in fact: "a decree went out from Emperor Augustus" and "was taken while Quirinius was governor of Syria" (Luke 2:1–2). And they are a propaedeutic to what is assuredly the biography of a real, historical figure, clearly unlike the narratives concerning Horus or Mars.

---

10. Hans Urs von Balthasar, *Credo: Meditations on the Apostles' Creed,* trans. David Kipp (San Francisco: Ignatius Press, 2005), 47–48.

But is this teaching, the critics insist, not simply repugnant to reason, even if we grant that it differs from similar accounts? That skeptical claim is grounded in the meta-assertion that the miraculous, strictly speaking, is impossible. However, once we affirm the existence of God, which, as we saw, can be done on rational grounds, this dismissal of the miraculous appears more or less arbitrary. To be sure, miracles are rare, for if they were not, we would not "wonder" at them, which is the state of mind implied in the word *mirari*. But what would prevent the creative source of all finite existence, who continually makes the world from nothing and sustains it from falling back into nonbeing, from producing a state of affairs outside of the normal course? What would be irrational about saying that God, on rare occasion and for his very particular purposes, might suspend or circumvent the natural regularities that he himself established? If God can bring something from nothing, he can surely cause a virgin to become pregnant.

Mary the Virgin also carries an extraordinarily powerful symbolic value for those with eyes to see. On the façade of Notre Dame Cathedral in Paris, there is a statue of Mary the Mother of God, and over her head is a depiction of the ark of the covenant, the holiest artifact in ancient Israel, the ceremonial container for the Ten Commandments and the rod of Aaron. The association is far from accidental, for Mary was seen as the fulfillment *par excellence* of the ark, since she herself bore the presence of God within her womb. And if we allow our symbolic and associative imaginations even wider play, we can see Mary, as the Church Fathers did, as evocative of the holy people Israel itself, who bore, over long centuries and through much suffering, the word of Yahweh. In light of these symbolic connections, Mary's words to Jesus at the wedding feast of Cana take on their full resonance: "They have no wine" (John 2:3). Here, she represents all of the patriarchs and prophets of Israel, crying to the God of Israel, "How long, O Lord? How your people yearn for the joy and salvation that only you can bring." And when she tells the waiters at the wedding, "Do whatever [Jesus] tells you" (John 2:5), she is, once again, all of the sages and seers of Israel, urging the holy people to follow the promptings of the Lord. It is from Mary's womb, and indeed from the womb of Israel, that the Messiah is born.

Having considered the two great agents of the Incarnation—Mary and the Holy Spirit—I want to look with careful attention at the extraordinary word that stands at the heart of this article and indeed of the Creed in its totality: *sarkothenta* (he became flesh). The Son of God, we are told, becomes incarnate (enfleshed) through the power of the Holy Spirit. It is crucially important to see how counterintuitive this assertion is to both the Greek and the Jewish mind. For biblical Jews, God is indeed the Creator of matter, and flesh is indeed good, but God himself is neither material nor fleshly. Jesus is operating out of a thoroughly Jewish framework when he tells the Samaritan woman at the well, "God is spirit, and those who worship him must worship in spirit and truth" (John 4:24). By the same token, those schooled in the classical philosophical tradition insisted that God is immaterial and that his nonmateriality is one of the marks of his ontological superiority. Precisely as finite, changeable, corruptible, and conditioned by both time and space, matter cannot belong to the divine manner of being.

But the Nicene Creed intimately associates the God of Israel, the Creator of the world, with matter, even to the point of speaking of his entry into flesh. What sense are we to make of this? First, we must avoid any temptation to say that the Incarnation involves God "turning into" matter, ceasing to be spiritual and becoming flesh, as though he changes from being one type of reality to another. All of that is ruled out by God's simplicity and immutability. Writing some 120 years after the Council of Nicaea, the fathers of the Council of Chalcedon insisted that the two "natures" that come together in Jesus do so "without confusion or change, without division or separation."[11] What is divine in Christ and what is human in him do not lose their respective integrity or bleed into one another.

When Nicaea speaks of God "becoming" human, therefore, it means that God the Son took to himself a human nature—which means a fully

11. Heinrich Denzinger et al., *Compendium of Creeds, Definitions, and Declarations on Matters of Faith and Morals*, 43rd ed. (San Francisco: Ignatius Press, 2012), nos. 302, 109.

constituted human manner of being—in order to use it as an icon of his presence and action. We recall that St. Paul, in his Letter to the Colossians, referred to Jesus as the "image of the invisible God," and the Greek term that stands behind "image" is none other than *eikon*. Those in the Eastern Christian tradition who pray in the presence of icons tell us that the sacred picture is much more than a mere representation; rather, it participates in the reality that it represents, drawing the viewer through itself to the invisible order. As became apparent to the disciples on the Mount of Transfiguration, Jesus' humanity functioned in precisely this way, as a radiant sign through which his divinity shone. Mind you, in using this comparison, I am by no means suggesting that the Lord's humanity is a flat and purely passive vehicle by which his divinity is made manifest. On the contrary, precisely in the measure that it is a complete human nature, it involves intellect, will, and freedom. It is by means of this richly complex humanity that Jesus' divinity expresses itself.

This was, by the way, the central issue of the so-called monothelite controversy in the seventh century. Eager to affirm the full divinity of Jesus, some theologians held that there was, in the Lord, only one will—namely, the divine will—and that this source of freedom and action effectively supplanted the properly human source of freedom and action. But Maximus the Confessor and others rose to meet this challenge, convinced that monothelitism denied the principle implied at Nicaea, and confirmed a century later at the Council of Chalcedon, that the natures subsist in their integrity and without mixing or mingling. Maximus and his colleagues insisted that there are, in Jesus, two wills, divine and human, just as there are, in him, two minds, divine and human. Thus, even as we speak of the humanity of Christ as an "icon" of his divinity, we by no means imply that it is a truncated or compromised humanity. In point of fact, the very unconditioned quality of God's way of being guarantees that these two freedoms can coexist noncompetitively within the unity of Jesus' person. It is worth dwelling a bit longer on this last point. Much of the modern and postmodern reaction against God is born of the conviction that an all-powerful and omniscient being would represent the ultimate threat to a self-determining human freedom. Jean-Paul Sartre made the charge in what he took to be an unanswerable syllogism: if God exists, I cannot be free; but I am free; therefore, God does not exist.[12] The coming together of a divine will and a human will in Jesus, made possible by the unique manner of God's being, shows why that syllogism collapses.

But does not this intimate association with a human nature change God? Certainly the great defenders of divine immutability in the classical philosophical tradition would never have imagined this possibility. Thomas Aquinas proves helpful here. The great medieval scholastic distinguishes what he calls "real" relations, which involve change and dependency, and relations that imply neither change nor dependency.[13] As an example of the first, we might cite a friendship, which clearly affects and changes both partners; and as an example of the second, we might cite Socrates being taller than Plato and then shorter than Plato, even while Socrates has undergone no change in height. As Plato grew taller, Socrates began to have a different relation to his student, even though Socrates' stature did not alter in any way. Something of this kind of relation obtains in regard to the Incarnation. God the Son begins to have a new relation to a human nature, but this implies no compromise of the Son of God's essential immutability.

Having stressed the integrity of the two natures in the Incarnation, we must now highlight the extraordinary truth that these two distinct manners of being *come together*, precisely in the unity of one divine person. Jesus is not two separate beings, nor is he a mere human person in an intimate rapport with God, in the manner of a great saint. Rather, in the unity of one person, he is both divine and human. To grasp how this is possible, we must remember what was said above about the unique nature of God. As the act of being itself (*ipsum esse*), God is not one being among many, competing for space on the same ontological grid as other beings. His otherness to the world, as we saw, is noncontrastive and noncompetitive. And this is why he is able to enter into union with a creaturely nature, without undermining his

12. See Jean-Paul Sartre, *Existentialism Is a Humanism*, trans. Carol Macomber, ed. John Kulka (New Haven, CT: Yale University Press, 2007), 28–29.

13. See, for example, Thomas Aquinas, *Summa theologiae* 1.28.1–2, 1.145.3, 3.35.5.

own nature or compromising the creature that he becomes. In the created order, one thing can become another only through aggression, supplanting, or surrender. Thus, the house becomes a pile of ash through being destroyed by fire; the zebra becomes the lion only by being devoured; one person "becomes" another only through domination and manipulation. But God does not relate to creaturely natures in this way. Rather, as we have seen, when God comes close to a creature, that finite thing becomes more truly itself.

Though I have followed the Creed in laying out the truths about God before expounding the truths about the Incarnation, I would hold that, in the order of discovery, things moved in the opposite direction. It was from the noncompetitiveness of the natures in Jesus that Christian theologians eventually concluded to God's strange and utterly unique quality of existence. When they mused on what God must be like if the Incarnation in fact took place, they understood that God is not a conventional supreme being but is rather best described as Being itself or "that than which nothing greater can be thought."[14] It is also important to look at the famous phrase "became man" from the other side. What does it mean for humanity that God became one of us? It implies that divinization is, for all of us, a real possibility. By this, the great tradition does not mean that we are absorbed into the divine being, for that would be misreading the Incarnation along the lines suggested above, but just from the human side of the equation. Nor does it mean that any of us is capable of becoming a son of God in the way that Jesus was. But the Fathers of both Eastern and Western Christianity came together in affirming that it does imply the possibility that our lowly nature can be so elevated as to be described as participating in the Trinitarian life.

The Greek-speaking theologians referred to this, unabashedly, as divinization (*theiosis* in Greek), and their Latin-speaking counterparts followed them in characterizing it as *divinisatio.* This is why the goal of the Christian spiritual life is never simply moral excellence, as indispensable as that is, but rather mystical participation in the divine life. One of the most surprising but consistent

14. Anselm, *Proslogion* 2–5, in *Anselm: Monologion and Proslogion*, trans. Thomas Williams (Indianapolis, IN: Hackett, 1996), 99–102.

affirmations of the early Church, formulated by theologians both East and West across many centuries, is *Deus fit homo ut homo fieret Deus*, which means, quite literally, "God became man that man might become God."[15] In many ways, the distinctiveness of Christianity, in comparison to any other religion or philosophy, is contained in that line. There is, frankly, no humanism, either ancient or modern, more dramatic and thoroughgoing than orthodox Christianity, which envisions, not simply moral achievement or political stability or economic advantage or psychological well-being as the goal of human life, but rather divinization.

III. The Descent

"For Our Sake He Was Crucified under Pontius Pilate"

There are precisely three human beings mentioned in the Nicene Creed: Jesus, Mary, and Pontius Pilate. The first two, quite obviously, are intimately involved in the Incarnation, which stands at the heart of the Creed. But why would Pontius Pilatus, the early first-century Roman governor of the province of Judea, play such a prominent role in this profession of Christian faith? One very simple and yet very significant service that the mention of Pilate performs is to ground Jesus unambiguously in history. No one wonders who the local magistrate was when Hercules cleaned the Aegean stables or who the ruler of Egypt was when Osiris rose from the dead. This is because those stories were and are recognized clearly as mythic in form. But in the case of Jesus, the first Christians were extremely interested in telling the world the name of the Roman authority who presided over the death of their Lord, lest one might be tempted to relegate the story they were telling to the generic realm of the mythical. The fact that there are coins, inscriptions, and documents from the period that clearly reference Pontius Pilatus confirms this instinct.

15. See, for example, Athanasius, *De incarnatione* 54 (PG 25:192). For an English translation of this work, see *On the Incarnation*, trans. and ed. a religious of C.S.M.V. (Crestwood, NY: St. Vladimir's Seminary, 1996).

But Pilate is present in the Creed for a deeper reason. He presided over the Crucifixion and death of Jesus, and upon this awful fact Christian preaching and teaching finally depend. As Paul put it in his first letter to the church in Corinth: "When I came to you, brothers and sisters, I did not come proclaiming the mystery of God to you in lofty words or wisdom. For I decided to know nothing among you except Jesus Christ, and him crucified" (1 Cor. 2:2). The terrible death of Jesus was not a mere tragedy, not an unpleasant fact that we must brush aside in order to get to the ethical substance of Jesus' message; somehow, it was (and is) the very heart of the matter, the hinge upon which all of Christian faith turns. And therefore it is exceptionally important that we know why Pontius Pilate and his many colleagues and collaborators, both Roman and Jewish, brought Jesus to the cross.

I would like to put this in the widest possible context. In many ways, the entire Bible is a book of battles. I am not speaking simply of the many military conflicts narrated therein; I am speaking of the almost constant struggle between the ways and purposes of God and those forces that stand opposed to the divine intention. From the opening lines of the Scriptures, we find the Spirit of God drawing life and order from the *tohu wabohu*, the watery chaos. Even in the Garden of Eden, we find the serpent, indeed the cleverest of God's creatures, but also a source of tremendous mischief. In the wake of original sin, Adam and Eve fall into conflict with one another and with the realm of nature. Cain hates his brother and murders him. By the time of Noah, sin had become so pervasive that the *tohu wabohu* returns in the form of an all-destroying flood.

Once established through a series of covenants, the holy people Israel is opposed on every front and from within. The Egyptians enslave Israel; Amalek and Philistia harass it; every power in the Promised Land stands opposed to it; Assyria, Persia, Babylon, Greece, and Rome conquer it. Its most sacred artifacts are destroyed; the temple itself, the dwelling of God on earth, is burned to the ground. And from the inside, Israel is constantly threatened as well: the sins of her own people, civil war, kingly rivalry, stupidity, resentment, violence, cruelty, the wanton disregard of the commandments of the Lord, the worship of false gods. In his magnificent homilies on the book of Exodus, Origen of Alexandria construes Israel as representative of all of those energies and instincts congruent with the will of God and the Egyptians as symbolic of all of those forces opposed to God.[16] How tragically telling, he observes, that Egypt has enslaved Israel, meaning that what is best in ourselves and in our societies is often in thrall to what is worst in ourselves and our societies. The Israelite slaves are compelled by their masters to build monuments and fortified cities for their oppressors; indeed, our intelligence, creativity, and energy are dedicated to the building of monuments to and fortifications for our selfishness, violence, and idolatry. Almost invariably, when God's spokespersons and representatives come on the scene, they are met with opposition. Think of the Israelites grumbling against Moses, or of the fierce military opposition faced by Joshua, or of Saul's deep resentment and constant harassment of David, or of the murderous opponents of Jeremiah the prophet, or of the Babylonian invaders who carried the prophet Ezekiel away.

All of this comes to full expression in the New Testament. From the very commencement of his life, Jesus, the one who speaks and acts in the very person of God, is opposed. When we read the familiar Lukan Christmas account through the right interpretive lenses, we see that it is far from a charming story that one might recite to children. Instead, it is marked, through and through, by the themes of conflict and opposition. The tale opens in the way that one might expect, by invoking great and mighty figures: Quirinius, the Roman governor of Syria, and Caesar Augustus, who effectively ruled the world. But Luke turns our expectations upside down when he makes it clear whom the narrative is about: not Caesar and Quirinius, but two obscure figures making their way to Bethlehem, prompted by Caesar's imperious call for a census of the whole world. The baby to whom the woman is about to give birth is the focus of Luke's attention.

16. Origen of Alexandria, "The Homilies on Exodus," in *Homilies on Genesis and Exodus*, trans. Ronald E. Heine (Washington, DC: The Catholic University of America Press, 1982), 227–387.

We must read the account, in point of fact, as a contrast between two ideas of kingship. The baby is born in a cave or a stable and placed in a dirty trough where animals eat. The best protected and best fed person in the ancient world would have been Caesar, and such advantages are normally seen as perquisites of the powerful. The baby is wrapped up in swaddling clothes, rendering him utterly incapable of movement. The most mobile and rangy person in the ancient world would have been Caesar Augustus, able to accomplish practically anything he wanted, and such a capacity is normally appreciated as a mark of the good life. Caesar had an enormous army, which is why he was capable of dominating his world. But the baby king, we discover, is the commander of a *stratias* (army) of angels, and this provides the hermeneutical key to the narrative. True world-conquering power is associated with humility, love, nonviolence, and poverty, not with the qualities valued by a fallen world. The Lukan Christmas story is something like an operatic overture, since it anticipates the central theme that will mark almost every aspect of the coming drama. Two kings, two ideas of kingship, two rival conceptions of power will battle against one another throughout the Gospel, and the *point* of the story is that one of them wins out.

Though his ultimate victory is indicated by the army of angels, the new King will endure, his whole life long, the opposition of the established powers of the world. Upon hearing of his birth, King Herod—a quasi-Jewish client of the Roman state—tries to stamp the child out. The breathtakingly brutal massacre of the children of Bethlehem displays the ruthlessness and cruelty of worldly power perhaps as clearly as it can be displayed. Jesus is forced to become an exile in order to escape the fury of Herod—and indeed of all Jerusalem, which "trembled" in unison with Herod upon hearing of the birth of his rival.

Just after his baptism and immediately before commencing his public life, Jesus has an encounter with the devil. This time of trial and temptation, mentioned by all three of the synoptic Gospels, manifests the *agon* (conflict) that stands behind all of the struggles that he will eventually have with earthly figures, both religious and political. At the foundation of the dysfunction of the world is a dark spiritual power that stands athwart the purposes of the Creator God. There is much that we could say about the way in which Jesus is tried by the devil, but for our purposes now I would like to concentrate on what Matthew presents as the third and final temptation. "Again, the devil took him to a very high mountain and showed him all the kingdoms of the world and their splendor; and he said to him, 'All these I will give you, if you fall down and worship me'" (Matt. 4:8–9). The salient point is that the devil is able to offer all of the political structures of the world, precisely because, in a fundamental sense, they belong to him. I do not know any more thoroughgoing critique of political power anywhere in the literature of the world.

As the Lord dismisses the devil, he uses the distinctive name *ho Satanas*: "Away with you, Satan!" (Matt. 4:10). The Greek term, grounded in the Hebrew *satan*, means "the adversary" or, in a legal context, "the accuser." What Luke is conveying, in no uncertain terms, is that all of the kingdoms of the world—that is to say, the way in which human beings organize themselves socially—belong to the Accuser. One does not have to subscribe to every detail of René Girard's theory to see here a basic agreement between the New Testament and the thought of the French literary theorist.[17] For Girard, all human social groupings, from the smallest to the grandest, are predicated upon what he called the scapegoating mechanism—that is, our tendency to dispel social tension through the identification and blaming of some individual or collective supposedly responsible for the negativity that obtains among us. In the ecstasy of common blaming, we find a sort of ersatz and deeply unstable peace, but this phony serenity is sufficient for us almost universally to sacralize the scapegoating mechanism, turning it into a fetish. This is why, Girard argues, in most cultures, the scapegoating instinct is ratified by the religious establishment. How powerful indeed it is, therefore, that Jesus, the Son of God, dismisses the Accuser and refuses

17. See René Girard, *The Scapegoat*, trans. Yvonne Freccero (Baltimore, MD: Johns Hopkins University Press, 1986); René Girard, *Things Hidden Since the Foundation of the World*, trans. Stephen Bann and Michael Metteer (Stanford, CA: Stanford University Press, 1987).

to bow down to him. He thereby de-sacralizes the scapegoating mechanism and opens the possibility of an entirely new way of grounding human society—not in collective blaming but in forgiveness and compassion for the other. That this exposing and disempowering of "the Satan" leads to intense, finally deadly, opposition to Jesus on the part of the Romans, many of his fellow Jews, and even his own disciples, is one of the central motifs of the Gospels.

Having battled with the Accuser, the dark spiritual animator behind the dysfunction of the world, Jesus is ready for his public work. Given our assumptions that the world is a disenchanted place, we might be distinctly uncomfortable with any talk of demons. Nevertheless, it is impossible to read the Gospels and not conclude that the exorcism of these fallen spiritual powers was central to Jesus' ministry. It is actually quite illuminating to examine the narratives of these exorcisms, for the devils reveal the key dynamics of the compromised world, on more immediate display in individuals and institutions. Alongside of "the Satan," the most common name for a fallen spirit in the New Testament is *ho diabolos*, which carries the sense of "the scatterer." In so many of the accounts of demonic possession, something of this splintering or dividing quality is on offer. For example, in the narrative of the exorcism of the Capernaum demoniac in Mark's Gospel, a single possessed man enters the synagogue, but he speaks to Jesus in the plural: "What have you to do with us, Jesus of Nazareth? Have you come to destroy us?" (Mark 1:23–24). Similarly, in the account of the Gerasene demoniac, we find a curious splitting and splintering within an individual. When Jesus asks the tortured man his name, the possessed one responds, "My name is Legion; for we are many" (Mark 5:9).

As we saw earlier, the act of right praise (orthodoxy) provides a center around which every aspect of one's personality can be gathered. When God is glorified in the highest, then a person's mind, will, imagination, public life, private life, play, and friendships find their harmonious and integrated place within him or her. When something other than the true God is given highest value, then the person inevitably splits, pluralizes from within, and he commences to say to God, "What do you have to do with *us*?" The struggle between Jesus and the demonic forces is an example of the problem of the one and the many in the spiritual order. A fine example of the fruit of Jesus' work and the very power of his person is found in the single-minded discipleship of Mary Magdalene, from whom the Lord, we hear, had driven out seven demons (see Mark 16:9).

The Sermon on the Mount in Matthew's Gospel and the similar Sermon on the Plain in Luke's Gospel provide a sort of summary of the typical teaching of Jesus. When he went about "proclaiming the Kingdom of God," we can assume that these two sermons represent, more or less, what he was saying. An adequate study of the themes of these sermons would take us way too far afield, but we can at least remark some major motifs that signal the astonishing novelty of Jesus' teaching and also why it conduced so quickly to a conflict with the powers that ruled his world. Whereas most forms of human organization are predicated upon displays of power, Jesus' kingdom belongs to the powerless: "Blessed are the meek, for they will inherit the earth." Whereas most kingdoms and nation states survive through war and the threat of war, Jesus' kingdom belongs to those who militate in favor of peace: "Blessed are the peacemakers, for they will be called children of God." Whereas most societies favor those who look out for themselves, Jesus' kingdom belongs to those who are focused on doing the will of God and imitating God's compassion: "Blessed are those who hunger and thirst for righteousness, for they will be filled," and "Blessed are the merciful, for they will receive mercy" (see Matt. 5:1–12).

And lest all of this sound like airy abstractions, Jesus makes things unnervingly concrete: "You have heard that it was said . . . 'You shall not murder'; and 'whoever murders shall be liable to judgment.' But I say to you that if you are angry with a brother or sister, you will be liable to judgment'" (Matt. 5:21–22). The participants in the kingdom of the God who is love right through must not be satisfied with mere external compliance with minimalistic moral regulations. Their mode of social organization must be conditioned by a repentance that reaches to the depths of their hearts.

The rhetorical and theological highpoint of the Sermon on the Mount is the teaching laid out in verses 38–48 of chapter 5 of Matthew's Gospel. In his doctrine on the love of enemies, Jesus articulates, in its most radical form, what an ethic predicated on *agape* (selfless love) looks like. "You have heard that it was said, 'An eye for an eye and a tooth for a tooth.' But I say to you, Do not resist an evildoer. But if anyone strikes you on the right cheek, turn the other also" (Matt. 5:38–39). Mind you, the *lex talionis* (law of retribution) that Jesus presents economically enough is not put forward as a perverted prescription to which the positive law of Jesus stands in contrast. On the contrary, the *lex talionis* had been a remarkable step in the direction of restraining the retaliatory violence of offended parties. By limiting the range of the vengeance—only one eye for one eye and one tooth for one tooth—it discouraged extremism and encouraged justice. But the doctrine of enemy love does indeed go beyond the justice of the *lex talionis.* If, according to the classical definition, justice is "rendering to each his due," love consists in rendering to others even what they are *not* owed, what they should *not*, in strict equity, receive. In Thomas Aquinas' typically laconic characterization, real love, as we saw earlier, is willing the good of the other as other—that is to say, really to want what is best for someone else, free of consideration of how one's goodness to another might redound to one's own advantage.[18] But if this is the case, then the truest test of love would be love of enemies, precisely because they can be counted upon not to return the generosity of the giver. Within this context, we can understand Jesus' admonition in Luke chapter 6: "If you love those who love you, what credit is that to you? For even sinners love those who love them. . . . If you lend to those from whom you hope to receive, what credit is that to you? . . . But love your enemies, do good, and lend, expecting nothing in return" (Luke 6:32–35). Once again, these prescriptions are meant radically to emphasize the "as other" tag at the end of the definition of love. They are designed to break us out of the economy

18. Thomas Aquinas, *Summa contra Gentiles* 1.91.2–3, trans. Anton C. Pegis (New York: Hanover House, 1955).

of exchange—giving that one might receive in return—which asserts itself almost inevitably, even among the most ethically alert.

The attentive reader will have noticed the correspondence between the ethical teaching of Jesus regarding the kingdom of God and the philosophical account of creation explored earlier. As we saw, God cannot have made the world out of need, since as unconditioned he has no needs; therefore, the very existence of the universe proves that it has been brought about as an act of sheer generosity. Jesus makes this connection explicit in the Sermon on the Mount as he closes the teaching on enemy love: "Love your enemies and pray for those who persecute you, so that you may be children of your Father in heaven; for he makes his sun to rise on the evil and the good, and sends rain on the righteous and on the unrighteous" (Matt. 5:44–45). Whatever is, is loved into existence. Therefore, it is a strictly correct metaphysical statement that God makes his grace to fall on the ugly and the beautiful, the lowly and the noble, the morally corrupt and the saintly. Those who are citizens of the kingdom of God, consequently, love in this same way.

It is most instructive, in light of the foregoing, to examine St. Augustine's late-career masterpiece *The City of God*. In his sweeping overview of world history, Augustine sees the *civitas Dei*, a society predicated upon love of God, as a tiny ship, a sort of Noah's Ark, tossed about on the waves of the *civitas terrena* (earthly city), a society predicated upon self-love.[19] Though he had been crucially shaped by the culture of ancient Rome, Augustine saw the late Roman Empire as a prime example of the "earthly city": unjust, cruel, lascivious, and above all, violent. He remarks that in the long history of the Roman Empire and Republic, the door to the temple of the god Janus had been closed only a handful of times, something that took place only when the entire Roman world was at peace. There was no more eloquent proof, he thought, that Roman authority rested primarily upon violence and the threat of violence. Little wonder that Augustine provides, as one of his principal definitions of sin, *libido dominandi* (the lust to dominate). But Rome, on Augustine's reading, is just the latest in a long line of dysfunctional

19. Augustine, *De civitate Dei* 15.26.

kingdoms, political arrangements that are, he famously asserted, no more than well-organized bands of thieves. Given this basic truth, it is absolutely no surprise that Jesus, the personal embodiment of the kingdom of God, was massively opposed by the political establishment of his time and that his Church, in the measure that it lives out the precepts of its founder, has been and will always be tossed on the waves of persecution.[20]

Now, Jesus' proclivity to speak of a "kingdom," his ability to stir up large crowds of followers, and perhaps especially his triumphal entry into Jerusalem in the manner of the Messiah-king predicted by the prophet Zechariah, was probably more than enough to excite the attention and opposition of Pontius Pilate. But it is likely that Pilate's interest was at the very least encouraged by the Jewish authorities of that time and place. Among the Jewish leadership were the so-called Sadducees, a party comprised mainly of members of the aristocracy who were closely tied to the temple and its rituals. Precisely as an "establishment" group, the Sadducees tended to collaborate with the occupiers, attempting to find a *modus vivendi* with Rome without completely compromising Jewish belief and practice. Likely, they shared Roman concerns about the purely political implications of Jesus' teaching and action.

But mainstream Judaism, led by the Pharisee party, had more properly theological objections to Jesus. With most of his teaching, they probably had little substantial quarrel, since much of it was anticipated in the Psalms and prophets. Their protest was against the extraordinary and, to them, frankly blasphemous claims that he made about himself. Since I rehearsed these above, I will not belabor the point. I will only indicate that to declare himself Lord of the sabbath (Matt. 12:8; Mark 2:28; Luke 6:5), greater than the temple, more authoritative than the Torah, and the highest good in person was to arrogate to himself the prerogatives of God alone—and this made Jesus, in their eyes, supremely dangerous. An extremely illuminating confirmation of this can be found in Rabbi Jacob Neusner's book *A Rabbi Talks to Jesus*. The contemporary Jewish scholar concedes that if he were in Jesus' audience in first-century Galilee, he would have found much of Jesus'

20. Augustine, *De civitate Dei* 2–3. For an English translation of this work, see *City of God*, trans. Henry Bettenson (London: Penguin Books, 2003).

teaching acceptable, even inspiring, but that he would have walked away when the speaker claimed authority that belonged uniquely to the Torah.[21]

Throughout the Gospels, we hear references to both the Jewish establishment and ordinary Israelites turning on Jesus: "After this Jesus went about Galilee. He did not wish to go about in Judea because the Jews were looking for an opportunity to kill him" (John 7:1); "They got up, drove him out of the town, and led him to the brow of the hill on which their town was built, so that they might hurl him off the cliff" (Luke 4:29); "When he went outside, the scribes and the Pharisees began to be very hostile to him . . . lying in wait for him, to catch him in something he might say" (Luke 11:53–54); "They said this to test him, so that they might have some charge to bring against him" (John 8:6); "Now the chief priests and the Pharisees had given orders that anyone who knew where Jesus was should let them know, so that they might arrest him" (John 11:57). And there are many more similar remarks that are sprinkled throughout the Gospels. The point is that both the Roman order and the Jewish order were, for mostly different reasons, though there was some overlap in their motivations, opposed to Jesus, even to the point of wanting to stamp him out.

I would like to make, at this juncture, something abundantly clear. None of this should be read in such a way as to single out any ethnic group for special blame for its opposition to Jesus. There is, quite obviously, a disastrous history of Christian anti-Semitism, prompted, it is tragic to say, by texts such as the ones I just quoted. But this is utterly unwarranted. By the end of his life, Jesus had been rejected by the Jewish establishment and by many ordinary Jews, by the Roman establishment, and indeed, by his own most intimate followers. With the exception of the Apostle John, every single one of his chosen twelve abandoned, betrayed, or denied him at his moment of greatest need. What I hope is clear is that the Gospel writers are emphasizing the *universality* of the rejection of Jesus. It was not "the Jews" or "the Romans" who turned on him; it was sinful humanity. Full stop.

---

21. Jacob Neusner, *A Rabbi Talks with Jesus: An Intermillennial, Interfaith Exchange* (New York: Image Books, 1993), 3–36.

As Karl Barth frequently argued, we do not really understand the nature and destructiveness of sin until Jesus appears, for it is only in contrast with his brilliance that the darkness of the world is made fully manifest.[22] This is why, furthermore, Barth insists that the Creed's statement that Jesus "suffered" under Pontius Pilate should be taken broadly indeed, so that the whole of Jesus' life might be seen under the rubric of suffering and opposition. Here the Protestant Barth agrees with the Catholic John Courtney Murray, who said that the Gospels recount the ever-increasing *agon* between Jesus and the world that he enters.[23] We also recall C.S. Lewis' marvelous remark to the effect that the Son of God came on the scene so quietly and unobtrusively, in a dusty corner of the Roman Empire, since he had to sneak clandestinely behind enemy lines.[24]

Now, all of the preceding was intended to provide the context for the claim that Jesus was crucified under Pontius Pilate. His condemnation was obviously not the result of an arbitrary whim of the Roman governor, but instead was conditioned, on the New Testament reading, by the entire history of humankind's rejection of God and the ways of God. For Søren Kierkegaard, the answer to the easy theological liberalism of his time, which blithely argued that the Incarnation corresponded to the deepest aspirations of the mind and heart, was the shock of the cross.[25] If we are all implicitly religious, and if Jesus is the teacher who gently shows us the deepest truth about ourselves, then why did we kill him when he came? Though there is much more that can and should be said about theological liberalism both Catholic and Protestant, the condemnation of Jesus at the hands of Pilate should indeed preclude any facilely optimistic theological anthropology. When the Truth appeared in person, all of our lies were exposed, all of our pretentions to spiritual achievement unmasked.

---

22. Karl Barth, *Church Dogmatics*, 4.1, *The Doctrine of Reconciliation* (Edinburgh: T&T Clark, 1988), 358–477.

23. John Courtney Murray, *An Eight Day Retreat*, unpublished manuscript.

24. Lewis, *Mere Christianity*, 45–46.

25. See Søren Kierkegaard, *Concluding Unscientific Postscript to* Philosophical Fragments, vol. 1, ed. and trans. Howard V. Hong and Edna H. Hong (Princeton, NJ: Princeton University Press, 1992).

With that, let us look at the meetings of Jesus and Pontius Pilate. Though some attempts have been made to rehabilitate Pilate, seeing him as a figure more pathetic than wicked, and though the Gospels do exhibit a certain sympathy toward him, we should be clear-eyed about him. He was a typical Roman functionary: efficient, concerned with order above all, brutal when he had to be. He was dismissed from office about five years after his condemnation of Jesus because he put down rebelliousness with a ferocity that was too much even for his Roman overseers. He was, to put it in Augustinian terms, a governor thoroughly and unapologetically motivated by the *libido dominandi.* In accord with his practical instincts, Pilate at first resisted passing sentence on Jesus, convinced that his case was a matter for the Jewish religious authorities. But when he heard of the Lord's claims to kingship, his interest was piqued. "Are you the King of the Jews? . . . Your own nation and the chief priests have handed you over to me. What have you done?" (John 18:33–35). To which Jesus answered, "My kingdom is not from this world. If my kingdom were from this world, my followers would be fighting to keep me from being handed over to the Jews. But as it is, my kingdom is not here" (John 18:36). He does not mean, of course, that his kingdom is an ethereal affair, with no relevance to human life here below; he means, rather, that his manner of ordering things has nothing to do with the violent, materialistic, self-absorbed, *libido dominandi* kingdom that Pilate represents. And as we would expect from the author of the Sermon on the Mount, *the* distinguishing mark of Jesus' kingdom is nonviolence: there is no fighting, even on behalf of the King himself.

As the dialogue continues, we see a crucially important condition for the possibility of the *libido dominandi* state—namely, the bracketing or subjectivizing of the very notion of truth. Jesus calmly tells Pilate that he, the Lord, came into the world "to testify to the truth" and that, accordingly, "everyone who belongs to the truth listens to my voice." To this declaration, the world-weary Roman governor responds, "What is truth?" (John 18:37–38). The assumption behind his sighing response appears to be that no one can ever really know the truth, that there are, in fact, a range of "truths," varying according to one's cultural situation. How oddly postmodern Pilate sounds here. He probably sniffs out behind a claim to represent the truth a dangerous fanaticism, an eagerness to impose one's point of view on others. Or perhaps he is just bored by the question, so abstract and philosophical, so removed from the *Realpolitik* of maintaining Roman order. But we can see precisely where this hostility/indifference to truth leads him. Though he clearly tells the prosecutors of Jesus that he finds no compelling case against him, he is altogether willing to play a political game in order to mollify a potentially rebellious crowd: "You have a custom that I release someone for you at the Passover. Do you want me to release for you the King of the Jews?" The people shouted back, "Not this man, but Barabbas," a bandit in Roman custody (John 18:39–40). The question of guilt and innocence—the truth of the matter—is completely irrelevant to the pragmatic Pilate. All that counts is power and the maintenance of power.

Hoping that a display of Roman brutality might satisfy the crowd, Pilate has Jesus lashed. Afterwards, he twice admits that he finds no guilt in the scourged man, but the anger of the mob frightens him: "We have a law, and according to that law he ought to die because he has claimed to be the Son of God" (John 19:7). Desperate to find a way out of his peril, he interrogates Jesus once more but receives no response. Frustrated, he cries, "Do you refuse to speak to me? Do you not know that I have power to release you, and power to crucify you?" Once more, power trumps truth—or better, power moves into the vacuum left behind by truth. Jesus' answer to Pilate is of profound metaphysical import: "You would have no power over me unless it had been given you from above" (John 19:10–11). What is insinuated here is the proper relationship between power and truth. To be properly exercised, power must be in right relation to the transcendent moral and spiritual truths that ought to guide it. Untethered from such truth, power becomes arbitrary and self-interested—precisely what is on display in Pilate's exercise of authority and what, frankly, is typically on offer in our society of self-invention.

As we saw earlier, God, as the unconditioned act of to-be itself, must be in possession of both intellect and will, and given his metaphysically simple nature, all of his attributes and powers must coincide. Thus, in God, truth and freedom are always co-implicated. A false theology, which has haunted Christianity from the earliest days to the present, is a voluntarism that so elevates the divine will that truth becomes a matter of arbitrary divine fiat. Thus Descartes himself, who advocated the position, can say that 2+3=5 because God so willed.[26] Presumably, if God decided otherwise, that mathematical equivalence would not hold. Thomas Aquinas had an abhorrence of voluntarism in regard to God or in regard to the human being. God's will is congruent with the dictate of his mind, which is equivalent to the divine essence, and the human being, following this prompt, should bring his will into conformity with his intellect, which is in touch with the structures of the real, which are, in turn, reflective of the divine being. It is to this metaphysical and anthropological state of affairs, which has crucial political implications, that Jesus refers when he reminds Pilate that the Roman governor's power comes "from above." That Pilate finally condemns to death a man he knows to be innocent is ample proof that the Roman governor's power has been frightfully abused. Pilate's washing his hands of all responsibility functions as a telling icon for all of those avatars of the City of Man up and down the centuries who would drive a wedge between freedom and truth.

"He Suffered Death and Was Buried"

As Fleming Rutledge points out, St. Paul's statement in the first chapter of Romans to the effect that he is not ashamed of the Gospel is a peculiar remark (Rom. 1:16).[27] Why, we wonder, would Paul have to reassure his listeners and readers that the content of his preaching is not a matter of shame? It would be difficult to imagine, say, the Buddha or Confucius or Muhammad saying something comparable about his own teaching. The simple reason is that the

26. See René Descartes, "First Letter to Mersenne" and "Second Letter to Mersenne," in *The Philosophical Writings of Descartes*, vol. 3, *The Correspondence*, trans. John Cottingham et al. (Cambridge: Cambridge University Press, 1991), 23–24.

27. Fleming Rutledge, *The Crucifixion: Understanding the Death of Jesus Christ* (Grand Rapids, MI: Eerdmans, 2015), 1–4.

central content of Paul's proclamation was a crucified criminal. We are so accustomed to seeing religious images of Jesus on the cross that much of the horror and humiliation of crucifixion is lost on us. But for a person of the first century, operating within the confines of the Roman Empire, crucifixion was about the worst thing he or she could imagine. So terrible was it in fact that Cicero, one of the most eloquent and articulate men of that age, would refer to the act of crucifixion only by means of a tortured circumlocution. For the first several centuries of the Christian era, there is, outside of a mocking graffito, no known depiction of the crucified Jesus. What was involved in that form of capital punishment was just too vividly present in the popular imagination.

The Romans, it is speculated, inherited the practice from ancient Persia, but it is fair to say that they perfected it. The condemned man was usually compelled to carry the cross beam to the place of execution, where it was fixed to an upright pole. The victim was stripped naked—the humiliation of this being part of his torture—and then fastened to the device, either by ropes or nails or perhaps both. (There is indeed archeological evidence of an ankle bone, from the first century, pierced through by an enormous nail.) He was subsequently left to die, exposed to the mocking of the crowds and to the cruelty of the elements and the wild animals. But the exquisite misery of the cross consisted in the slow asphyxiation that it produced in the one who hung thereupon. And if the victim were nailed through wrists and ankles, the constant rocking up and down in order to breathe would give rise to excruciating (*ex cruce*, literally "from the cross") agony. Depending on the age and health of the condemned, the process of dying could last hours or, in many cases, several days and nights. And when the ordeal was finally over, the body was typically left on the cross until the carrion devoured it, as a very public disincentive to run afoul of the Roman authorities.

Due to its horrific nature, death by crucifixion was reserved to the worst enemies of the state and to those of lowest social status: brigands, prisoners of war, traitors, and slaves. It is instructive to note that St. Paul, in virtue of his Roman citizenship, was given the far nobler death by quick decapitation, whereas St. Peter, enjoying no such privilege, was, at least according to tradition, crucified upside down. No one should be surprised to read that, even for Jews, death in this manner was appreciated as a sign of divine disfavor: "For anyone hung on a tree is under God's curse" (Deut. 21:23). Moreover, for the first followers of Jesus, his death by crucifixion was a source not only of intense personal sadness but also of deep embarrassment, since there was, for a Jew of that time, no more evident sign that someone was not the Messiah of Israel than his violent death at the hands of the enemies of Israel. For the *Mashiach* was meant to be a new David, who would deal definitively with the nation's foes and reign as the Lord of the world. Therefore, seeing the one they took to be the Messiah writhing on this instrument of torture and death, the disciples must have thought that their commitment and proclamation had been a pathetic waste of time. The whole awful process was undoubtedly a source of shame.

And yet these same disciples went careering around the world declaring precisely this crucified man as Lord and Messiah! As N.T. Wright has frequently insisted, even from a strictly historical standpoint, the emergence of Christianity as a *messianic* movement is, to say the very least, an anomaly.[28] They did not hide the fact of the Crucifixion; they brought it to the fore. Paul says to the Galatians, "It was before your eyes that Jesus Christ was publicly exhibited as crucified!" (Gal. 3:1). And to the Corinthian Christians, he declares, "For the message about the cross is foolishness to those who are perishing, but to us who are being saved it is the power of God" (1 Cor. 1:18). And to the Colossians he can say, "For in [Christ Jesus] all the fullness of God was pleased to dwell, and through him God was pleased to reconcile to himself all things, whether on earth or in heaven, by making peace through the blood of the cross" (Col. 1:19–20). Once again, given what we know about the meaning of crucifixion in the ancient world, the association of the cross of Jesus with anything like reconciliation, power, and peace is just head-shakingly bizarre.

28. N.T. Wright, *Surprised by Scripture* (New York: HarperOne, 2014), 49–52.

The only way that we can make sense of this is to affirm the Resurrection of Jesus from the dead. If the crucified and buried Jesus had simply stayed in his grave, he would have been, like any number of messianic pretenders, promptly forgotten. We will have much more to say about the Resurrection in due course, but for the moment, I want to make clear simply that the first proclaimers of Jesus understood his awful death in light of the world-changing and utterly unexpected fact that he did not remain in his grave, that he in fact appeared alive again to those who had denied, abandoned, and betrayed him. Seen through the lens of the Resurrection, the calamity of his death was reinterpreted as indeed the source of power, peace, and salvation. To grasp this is to grasp the nettle of Christianity. To miss it is to miss everything and to allow Jesus to devolve to the level of a vague spiritual teacher or stirring ethical example.

So why did they announce a crucified Messiah, and how did they come to understand the meaning of his death? The Creed cites the death of Jesus laconically enough, but the great tradition has provided a number of templates and models for interpreting it. I will explore just two of them—namely, Jesus as victor and Jesus as sacrifice. Let us take the first one first. We have already made reference to Jesus as the Christ—which is to say, the anointed successor of David. And to say this is to insinuate that Jesus imitated and indeed surpassed David by dealing with the enemies of Israel and establishing an empire centered around the worship of Israel's God. As we saw, much of his life can legitimately be considered under the rubric of opposition and confrontation. From the beginning, Jesus did battle with the powers of the world, which in turn were grounded in a dark spiritual power unseen. In light of this, we can appreciate the Crucifixion as the climactic struggle in the great *agon*.

The political and religious leadership of the time was arrayed against him and brought him to capital punishment, but if we read the artfully crafted Passion narratives in each of the four Gospels, we see that the entire array of God's enemies, the full tide of the *tohu wabohu*, in fact swept him to his cross. The betrayal visited upon him by one of his most intimate followers, the general stupidity and cowardice of his disciples, the denial enunciated by his friend Peter, the corruption and blindness of the Jewish Sanhedrin, the scapegoating violence of Caiaphas the High Priest, the irresponsibility of Herod, the indifference to truth displayed by Pilate, the bloodthirsty cruelty of the Roman soldiery, the mockery of the passersby—all of it came after him, inundated him, overwhelmed him. On the cross, Jesus was David against Goliath, a naked and defenseless young man facing the giant bearing scimitar and spear and clothed in armor.

But he fought, not in the conventional manner, not meeting force with force, not answering fire with fire, but rather, in accord with his own teaching from the Sermon on the Mount, with nonviolence, turning the other cheek, saying, "Father, forgive them; for they do not know what they are doing" (Luke 23:34). It is crucially important to bear in mind that we are dealing here not simply with a heroic human being, but rather with the Son of God, the one who is "God from God, Light from Light, true God from true God." *God* is fighting those forces opposed to him, and he is doing it in a way congruent with his own nature. Bob Dylan said, "The enemy I see wears the cloak of decency," and this is exactly why part of the saving work of the Son of God was to draw the dark powers, which typically hide themselves behind a cloak of respectability, out into the open.[29] In sharp contrast to the speech, action, and purpose of the Son of God, the enemies of Jesus show themselves for what they are.

Properly unmasked, the very worst of the dark powers, both visible and invisible, were hurled at him, and he responded by swallowing them up in the ever greater, ever more powerful, divine mercy. The "world" is allowed to do its worst, spending itself on him, and he wears it down. There is a martial art called aikido, which does not so much match one's opponent with force, but rather uses the force of the opponent against him. Thus, for instance, the practitioner of aikido will take advantage of his partner's momentum in order to throw him to the floor. The purpose of this fighting art is not to harm the opponent but to frustrate his efforts, eventually convincing him

29. Bob Dylan, "Slow Train," track 4 on *Slow Train Coming*, Columbia, 1979.

that he cannot win. There is a good deal of aikido in Jesus' victorious struggle on the cross: his nonviolence and infinite divine forgiveness effectively undermine wickedness, giving it nothing from which it could draw further energy, absorbing all of its momentum. Thus, in a very real sense, Jesus on the cross "takes away the sin of the world" (John 1:29).

Many of the Fathers of the Church attempted to express the significance of Jesus' death through the metaphor of battle, giving rise to what came to be characterized as the *Christus Victor* theory.[30] In one version of this scenario, the devil is pictured as a great fish and the humanity of Jesus as the bait on a hook. When the devil, enticed by the opportunity of conquering this particularly heroic man, takes the bait, he is caught on the hook, which is evocative of the hidden divinity of the Lord. A tad fanciful, but still telling. The powers of the world did indeed perceive Jesus as one man among many and did indeed try to stamp him out, but what they did not see was the capaciousness of the divine forgiveness concealed behind the icon of Jesus' humanity. In devouring him, they found their own wickedness devoured.

In another version of the *Christus Victor* scenario, the devil is imagined as a kidnapper, who has absconded with the human race and holds every person tightly in his arms. Jesus appears as the perfect, untrammeled man and offers himself to the devil in exchange for his prisoners. So beguiled by the prospect of catching this supreme prize, the evil one opens his arms, releasing the entire human race, and makes to seize the Lord. At this point, Jesus reveals his hidden divinity, which is more than powerful enough to overwhelm the devil, who finds himself now utterly bereft and defeated. Again, this is a highly imaginative, even comical, picture, but it speaks a rather profound truth. Human beings are meant to belong to God and to serve his purposes. Through sin, they have effectively handed themselves over to an alien lord; they have become slaves of a ruthless taskmaster. The very purity and perfection of Jesus' humanity beguiles the forces of darkness and draws them out. In the very act of taking him, they let go of what they had held captive.

---

30. Gustaf Aulén, *Christus Victor: An Historical Study of the Three Main Types of the Idea of Atonement*, trans. A.G. Herbert (Eugene, OR: Wipf & Stock, 2003).

A remarkable contemporary presentation of this form of the *Christus Victor* theory is Clint Eastwood's 2008 film *Gran Torino.* The main character, Walt Kowalski, is a retired Detroit autoworker, who has come to befriend a young man from the Hmong community named Thao, who had moved into the house next door. Though he has no interest in joining their number, Thao is terrified into cooperating with a local gang of Hmong thugs. When he attempts to escape their influence, they shoot up his house, putting his family in mortal peril. Sensing that his young friend is caught in a hopeless situation that will effectively compromise the rest of his life, Walt decides to act. One night, he makes his way to the gang headquarters and, from the street, loudly berates them and names their crimes. This harangue brings the gang members out into the open and also prompts a number of neighbors to see what is happening. After indicating each of the belligerents with his finger, Walt pulls a lighter out of his coat pocket, but he does so in such a way as to suggest he is drawing a gun. In their alarm, the young men open fire and shoot Walt to death. As the camera pulls up and away from his body, we can see that he lies in the attitude of the crucified Jesus, the lighter resting in his limp right hand. The essential features of the *Christus Victor* are all in place: a human being held captive by wicked forces; no escape from the imprisonment through the effort of the imprisoned; an act of self-sacrificial love that both exposes the wickedness of the wicked and liberates the imprisoned. If the Church Fathers' narrative seems a bit contrived, watch this film and you will find the dynamics beautifully laid out.

The human race is indeed like Thao, held bound by an entire nexus of dysfunction, and we have no conventional way out of our dilemma. Jesus, by a great act of self-sacrificial love, both exposed the enemies of the human race for what they are and liberated those held prisoner. An ancient Advent hymn expresses the feeling-tone that surrounds this theory: "O Come, O Come, Emmanuel, and ransom captive Israel, that mourns in lonely exile here, until the Son of God appear." The *Christus Victor* approach helps us to see how the cross of Jesus has functioned, up and down the centuries, as a sort of taunt to the powers of the world. As we saw, for Jesus' contemporaries, there was nothing more terrifying than a Roman cross—and yet the first Christians held it up, celebrated it, proclaimed it. What was meant to be an inconvertible sign of Roman power became the inconvertible sign of its defeat. And so it has functioned to the present day as a warning to the avatars of sin and a beacon to those whom sin has imprisoned.

Here we call to mind N.T. Wright's insistence that one of the principal tasks of the Messiah was to deal definitively with Israel's enemies.[31] Jesus did indeed battle them all the way down, entering into a kind of hand-to-hand combat with them. But he did not employ the weapons of the world. Isaiah 52 speaks of Yahweh "[baring] his holy arm before the eyes of all the nations," so that everyone might see "the salvation of our God" (Isa. 52:10). Who would have guessed that the bared holy arm of Yahweh would be the naked arm of Jesus, nailed to a cross? But the whole world did indeed come to see the salvation effected by the God of Israel, for over that cross Pontius Pilate, with unintended irony, placed a sign declaring in the three great languages of that time and place—Hebrew, Latin, and Greek—that the crucified Jesus was "the King of the Jews."

A second great template for understanding the meaning of Jesus' death is that of sacrifice. Admittedly, the idea of making a sacrifice in order to placate divine powers is, to say the least, alien to our contemporary consciousness. And the classical idea that Jesus performed on the cross a bloody sacrifice that was somehow demanded by his Father strikes many people today as, at best, incredible, and at worst, the archetype of both patriarchal oppression and child abuse. I can testify that when I was going through university and seminary studies, the notion, usually associated with St. Anselm, that Jesus' death involved a sacrificial atonement for sin was customarily dismissed in favor of Abelard's far gentler theory that the supreme love exhibited on the cross in turn awakened love in us. At the same time, I will admit that, even as I took in these explanations, it occurred to me that Abelard's theory would not make sense unless it were, in some sense, tied to Anselm's explanation,

31. N.T. Wright, *Simply Christian: Why Christianity Makes Sense* (New York: HarperOne, 2006), 105–108.

for otherwise, how would a figure dying pathetically on a Roman cross be seen as performing an act of love?

Of course, an even more fundamental problem with dismissing the Anselmian theory out of hand is that, in its basic outlines, it is grounded unambiguously in the Scriptures. In describing the contours of his mission, Jesus himself says, "The Son of Man came not to be served but to serve, and to give his life a ransom for many" (Mark 10:45). And the night before his death, in reference to the Passover bread and cup, he clearly gave a sacrificial interpretation to the cross that he would endure the following day: "This is my body, which is given for you"; and even more tellingly, "This cup that is poured out for you is the new covenant in my blood" (Luke 22:19–20). Moreover, in Ephesians, we find what is unmistakably temple talk: "Therefore be imitators of God, as beloved children, and live in love, as Christ loved us and gave himself up for us, a fragrant offering and sacrifice to God" (Eph. 5:1–2). And in Romans, Paul says, "They are now justified by his grace as a gift, through the redemption that is in Christ Jesus, whom God put forward as a sacrifice of atonement" (Rom. 3:24–25), and in First Corinthians, he recommends, "Clean out the old yeast so that you may be a new batch, as you really are unleavened. For our paschal lamb, Christ, has been sacrificed" (1 Cor. 5:7). And there are many more such passages from the New Testament that we could cite. Therefore, it is certainly facile to argue that the Anselmian theory represents simply a medieval accretion.

In order to understand this approach to the death of Jesus, it is best to commence with the biblical idea of sacrifice, the basic logic of which is actually quite straightforward. The religious devotee would take some aspect of God's creation—the first fruits of his harvest, food products, unblemished animals, etc.—and he would offer them back to God in order to indicate thanksgiving, reparation, petition, or sorrow for sins. The Bible is eminently clear—and this is backed up by good metaphysics—that the true God has no *need* of such offerings, for indeed how could the Creator of the totality of the universe ever benefit from what he himself already gave in its entirety? The author of Psalm 50 puts these words in the mouth of God, upbraiding his people lest they think the Lord gains something from their sacrifices: "For every wild animal of the forest is mine, the cattle on a thousand hills. I know all the birds of the air, and all that moves in the field is mine . . . for the world and all that is in it is mine" (Ps. 50:10–12).

Nevertheless, such sacrificial gestures are for the good of the one who makes them, bringing him or her on line with God, re-establishing right relationship with the Creator. In that sense, God is "pleased" with our offerings, since his delight is in what redounds to our benefit. In terms of the Crucifixion of Jesus, the type of sacrifice that comes to the fore is the sacrifice of expiation or reparation. When someone presented himself at the Jerusalem temple to make this sort of sacrifice, he would bring an unblemished animal—bull, sheep, goat, or dove—and would, with the assistance of the priest, slit the animal's throat while the priest caught the blood in a bowl. Then the beast would be burned, either whole (a holocaust) or partially, returning it thereby to God. The spiritual psychology behind the gesture seems to have been this: what is happening to this animal should, by rights, be happening to me. The goat or bull was, as it were, standing in for the person who offered it, representing him in a quasi-sacramental manner.

This substitutionary dynamic was on particularly clear display on the Day of Atonement, the one day in the Jewish liturgical year when the high priest was allowed to enter the Holy of Holies in the temple. He slaughtered and sacrificed a number of animals in the course of the day, but the spiritual highpoint was the symbolic imposition of the sins of Israel onto the scapegoat within the Holy of Holies. The animal so burdened was then driven from the temple and, led by a priest, brought deep into the desert where he was abandoned to certain death. Symbolically, he thereby bore away the sins of the people, representing both their degradation and their repentance before God. Again, though unfamiliar to us, this sort of representational thinking was absolutely standard within the cultural framework of the biblical authors. The idea perdured to the dawn of modern times in the figure of the monarch, who, in a very real way, represented all the people; we can also see it in the story of David and Goliath, in which two individuals fought in the name of their respective armies.

There was, even within the Old Testament, furthermore, an analogy between the animal sacrifice offered in the temple and a sin-offering sacrifice made directly by a human being, representative of the entire nation. I am referring, of course, to a series of mysterious and extraordinary texts in the fifty-second and fifty-third chapters of the book of the prophet Isaiah. As we saw, the prophet envisions a time when the God of Israel would be victorious, but then he segues almost immediately into the surprising description of the one through whom that victory would be won: "See, my servant shall prosper; he shall be exalted and lifted up, and shall be very high. Just as there were many who were astonished at him—so marred was his appearance, beyond human semblance, and his form beyond that of mortals—so he shall startle many nations" (Isa. 52:13–15).

But why is his appearance so repellant? "He was despised and rejected by others; a man of suffering and acquainted with infirmity. . . . Surely he has borne our infirmities and carried our diseases. . . . He was wounded for our transgressions, crushed for our iniquities; upon him was the punishment that made us whole, and by his bruises we are healed" (Isa. 53:4–5). His degradation, in a word, was the direct result of his functioning as the lamb of sacrifice and the scapegoat for the entire people. What would happen to him should by rights be happening to the whole of Israel; the sins of the entire nation would be placed upon his shoulders so that he could bear them away. Though, as we have said, this kind of representational thinking is rather foreign to our individualistic social psychology, it was altogether standard for ancient Israel.

Just as the animals brought to the temple for sacrifice should be unblemished, so this suffering servant would be a man of righteousness and innocence: "He was oppressed, and he was afflicted, yet he did not open his mouth; like a lamb that is led to the slaughter, and like a sheep that before its shearers is silent, so he did not open his mouth" (Isa. 53:7). After his death, they would bury him with the wicked, "although he had done no violence, and there was no deceit in his mouth" (Isa. 53:9). His complete moral integrity would appear to be a condition for the possibility of his performing his sacrificial function, since otherwise he would presumably have to make reparation for his own sins. To bear the sins of the whole nation, he would have to be sinless: "The righteous one, my servant, shall make many righteous" (Isa. 53:11). In light of temple practice and these extraordinary texts, it is not difficult to see why the first Christians reached for sacrificial language when attempting to explain the significance of Jesus' terrible death. They saw an innocent man, their sinless Lord, indeed someone who, even in the midst of the agony of crucifixion, uttered not a curse but a blessing on those who were killing him, taking upon himself a thoroughly undeserved punishment. Like the lamb of sacrifice, they thought, his blood was being poured out as a substitute for our blood; like the scapegoat, he was being driven into the wilderness to die, as by rights we should.

At this point, I should like to return to St. Anselm's theory and look at it with fresh eyes. In accord with his rationalistic tendencies and under the influence of his feudalistic culture, Anselm speaks of the offended honor of God the Father and of the requirement, in strict justice, that a price be paid to restore that honor.[32] Since the offense of sin belongs to the human race, a human being had to be involved in the payment, but since the offense to the honor of God is infinite, only God could *adequately* pay it. Therefore, the righteous anger of the Father could be quieted only by the suffering and death of someone who is both God and man.[33] This bit of theological reasoning, which explained with admirable economy *cur Deus homo* (why God became man), was one of the great intellectual achievements of the Middle Ages. And its principal virtue is that it takes the real damage of sin—what Anselm calls the *pondus peccati* (the weight of sin)—seriously.[34]

32. Anselm, *Why God Became Man* 1.11, in *Anselm of Canterbury: The Major Works* (New York: Oxford World's Classics, 2008), 282–284.

33. Anselm, 2.6, 319–320.

34. Anselm, *Cur Deus homo* 21 (PL 158:393–394), *Why God Became Man*, 305–306.

Why could not God simply forgive human wickedness with a wave of his hand, with a stentorian decree? Of course, as Thomas Aquinas indicates, God could have done so, but such a detached pronouncement would not have *dealt* with sin. It would not have *repaired* what needed repairing.[35] Anselm taught that humanity is like a beautiful pearl that had fallen into the muck, indeed to the very bottom of it. God might have declared the pearl clean, but this would have done nothing to restore it to its pristine beauty. Instead, God had to descend into the muck, indeed to the very bottom of it, in order to seize the pearl, and then he had to draw it out and clean it off.[36] I would urge us not to think of the restoration of the Father's honor as something taking place within the psychology of the Father, but rather something taking place in us and for us, since God's honor or glory is precisely that we be fully alive. God is "offended" by sin, not in the sense that his subjective well-being is compromised, but in the sense that he hates and wants to eliminate whatever harms his beloved creatures. I will confess that here is where Anselm's language, especially for contemporary audiences, remains problematic. To speak of a blood sacrifice required to calm an exquisitely offended sense of honor does seem to project onto God the Father a good deal of psychological dysfunction. But if we recontextualize it a bit, we can appreciate that Anselm is imagining Isaiah's suffering servant, not simply as a human hero willing to represent the entire race, but as the God-man taking upon himself the sins of the world in order to take them away, to pay the price, to set things right.

Further light might be shed on both templates if we consider the theorizing of Hans Urs von Balthasar regarding the cross of Jesus as the furthest trajectory of the Incarnation.[37] Following the prompt provided by the famous hymn in the second chapter of Paul's Letter to the Philippians, Balthasar appreciates the Incarnation as a downward movement, from equality with God, to identity with the human race: "Though he was in the form of God, [Jesus] did not regard equality with God as something to be exploited, but emptied himself,

35. Thomas Aquinas, *Summa theologiae* 3.1.2.

36. Anselm, *Why God Became Man*, 301.

37. Hans Urs von Balthasar, *Mysterium Paschale*, trans. Aidan Nichols (San Francisco: Ignatius Press, 2000).

taking the form of a slave, being born in human likeness" (Phil. 2:6–7). But the descent of the Son of God did not stop with his becoming human, for "being found in human form, he humbled himself and became obedient to the point of death—even death on a cross" (Phil. 2:6–8). How wonderfully that last phrase sums up everything we said above about the horror of crucifixion. The point is that God went all the way down, as far as he could go in the direction of godforsakenness, taking on pain, sickness, psychological and spiritual distress, even the agony of total isolation from God. He thereby made all of them potentially a route of access to the Father, effectively sanctifying them. Or, if we wish to shift the metaphor, he "conquered" them, robbing them of their power permanently to separate us from God. Or, to put it in the sacrificial context, he took them on in order to take them away.

One might summarize this theology of the cross as follows. The Son of God went to the limits of alienation from God so that even as the worst sinner runs with all of her energy away from the Father, she finds herself running into the arms of the Son. Here we can see the deep soteriological implications of the Trinitarian doctrine. It is only because God can, so to speak, open himself up, become other to himself while remaining one in essence, that he can embrace all of sin, even the most thoroughgoing rebellion. This is the condition for the possibility of the victorious battle of the cross and of the efficacious sacrifice of the cross.

Within sight of the temple, the Crucifixion of Jesus, involving victim and shed blood, was the work of a high priest. We recall that the vocation of Adam and hence of all humanity after him is, on the biblical reading, to be priest of creation—that is to say, the one who offers right praise to God on behalf of all creatures. Sin is a compromising of this vocation. Israel was founded as a priestly people, the nation whose praise was to bring all of humanity, in time, back on line. Precisely because of sin, the act of worshiping God had become painful, sacrificial, for it involved, necessarily, a twisting back into shape what had been twisted out of shape. All of this is summed up and brought to full expression in the consummately priestly act of Jesus on the cross, as he gives right praise to the Father, even while bearing the sins of the world.

Pilate's sign, affixed to the cross of Jesus, announcing the crucified one as King of the Jews was, by implication, a declaration that he was King of the world, for this association was basic to the messianic expectation. So the cross is an altar where an offering is made; it is also a throne from which a King reigns. Spreading the news of this kingship was precisely the work of St. Paul, who refers, again and again, to "Jesus the Lord," *Iesous Kyrios*, an intentional play on *Kaiser kyrios* (Caesar is Lord), a common acknowledgement of the authority of the Roman emperor. Like Pilate, Paul announced to the dominant cultures of his time that a new allegiance was owed.

After mentioning the death that Jesus suffered, the Creed adds, simply enough, "and was buried." Is there anything that signals the finality and irreversibility of death more than burial? While the wake and funeral services for a loved one are ongoing, there is still a sense that they are with us; but when the body is lowered into the grave and covered over by earth, we know that they have left us forever, that they are, as the ancient Romans put it, no longer *inter homines* (among human beings). In his meditation on the burial of Jesus, Karl Barth invites us to call to mind a scene when all of our family members and friends are gathered around a grave, prayers are said, and then everyone returns home for a meal.[38] But you are not with them. You are the one left behind. To affirm, therefore, that Jesus was buried is to affirm that he was truly dead. Over the centuries, there have been fanciful attempts to show that Jesus did not die on the cross but swooned, only to be revived later. That a dreadfully wounded man, staggering half-dead out of his tomb, would ever be mistaken for the risen Lord is, of course, beyond ludicrous. The Romans were skilled executioners, and if there were any doubt that the cross had done its terrible work, the lance-thrust into the heart of Jesus should have eliminated it. It is interesting to note that the Gospels themselves and numerous summary statements of the Paschal Mystery throughout the New Testament make special reference to the burial of the Lord, presumably to hammer home the facticity of his death.

38. Karl Barth, *Dogmatics in Outline*, trans. G.T. Thomson (New York: Harper & Row, 1959), 114–120.

In his study of this article of the Creed, Balthasar speaks of the *Todsein Gottes*, literally the "being dead" of God.[39] He means that the downward trajectory of the Incarnation reaches its limit here, in the tomb of Jesus, when the Son of God enters into the experience of having no experience, into the negation, the nonbeing, of death. Having hit rock-bottom, the Son of God finds solidarity with all those human beings who have come to that same awful place. The *Catechism of the Catholic Church* cites an ancient homily on Holy Saturday, which highlights the silence and passivity of the buried Christ: "Today a great silence reigns on earth, a great silence and a great stillness. A great silence because the King is asleep."[40] In this context, Balthasar makes reference to Hans Holbein's ghastly depiction of the dead Christ, in the presence of which Dostoevsky himself fell into a state of agitation, a scene reproduced in his novel *The Idiot.* Most depictions of the dead Jesus are placid and serene, the Lord appearing to be asleep, the Resurrection a sure expectation. But Holbein's picture, clearly based upon his observations of a real corpse, is horrific. The wounds of Jesus are large and discolored, his eyes are half-opened, his chin up-turned and distended, his entire body turning a sickly blue, and rigor mortis rather obviously setting in. Prince Myshkin, the main character in Dostoevsky's story, cries out upon seeing Holbein's canvas: "Why, a man's faith might be ruined by looking at that picture!"[41] Unless and until we feel something along those lines, we probably have not come to grips with what it means to say that Christ was buried. Indeed, a superficial faith might be wrecked by coming into contact with Christ truly dead and buried, but a robust faith accepts this truth as integral to the entire event of the enfleshment of the Son of God, his identification with the whole of what it means to be human.

Though the Nicene Creed simply says "and was buried," the Apostles' Creed, after mentioning his burial, says of the dead Jesus that he "descended into hell." There are, most likely, two biblical references that stand behind

39. Balthasar, *Mysterium Paschale*, 168–188.
40. *Catechism of the Catholic Church* 635.
41. Fyodor Dostoevsky, *The Idiot*, trans. Eva M. Martin (Overland Park, KS: Digireads, 2018), 172.

this claim. The first is the assertion, expressed in numerous places in the Old Testament, that the dead go to a shadowy underworld called *Sheol.* This is not a place of heavenly refreshment or spiritual fulfillment; it is instead a dismal and dissatisfying realm, where shades of human beings live a sort of half-life, cut off from community and, most painfully, the praise of God. A particularly telling description of *Sheol* can be found in Psalm 88: "I am counted among those who go down to the Pit; I am like those who have no help, like those forsaken among the dead, like the slain that lie in the grave, like those whom you remember no more, for they are cut off from your hand" (Ps. 88:4–5). Jesus' descent into hell means that he has entered into solidarity with those at the furthest possible remove from the mercy of God. Though it is odd to say, it coheres with a Trinitarian logic: God goes to those cut off from God and overcomes thereby a separation that could never be overcome from the human side.

And this brings us to the second scriptural inspiration behind the doctrine of Christ's descent into hell—namely, 1 Peter 3:18–19: "He was put to death in the flesh, but made alive in the spirit, in which also he went and made a proclamation to the spirits in prison, who in former times did not obey." The prison in question here is undoubtedly *Sheol*, and the prisoners are those dead who, in their lifetimes, had wandered from the path of God. That Jesus preached the Gospel, or better, revealed it in his very person, to these long-forgotten people, is a source of tremendous consolation. How else could we possibly claim the possibility of salvation for those who had lived and died before the saving event of the Incarnation? This passage helps us see that what happened in Jesus, since it was grounded in a properly divine subject, has a ramification across all of space and time. Might we follow the prompts of *Lumen Gentium*, one of the most striking of the documents of the Second Vatican Council, and speak of the possibility that non-Christians, even nonbelievers, across the ages, *can* be saved? If they are, *Lumen Gentium* argues, they are saved through some participation in the grace of Christ, some light that comes from Jesus, though they might not be aware of it.[42] In the case of nonbelievers, it would happen through following, honestly and courageously, the dictates of the conscience, which John Henry Newman helpfully described as the "aboriginal Vicar of Christ" in the soul.[43] The great English master was anticipating the teaching of Vatican II by insisting that the voice of conscience is, in point of fact, the voice of Christ, though anonymously so. If Jesus were but one spiritual teacher among many, this would not hold, but since he is, in person, the very Word of the Father, the dictate of conscience *is* his dictate. Thus, the "being dead" of the Son of God is not a desperate state of affairs, but rather the ground of our most extravagant hope.

IV. The Rise

"And Rose Again on the Third Day"

The Resurrection of Jesus Christ from the dead is the fulcrum on which all of Christian faith turns. If Jesus did not rise, everything in Christian theology, philosophy, social action, art, spirituality, and morality loses its *raison d'être.* As St. Paul put it, bluntly enough, "If Christ has not been raised, your faith is futile and you are still in your sins" (1 Cor. 15:17). Without faith in the Resurrection of Jesus, Christianity devolves, immediately, into a vague mythic system, religious philosophy, or generic spirituality. There has been, from the beginning of Christianity, a temptation to de-mythologize the Resurrection, turning it into a symbol or cipher. But if Jesus did not truly rise, then his claims to be speaking and acting in the person of God would be invalidated; and if these are invalidated, then all talk of Incarnation is negated; and if Incarnation does not hold, then the dogma of the Trinity falls away. And if the Trinity collapses, all speech about the Holy Spirit is nugatory. And if there is no Holy Spirit, it makes no

42. *Lumen Gentium* 16, in *The Word on Fire Vatican II Collection*, ed. Matthew Levering (Park Ridge, IL: Word on Fire Institute, 2021), 66–68.

43. John Henry Newman, "A Letter Addressed to the Duke of Norfolk," in *Certain Difficulties Felt by Anglicans in Catholic Teaching*, vol. 2 (London: Longmans & Green, 1900), 248.

sense to refer to the Church or to its sacraments. Finally, if Christ has not been raised, then we have no reasonable hope of personal resurrection. What I have just demonstrated is that 90% of the Creed craters in upon itself if Resurrection faith disappears. So wrestling with this strange "be-all and end-all" teaching is required work for every generation of Christian believers.

To be fair, the de-literalizing tendency, found in both the ancient Gnostics and in too much of contemporary theology, is, in a way, understandable, for this proposition has always been, to put it mildly, hard to believe. It is a gross misrepresentation to argue, as some do today, that ancient people, in their prescientific naïveté, were apt to believe any wild claim. They might have been prescientific, but they were not foolish. The assertion that a dead man had come back to life and had been seen by eyewitnesses was as staggering and improbable then as now. For just one bit of evidence in this regard, consider the scoffing reaction of the sophisticated Athenian crowd when Paul proclaimed the Resurrection of Jesus, as reported in Acts 17. But as Søren Kierkegaard said, the purpose of Christian theology is to make Christianity *hard* to believe.[44] As counter-intuitive as this seems, this move is indispensable lest the faith decline into a mere echo of the culturally regnant philosophy or psychology—in other words, into something not worth believing. The *hardest* doctrine to accept—and hence the most important doctrine of all—is the Resurrection.

Following the lead of N.T. Wright and many others, I would like to get at the Resurrection through a sort of *via negativa*, delineating, first, how it should not be understood.[45] In the ancient world, there were many views in the marketplace of ideas regarding what happened to someone after she died. We might start with the Jewish thought world. There are numerous texts in the Old Testament that regard death as simply the end, full stop. With physical death, the person decays and returns to dust, a philosophy defended by the Sadducees in the time of Jesus. As we saw when we examined the issue of Jesus' descent into hell, there are other texts in the Hebrew Scriptures that indicate the existence of shadowy *Sheol*, a place of virtual nonexistence,

44. See, for example, Kierkegaard, *Concluding Unscientific Postscript to* Philosophical Fragments, 186–187.

45. N.T. Wright, *The Resurrection of the Son of God* (Minneapolis, MN: Fortress, 2003), 1–206.

where the shades of the dead continue, in a deeply mitigated condition, to be. By the time of Jesus, a third proposition had gained a wide acceptance—namely, that the righteous dead would be raised bodily at the end of time, in a sort of general resurrection of the dead. In the story of the raising of Lazarus, Martha gives voice to this conviction: "I know that [Lazarus] will rise again in the resurrection on the last day" (John 11:24). The Pharisees were famous for holding this view in the first century.

But none of these frameworks applies when we examine the New Testament texts on the Resurrection of Jesus. Quite obviously, they do not cohere with the conviction that death is simply the end. But just as obviously, they have nothing to do with the belief that Jesus' soul or shade continues to exist in *Sheol.* On the contrary, they say that Jesus presented himself alive again, in his body and very much in this world. Neither are they contending that Jesus, along with all of the righteous, would rise at the end of time. Therefore, nothing from the matrix of Jewish reflection on the state of the dead is adequate to what the first witnesses of the Resurrection were reporting.

Certainly by the time of the New Testament, the classical Greek philosophical understanding of the survival of the soul was well known, especially in those parts of Mediterranean society under Hellenizing influence. Following the lead of Socrates and Plato, Greek thinkers opined that the soul, given its essentially immaterial nature, would survive the death of the body and go, happily enough, to a realm more agreeable to it, away from the particularity and changeability of matter. This point of view, though emerging from a purely philosophical context, has proven to have had an enormous influence within religious circles. I would hazard a guess that a majority of Christians hold at least a quasi-Platonic notion of what happens after we die—namely, that our disembodied souls go to heaven. But whatever can be said for the dualist view—and lots of serious people have defended it over the centuries—it does not in fact shed much light on the Resurrection of Jesus. From all of the texts that we have, it is abundantly clear that the first believers were not declaring that Jesus' disincarnate soul had left this vale of tears and gone to heaven. In the first place, though the word "soul" can be found in the Old Testament, it does not quite have, for biblically formed people, the Greek connotation of a substance separate from the body; rather, it is the life force of a living body. Secondly, all of the accounts of the Resurrection that we have in the New Testament insist on the materiality of the risen Lord. He speaks, he eats, he presents himself as concretely alive.

Of course, the philosophical was not the only thought-form for the ancient Greeks. Even more influential than Plato was the great epic poet Homer, whose account of life after death profoundly shaped the thinking of both ordinary people and sophisticates. As is evident from accounts of the afterlife state of Achilles, Patroclus, and others, the dead live in a realm not unlike the *Sheol* of the Old Testament. In this depressing underworld, the dead become "shades" or "phantoms" or "ghosts," pale simulacra of what they once were in this life. In their sadness and desperation, they sometimes reach out to the living, even sucking on the blood of sacrifices poured into the ground, but there is nothing noble or hopeful about their manner of existence—just the contrary.

Within the Roman cultural context, one certainly found the Platonic understanding of life after death. Cicero, for example, would have held to a version of it. On the more popular (and political) level, we encounter the expectation of deification (*apotheosis*) for military heroes, certain political figures, and most especially for Roman emperors. Wright cites the delicious quote attributed to the Roman emperor Vespasian while languishing on his death bed: "Oh dear, I think I'm becoming a god."[46] Such elevated figures would take their place alongside of the established deities and would live an exalted version of life here below. Still others within the Greco-Roman world—and to a degree, even within the Jewish context—believed in some version of metempsychosis, the return of the soul to a different incarnation. As in some forms of Hinduism and Buddhism, the ultimate spiritual purpose was not to come back in another form, but rather to break free of the process altogether and live in some sort of disincarnate state.

---

46. Wright, 55.

Once again, none of these frameworks apply to the New Testament accounts of Jesus' Resurrection. None of the first Christians claim that their Lord had been apotheosized in the manner of Julius Caesar or that he, like the Dalai Lama, had returned to assume another physical form. Rather, this Jesus, whom they knew and who had been crucified, appeared alive again in an embodied state. Who cannot be moved by the stunning and disconcerting description in the tenth chapter of the Acts of the Apostles? Speaking to Cornelius and his family, St. Peter blithely remarks: "But God raised him on the third day and allowed him to appear, not to all the people but to us who were chosen by God as witnesses, and who *ate and drank with him after he rose from the dead*" (Acts 10:40–41; emphasis added).

So what precisely do they claim about the resurrected Jesus? Perhaps the best way to put it is this: what some Jews expected of all the righteous dead at the end of time has happened within time to this singular figure, Jesus of Nazareth, within time. This one man has risen, even now, *ek tōn nekrōn* (literally, "from out of the dead ones") and moved once again among us. Now, having made these remarks about the objectivity and corporeality of the Resurrection, it is singularly important to emphasize that the resurrected Jesus is not like those personages described in the New Testament—the daughter of Jairus, the son of the widow of Nain, Lazarus—who came back from death but to an absolutely ordinary existence in this world and who were destined to die again. As extraordinary as those events were, they could best be described as "resuscitations," not entirely unlike what happens to those who had near-death experiences and subsequently returned to tell the tale.

Though the risen Christ is, in one sense, the same Jesus who walked the hills of Galilee and died on a Roman cross outside Jerusalem, in another sense, he is transformed, strange, not entirely of this world. This otherness is signaled, in almost all of the accounts of his post-Resurrection appearances, by the fact that the witnesses remain confused, hesitant. "Now the eleven disciples went to Galilee, to the mountain to which Jesus had directed them. When they saw him, they worshiped him; but some doubted" (Matt. 28:16–17); "While they were talking and discussing, Jesus himself came near and went with them, but their eyes were kept from recognizing him" (Luke 24:15–16); "While in their joy they were disbelieving and still wondering" (Luke 24:41); "Jesus said to them, 'Come and have breakfast.' Now none of the disciples dared to ask him, 'Who are you?' because they knew it was the Lord" (John 21:12). The consistency of this theme—especially in documents whose central purpose was to convince skeptics of the truth of the Resurrection—is striking and certainly reflects the vivid memories of those who encountered Jesus after the Resurrection. They were trying to take in something quite new, but that was appearing within the context of their ordinary experience. If I can borrow an idea from speculative physics, they were attempting to articulate what it was like to sense a phenomenon on an event horizon, on the borderline between two different dimensional systems. Signs of the uncanniness of the risen Jesus include his ability to pass through walls, to appear and disappear suddenly, and to know states of affairs even when he is not physically present.

I have been speaking at length of the apparitions of the risen Jesus, and indeed, without these, Resurrection faith would never have emerged. Attempts to argue that the Resurrection is merely a symbol for inner convictions of the Apostles—for example, their feeling of being forgiven by him or their sense that his cause would go on—are simply untenable, given the extraordinary stress on the objectivity and materiality of the risen Lord. They are also utterly incredible in an ancient Jewish context. No Jew of the first century would have used the term "resurrection" to designate something as interior as a subjective state; by that word they could only mean something that happened to a body. And it simply beggars belief that the first Christians would have had any impact if they bore the message that the spiritual cause of a crucified criminal is worthwhile, or that they felt pardoned by a dead man. Even more incredible: that many of the witnesses to the Resurrection would have gone to their deaths defending it, if all they meant is that they felt forgiven by Jesus!

But having said this, we must also acknowledge that the second indispensable element in the emergence of Resurrection faith is the empty tomb of Jesus. If the body of the Lord were still in the sarcophagus in the garden adjacent to Calvary, no number of appearances would have convinced a first-century Jew that Jesus had risen from the dead. They would have written those off as hallucinations or fantasies. Once again, given the normal connotation of "resurrection," an enemy of the faith would simply have to indicate the presence of the moldering body of Jesus in order to refute the claim that Jesus had risen from the dead. Proposals made by some contemporary writers that no one would have known the location of the tomb of Jesus since, like most common criminals, his body would have been hurled into a mass grave or simply devoured by wild animals, strain credulity. It is not the least unlikely that a figure as prominent and as revered as Jesus would have had a wealthy follower such as Joseph of Arimathea, who might well have provided a tomb for his Lord. And thus there is no reasonable ground for doubting the consistent Gospel assertion that the site of his burial was well known.

It is therefore of considerable interest that all four Gospels draw attention to the fact that Jesus' tomb was empty, St. John going so far as to describe the burial cloths left behind, even the manner of their disposition. To be sure, an empty tomb by itself would not have provided sufficient ground for belief in the Resurrection, for the body might easily enough have been stolen or moved. But when the fact of the empty tomb is combined with the numerous accounts of Jesus appearing alive again to his disciples, Resurrection faith finds firm ground.

Having determined, at least to a sufficient degree, the nature of the Resurrection, what is its significance? As we have hinted already twice, the first great implication of the Resurrection is the ratification of Jesus' daring claim to speak and act in the very person of God. Had he remained in his grave, he would have been remembered by history as at best a tragically heroic figure, but more likely, as a bit of a madman. However, having risen from his grave, he received, the first Christians were convinced, the most extraordinary confirmation possible of his identity and mission. Having seen their crucified Lord alive again, how could the disciples doubt that he was the One Sent, the unique Son of the Father? To put this in the properly Jewish context, the Resurrection was vivid proof that Jesus was indeed the Messiah of Israel, the culmination of the story of salvation. He was the fulfillment of covenant, temple, prophecy, and Torah—all of the great institutions of Israel. As St. Paul would put it, Jesus is the "yes" to all the promises God made to his holy people (2 Cor. 1:20), though that "yes" came in a remarkably unexpected way.

Secondly, the Resurrection provided an entirely new interpretive lens for the reading of Jesus' Crucifixion. As we saw, dying on a cross was, in the old dispensation, a perfect indication of failure on the part of the victim, and victory on the part of the political establishment that passed the terrible sentence. But the rising of Jesus proved beyond doubt that the power of God is greater than the power of Caesar, greater than the power of Rome—and indeed, as we read in St. John's Gospel, "greater than all else" (John 10:29). The Messiah, the new David, was indeed victorious, but in a manner that no one envisioned. When Jesus appeared alive again to those who had betrayed, denied, and abandoned him at his moment of greatest need, he did indeed show his wounds in order to remind them of what "the world" had done to him. However, he then uttered not a word of condemnation or recrimination, but rather the word *shalom* (peace), which sums up the hope of Israel and the intention of God toward his people and toward his entire creation. The nonviolence and forgiveness of God swallowed up the violence and wickedness of the dysfunctional human family. The epic war with death and the ways of death, whose climactic battle was fought on the cross, has ended with God's victory. To be sure, death and its effects and accompaniments have not disappeared, but their tyranny is over, for Jesus is Lord. The mop-up work belongs to the Church—but more on that anon.

I mentioned above that the kingship of Christ was declared, ironically enough, by Pontius Pilate. If Jesus had not risen from the dead, Pilate's mocking sign would have remained just one more affirmation of Roman power; but given the Resurrection, it became the first great act of evangelization. The term *euangelion* (glad tidings) is indeed redolent of the book of the prophet Isaiah—"How beautiful upon the mountains are the feet of the messenger . . . who brings good news" (Isa. 52:7)—but it was also, in Jesus' time and place, a word with strong political overtones. When Caesar won a victory, evangelists were sent out with the *euangelion*, the glad tidings that Rome had triumphed. How wonderful that the first Christians played with this term, turning it around for their own purpose, declaring a victory not of Caesar but of Christ. The opening line of the Gospel of Mark, which by common scholarly consensus was the first Gospel written, expresses this admirably: "The beginning of the good news of Jesus Christ, the Son of God." Not only has the word *euangelion* been co-opted, but so has the title "Son of God," which was, from the time of the Emperor Augustus, an imperial prerogative. What Mark is not so subtly insinuating is that there is a new Emperor, who has supplanted the old one through winning a great victory, and that he, Mark, is the proud evangelist, bearing this Good News. Given all of this, it is easy to see why the powers that be have always trembled at a bold and realistic declaration of the Resurrection. If God has truly raised a victim of a corrupt government to life again, then his judgment has fallen on institutional injustice. Vaguely metaphorical and symbolic explications of the Resurrection pose no such difficulty to the status quo—and hence are encouraged and subsidized.

Next, the Resurrection demonstrated that the sacrifice of the cross had been accepted. As I clarified above, this has nothing to do with the successful mollification of a dysfunctional father's anger. Rather, it means that the work of reparation on behalf of the entire human race has been done. Something has been offered back to the Father—namely, the loving obedience of the Son—which is so pleasing to God that it effectively rights the wrongs of the world, wiping away the debt of sin. What appears in the Resurrection of Jesus are the fruits of that reparation, the effects of that sacrifice. The Son of God journeyed to the furthest extreme of alienation from God—he made that supreme sacrifice—in order that he might reach even the most desperate sinner and open up a path of return.

If Jesus had simply stayed in his tomb, that path would not have opened up, and his sacrifice would have been a meaningless gesture. But when he returns from utter desolation with the divine forgiveness on his lips, he gives hope to every sinner. In an ecstatic outburst in the eighth chapter of his Letter to the Romans, St. Paul expresses the implication of Christ's sacrificial death and glorious Resurrection: "For I am convinced that neither death, nor life, nor angels, nor rulers, nor things present, nor things to come, nor powers, nor height, nor depth, nor anything else in all creation, will be able to separate us from the love of God in Christ Jesus our Lord" (Rom. 8:37–39). Paul knows this precisely because we killed God, and God returned in forgiving love. If Jesus had been simply a heroic human being who had sacrificed himself for others and if, through a great miracle, he returned, like Lazarus, to life, we would have been astounded—but we would not have been saved. Only when the most nefarious possible sin—the killing of God—was answered with God's compassion did we come to know what Paul expresses in Romans chapter 8. As the Apostle put it in verse 31 of that same crucial chapter of Romans: "If God is for us, who is against us?"

The two implications that we have drawn so far are conditioned by a more "Thomist" understanding of the Incarnation—namely, that God became flesh so as to address the problem of sin and death. But if we look at the Resurrection in a more "Scotist" mode, another dimension opens up rather dramatically. We recall that Duns Scotus had argued that the Son of God would have become incarnate even if we had never sinned, since the ultimate purpose of the enfleshment of God is not to repair dysfunction but to bring creation to its glorious fulfillment. St. Paul spoke often of Christ within this cosmic perspective as the one who would "recapitulate" all of nature and history—that is to say, to draw them under his headship and cause them to realize their deepest meaning and potential. The Resurrection of Jesus from the dead indicates, as dramatically as possible, that God has not given up on his creation, and that his intent is to bring all of it, even lowly matter, to a glorious state of being. Just as God created all of matter—even the humblest instantiations of it—so he intends to save all matter. Platonic salvation is indeed about the escape of the soul from the prison of the body, but biblical salvation *always* involves the body.

The stress upon the physicality of the resurrected Jesus in the Gospel accounts is not simply to emphasize the objectivity of it, but also the *materiality* of it. Jesus' body, indeed still bearing the scars of his Crucifixion, has been elevated and perfected. In what does this elevation consist? St. Paul made bold to speak of a *soma pneumatikon* (a spiritual body; 1 Cor. 15:42–44) that we will one day receive and that will bring us into conformity with Jesus' risen flesh; but what does this mean precisely? Though we will never fully know this side of death, the body of the resurrected Jesus gives us, the tradition holds, some clues. Thomas Aquinas is particularly instructive in this regard. Thomas speaks of four qualities of the spiritual body: subtlety, agility, impassibility, and clarity.[47]

By the first he means the capacity to pass through other bodies, the prime example being the risen Jesus' ability to traverse walls and doors. It is fascinating to note that those who report near-death experiences often speak of possessing precisely this power to pass effortlessly from place to place and to move through barriers and boundaries. In a famous case, a person felt herself floating above her body, which lay motionless on the operating table, and then she moved out of the room and outside the walls of the hospital, where she spied a very particular item perched on a ledge on the exterior of the building.[48] Would subtlety even have to do with the capacity to enter into the body of another—not aggressively but as an expression of intimacy and communion?

By "agility," Thomas means a coordination of body and soul so complete that whatever the soul desires, the body can perform. If the mind and heart can envision it, the agile body can do it. We get a hint at what agility means by looking at highly trained athletes, who can perform extraordinary feats, precisely in the measure that their training, their desire, their imagination, and their will are so developed, so refined, that their bodies, almost automatically, follow the prompts of their souls. Perhaps this helps to explain why we so love to watch athletes, musicians, and dancers at the top of their

47. Thomas Aquinas, *Summa theologiae* Suppl. 3.82–85.

48. Kimberly Clark Sharp, "Clinical Interventions with Near-Death Experiences," in *The Near-Death Experience: Problems, Prospects, Perspectives*, ed. Bruce Greyson and Charles P. Flynn (Springfield, IL: Charles C. Thomas, 1984), 242–255.

game: they are expressing as fully as one can here below what the body/soul relationship will be like for all of us in the life on high.

By "impassibility," Aquinas means that the resurrected body will not be subject to the pains, injuries, and diminishment that are simply unavoidable within this dimension. Every body here below, no matter how beautiful and strong it is, will eventually wear out, until it finally dies and deteriorates. Much of the drama, poignancy, and suffering of human life is consequent upon this awful but finally inevitable state of affairs. But none of this will obtain in the life to come. Our beauty and strength will not fade and will not be dependent upon the constant renewal that comes through food and drink, for we will be animated, so to speak, directly by the source of Life, which is God. As we saw, again and again, the New Testament writers remind us that Jesus' Resurrection is not a simple return to this life but a translation to a new pitch of existence: "But God raised him up, having freed him from death, because it was impossible for him to be held in its power" (Acts 2:24).

Finally, Thomas Aquinas speaks of the "clarity" of the risen body. In his aesthetics, Aquinas opines that the beautiful occurs at the intersection of wholeness, harmony, and *claritas* (radiance, light). Beautiful objects or faces or golf swings have integrity (they are about one thing); they have consonance (each part in balance with every other part); and they have luminosity (they shine forth). Now, we might take this third quality literally and admit that often we admire the beauty of physically bright things, but we might also read it more metaphysically to mean the luminosity of form. Of a beautiful thing or movement, we tend to say, "That is how it is supposed to be," meaning that this particular shows forth its form, or essential pattern, with striking aptness. Thomas seems to intend both of these meanings when he speaks of the *claritas* of the risen body. The brightness comes, he says, from the overflow of the luminosity of the soul into the matter of the body, the integrity of mind and will flooding flesh with light. If we want a biblical warrant for this, we should look no further than the Gospel accounts of the Transfiguration of the Lord, during which Jesus' "clothes became dazzling white, such as no one on earth could bleach them" (Mark 9:3).

In this context, I think of a peculiar remark of the great American Catholic writer Flannery O'Connor. In the face of rationalist critiques of the miraculous, O'Connor said that the Virgin Birth, the Immaculate Conception, Jesus walking on the water, and the Resurrection should be seen not as one-off exceptions to the laws of nature but revelations of the true laws of nature, of nature as it is intended to be.[49] The Resurrection of Jesus is a proleptic breakthrough even now in the midst of history of what God purposes for his creation—both spiritual and material—at the end of time. He is, as Paul puts it, "the first fruits of those who have fallen asleep" (1 Cor. 15:20), and hence his body—radiant, agile, impassible, and subtle—is an indication of what we can all hope for.

"He Ascended into Heaven"

We recall that after having clarified the nature of the Son of God, the Creed states, simply enough, "He came down from heaven," implying that he came among us not by abandoning his transcendent state but by taking to himself a human manner of existence. Just after the statement of Resurrection faith, the Creed says, completing the cycle, "He ascended into heaven." This is the *exitus-reditus* (going out and coming back) rhythm of the Incarnation: he came down and he went back up. The implication is that the humanity that he came down to embrace, he now brings up for deification. The Creed in this regard is simply imitating the hymn in the second chapter of the Letter of Paul to the Philippians: "[He] emptied himself and took the form of a slave, being born in the likeness of men. . . . God highly exalted him and gave him the name that is above every name" (Phil. 2:7, 9). The downward trajectory is the condition for the possibility of an upward trajectory; heaven came to meet earth, so that the earthly could become the heavenly; or according to the patristic formula cited above, "God became man that man might become God."

49. Flannery O'Connor, *The Habit of Being: Letters of Flannery O'Connor* (New York: Farrar, Straus & Giroux, 1979), 100. Quoted in *Flannery O'Connor Collection*, ed. Matthew Becklo (Park Ridge, IL: Word on Fire Classics, 2019), 64–65.

If we consult the very few texts in the New Testament that describe the Ascension itself—in the Gospels of Mark and Luke and in the Acts of the Apostles—we will most likely be disappointed by their lack of detail and their somewhat tensive relationship with one another. The so-called longer ending of Mark, which probably does not go back to the evangelist himself, says only, "So then the Lord Jesus, after he had spoken to them, was taken up into heaven and sat down at the right hand of God" (Mark 16:19). And St. Luke's Gospel tells us that Jesus led the disciples out to Bethany, blessed them, and then "withdrew from them and was carried up into heaven" (Luke 24:51); whereas the Acts of the Apostles, written by the same Luke, makes no mention of Bethany, but seems to situate Jesus and his disciples in Jerusalem, whence Jesus "was lifted up, and a cloud took him out of their sight" (Acts 1:9). For most of the history of Christianity, these were indeed taken as more or less literal accounts describing some "vertical movement" on the part of Jesus as he left this world. However, I do think it is fair to say that these brief statements are meant, above all, to convey the theological meaning of Jesus' definitive entry into the realm of God. It is according to that hermeneutic that I would like to address them.

In my discussion of the Resurrection, I averred that the appearances of the risen Christ might be construed as happenings along an event horizon. Though belonging substantially to the dimension of God, Jesus still communed with this world of space and time. By all accounts, these appearances continued for a time—the standard biblical frame is forty days—and then stopped. The Ascension of Jesus signals the definitive end of these post-Resurrection appearances and the commencement of Jesus' operation from the properly heavenly sphere. It is crucial to remember, however, that this distantiation by no means amounts to an abandonment, but rather to an even more intense form of intimacy. To move into heaven, or the divine manner of existence, is not to move to another place, but to that arena of existence that stands outside of space. Paul Tillich refers to God's *Überräumlichkeit* (over-spacedness), and he insists that this transcendence to any particular space implies the capacity to be present to every space. This is what we mean when we say that God is "everywhere" or ubiquitous.

Therefore, to say that Jesus has "ascended" to that sphere of existence is not to say that he has "gone away." It is to assert, if I can adopt a military metaphor, that he has journeyed to a higher point of vantage where he can see the entire field of battle and direct operations more efficaciously. With this comparison in mind, we can understand why the Creed tightly juxtaposes the affirmation of the Ascension with the claim that Jesus "is seated at the right hand of the Father." To be at the right hand of the king and to be in the seated position is to have assumed the role of plenipotentiary, something like a prime minister or chief vizier. The point is that Jesus is ruling his Church, indeed ruling the entire world, with the full authority of the Father. From his heavenly throne, he sees all, directs all, and intends to draw all to himself.

Though the explicit descriptions of the moment of Ascension are, as we saw, only few, there are numerous biblical references to the reign of Jesus. When asked at his trial whether he is the Messiah, Jesus responded: "I am; and 'you will see the Son of Man seated at the right hand of the Power,' and 'coming with the clouds of heaven'" (Mark 14:62). In Peter's great kerygmatic sermon on the morning of the first Pentecost, we hear: "This Jesus God raised up, and of that all of us are witnesses. Being therefore exalted at the right hand of God, and having received from the Father the promise of the Holy Spirit, he has poured out this that you both see and hear" (Acts 2:32–33). In the ecstatic poem that makes up much of the first chapter of Paul to the Ephesians, we read, "God put this power to work in Christ when he raised him from the dead and seated him at his right hand in the heavenly places. . . . He has put all things under his feet and has made him the head over all things for the church, which is his body, the fullness of him who fills all in all" (Eph. 1:20, 22–23). And to give just one more example, the Letter to the Hebrews is explicitly clear regarding both the ontological status of Jesus and his capacity to rule: "[Jesus] is the reflection of God's glory and the exact imprint of God's very being, and he sustains all things by his powerful word. When he had made purification for sins, he sat down at the right hand of the Majesty on high" (Heb. 1:3).

I fully realize that many contemporary readers become uneasy whenever talk turns to the absolute and all-embracing power of a king. This Jesus, reigning from on high, might appear to many as a threat to freedom, but it is most important to see that the ascended Jesus is in fact a judgment on all corrupt and oppressive forms of human authority. The one who reigns at the right hand of the Father, the one who is directing the work of his Church for the sake of the transformation of the world, is none other than the crucified Jesus of Nazareth, the nonviolent victim of corrupt power. He was a threat to the worldly authorities of his time, and he was the scourge of the supernatural Accuser who controlled (and controls) all forms of human organization. As the plenipotentiary of the Father, the exact imprint of the Father's being, he represents the divine law of love and hence functions as a criterion by which all authority here below ought to be exercised. And mind you, the ascended Jesus is not simply "God" ruling the world, but precisely the God-man. This means that something of the human has found its way into the realm of God—that is to say, God's manner of reigning. Therefore, all earthly rulers can find in the ascended Lord a model, a spur, an inspiration.

Though I have stressed that the Ascension of Jesus does not mean that the Lord has "gone away," I would like equally to stress that, in another sense, his Ascension does represent a kind of clearing of space for others to do his work here below. Precisely as embodied, Jesus does indeed exist in a kind of mutually exclusive relationship to other bodies. Thus, if he were still present on earth, he would crowd anyone else out of the position that he holds. Imagine what the political arena would be like if Lincoln, Churchill, Roosevelt, and Napoleon still strode the stage: there would be room for no one else. In this sense, the "disappearance" of the Lord from the stage of history enables others to imitate him in creative ways. It opens up the arena for the saints, who participate in his governance, each in a distinctive way.

So far, we have been discussing the Ascension of Jesus under the more or less "political" rubric of his reign, his active direction of his Church. But there is an equally important dimension of the ascended Christ's action—namely, the liturgical. We saw that the cross of Jesus must be understood as an act of priestly sacrifice. Representing the entire human race, Jesus offers his own body and blood to the Father; taking the role of the scapegoat, Jesus allows all of the sins of the world to be placed on his back in order that he might carry them away. When he passes judgment on the corrupt Jerusalem temple, just days before his death, he predicts that that great center of Jewish worship would be torn down but that he himself would rebuild it in three days. John's Gospel adds the interpretive gloss that he was speaking of the temple of his body. We must conclude that Jesus' crucified body is the new place where heaven and earth meet, and that the Lord acts as both sacrificing priest and sacrificed lamb.

The author of the Letter to the Hebrews, whose name and identity have been lost to us, was undoubtedly either a priest of the temple or someone intimately associated with the temple and its rituals, for he provides a richly liturgical interpretation of the essential activity undertaken by the ascended Christ. He signals his principal theme in chapter 4: "Since, then, we have a great high priest who has passed through the heavens, Jesus, the Son of God, let us hold fast to our confession" (Heb. 4:14). Having ascended to a transcendent realm (through the heavens), he functions in the manner of the high priest in the temple—which is to say, offering sacrifice for the reconciliation of God and his people. He performs this function precisely because the priesthood here below was inadequate to its task: "Now if perfection had been attainable through the levitical priesthood . . . what further need would there have been to speak of another priest arising" (Heb. 7:11). But why was the reconciling work of the levitical priesthood imperfect? The author of Hebrews gives two reasons. First, the priests were morally and spiritually impure and hence were required to offer sacrifice for themselves as well as for the people. And second, they presented only the blood of animals, which were but rather pathetic symbolic substitutes for the required sacrifice.

But now, in the resurrected and ascended Jesus, we have a morally and spiritually immaculate representative: "For it was fitting that we should have such a high priest, holy, blameless, undefiled, separated from sinners, and exalted above the heavens" (Heb. 7:26). Unlike the corrupt priests here below, this heavenly figure "has no need to offer sacrifices day after day, first for his own sins, and then for those of the people" (Heb. 7:27). He has, in point of fact, offered the perfect sacrifice on the cross once and for all—and this indeed historical act, since it belonged to a divine person, subsists in the eternal realm, beyond space and time and hence applicable to all space and all time. Secondly, this perfect high priest, having ascended to the heavenly temple, brings into the true Holy of Holies that of which the blood of thousands of sacrificed animals were but the symbol: "He entered once for all into the Holy Place, not with the blood of goats and calves, but with his own blood, thus obtaining eternal redemption. For if the blood of goats and bulls . . . sanctifies those who have been defiled . . . how much more will the blood of Christ . . . purify our conscience from dead works to worship the living God!" (Heb. 9:12–14). In a word, the Son's great act of obedience that took place on the cross now stands permanently in the presence of the Father as a sweet offering, effecting reconciliation. Jesus is the high priest on the Day of Atonement, but his sacrifice is perfect and has eternal validity, and the Holy of Holies that he has entered on our behalf is not an earthly simulacrum but the very dwelling place of God.

This same idea finds an imagistic counterpart in the book of Revelation. In chapter 4, the visionary author reports that "there in heaven a door stood open!" (Rev. 4:1). When he passes through, he sees a throne room that also seems to function as a sort of temple, for around the throne are gathered white-robed elders (the word here is *presbyteroi*, from which "priest" is derived), who engage in gestures and songs of worship: "Whenever the living creatures give glory and honor and thanks to the one who is seated on the throne . . . the twenty-four elders fall before the one who is seated on the throne and worship the one who lives forever and ever" (Rev. 4:9). In the right hand of the one seated upon the throne, the visionary spies "a scroll written on the inside and on the back, sealed with seven seals" (Rev. 5:1). This might be construed as an account of all of history or the Scriptures themselves. A voice is heard asking, "Who is worthy to open the scroll and break its seals?" (Rev. 5:2). In other words, who can possibly provide the interpretive key to the mysteries of revelation and of history?

No one presents himself, and there is sadness in heaven, until there finally appears a peculiar figure, "a Lamb standing as if it had been slaughtered" (Rev. 5:6). This weakest of animals, this typical sacrificial victim, is evocative of Jesus, the one slain upon the cross for the sake of the world. But anomalously, he *stands*, indicating the enduring power of what he had accomplished. This lamb, standing though slain, takes the scroll from the hand of the King, and all of the heavenly court gathers around him, singing a hymn of praise: "You are worthy to take the scroll and to open its seals, for you were slaughtered and by your blood you ransomed for God saints from every tribe and language and people and nation; you have made them to be a kingdom and priests serving our God, and they will reign on earth" (Rev. 5:9–10). I have quoted this extraordinary passage at length, for it gathers, marvelously, so many of the themes that we have explored in relation to the cross, Resurrection, and Ascension of Jesus. The Crucifixion was indeed an act of reparation by which a ransom was paid and the people set free. It was also the final great act of a King, who thereby gathered to himself people of every nation. And this priestly and kingly accomplishment, because it was achieved by a divine person, is now elevated to the eternal dimension, where it has become the focal point of the praise offered by the citizens of both heaven and earth.

And this brings us to the liturgical praise offered by the Church here below. From the beginning, Christian worship has had a transcendent orientation and a mystical meaning. That is to say, it is infinitely more than the gathering of like-minded people for the purpose of mutual support and shared praise; it is an act performed in conscious union with the saints and angels in heaven and under the headship of the ascended Christ. In the prayers of the Catholic liturgy, uttered just before the climactic Eucharistic Prayer, we find this language: "May our voices, we pray, join with [the angels] in one chorus of exultant praise." What follows is "Holy, Holy, Holy, Lord God of hosts. Heaven and earth are full of your glory. Hosanna in the highest."[50] The triple holy is meant to evoke two great biblical texts, one from the Old Testament and one from the New Testament. The first is from the story in the sixth chapter of the book of the prophet Isaiah concerning the call of the prophet. While praying in the temple, he sees the glory of the Lord filling the place and he spies Seraphs, the highest type of angels, singing to one another: "Holy, holy, holy is the Lord of hosts" (Isa. 6:3). The second reference is to the fourth chapter of Revelation, which describes the four living creatures around the throne echoing their counterparts in Isaiah: "Holy, holy, holy, the Lord God the Almighty, who was and is and is to come" (Rev. 4:8). Again, the prayers of worshipers here below are meant to "be one" with these prayers offered on high, the harmonious singing of heaven awakening the harmonious singing of the Church on earth. And that we might keep the kingly and priestly dimensions connected, we should never forget that this liturgical *communio* is meant to be the model and source of political, economic, and social *communio,* the prayer of the Church functioning, as Thomas Merton put it, as the "axle around which the whole country blindly turns."[51]

Some may wonder why St. Augustine spends so much time in *The City of God* discussing the gods and goddesses worshiped by ancient Rome. He does so because of a fundamental biblical conviction that we tend to become what we worship, our political lives reflecting the manner of being of those realities we consider of highest value. Therefore, to show the venality, violence, pettiness, and jealousy of the Roman deities was indeed to show the typical vices that mark—and eventually came to undermine—Roman society. One could argue that Augustine's ultimate point in *The City of God* is that the right worship offered by the Christian Church—praise directed to the God of love and forgiveness—would be the key to the creation of a just social order here below and ultimately an anticipation of the life that the blessed will live on high forever with God.

50. "Preface III of the Sundays in Ordinary Time" and "Preface Acclamation," in *Roman Missal* (ICEL, 2010).

51. Thomas Merton, *Run to the Mountain: The Story of a Vocation*, ed. Patrick Hart (San Francisco: Harper, 1995), 333.

"He Will Come Again in Glory to Judge the Living and the Dead"

I spoke earlier of the *exitus-reditus* rhythm of the Incarnation, but I wonder whether an exhaustive account would not include a second *exitus*: the Son of God goes out, comes back, and then goes out again. He came once to earth (taking to himself a human nature), brought that nature glorified to heaven, and then will come again in order to glorify all of matter, all of space, and all of time. If the metaphor of coming and going and coming again is getting a little awkward, we could speak of the ascended Jesus, who is God and man, finally drawing all things to himself, so that earth and heaven meet in a marvelous *conubium* (marriage). Remember that at the heart of the prayer that Jesus taught his disciples is the petition that the will of God be done "on earth as it is in heaven" (Matt. 6:10). This implies not an escape from the earth to heaven but a coming together of the two dimensions in a kind of embrace.

This anticipation of a definitive salvation of creation itself is mentioned again and again in the New Testament. In a series of supremely mysterious texts, St. Paul speaks, in his Letter to the Romans, of the longing of the universe for redemption: "We know that the whole creation has been groaning in labor pains until now" (Rom. 8:22). All of matter, under the influence of the Spirit of Christ, is preparing to bring forth something altogether new. What will this be like? "For the creation was subjected to futility, not of its own will but by the will of the one who subjected it, in hope that the creation itself will be set free from its bondage to decay and will obtain the freedom of the glory of the children of God" (Rom. 8:20–21). Yes, the world as we know it, in its essential beauty and intelligibility, is good, yet it is marked, in every corner, by suffering, conflict, decay, imperfection. It is indeed "subject to futility," and therefore cannot be as God fully wants it to be. We find something similar in 2 Peter 3, where the author speaks of "the coming of the day of God," which will result in a passing away of the old order and the arrival of "new heavens and a new earth, where righteousness is at home" (2 Pet. 3:12–13). In the twenty-first chapter of the book of Revelation, we are told of the descent of the heavenly Jerusalem, the glorified city where perfect praise of God obtains in its every aspect, and accompanying this arrival is "a new heaven and a new earth" (Rev. 21:1).

That this cosmic renewal is centered around the very particular Jesus of Nazareth is made abundantly clear in Paul's Letter to the Colossians. In an astonishing hymn of praise in the opening chapter of that letter, Paul signals that Jesus is the one through whom the universe was made: "He is the image of the invisible God, the firstborn of all creation; for in him all things in heaven and on earth were created" (Col. 1:15–16); the one in whom it subsists: "He himself is before all things and in him all things hold together" (Col. 1:17); and the one by whom it will be brought to fulfillment: "For in him all the fullness of God was pleased to dwell, and through him God was pleased to reconcile to himself all things, whether on earth or in heaven" (Col. 1:19). The very same idea of universal reconciliation through Christ is unambiguously laid out in the opening chapter of Paul's missive to the church in Ephesus: "With all wisdom and insight he has made known to us the mystery of his will, according to his good pleasure that he set forth in Christ, as a plan for the fullness of time, to gather up all things in him, things in heaven and things on earth" (Eph. 1:8–10).

There are many other such texts that I could cite, but I trust the point has been made. The "coming again" of Jesus, for which the author of Revelation in practically the very last words of the Bible prays ("Come, Lord Jesus"), involves the elevation and glorification of the whole of God's creation. The Gnostic dream of escape from matter is just not at all what the Scriptures are interested in. Now, what will this new heavens and new earth be like? No one knows with certitude. But can the resurrected Jesus give us at least a frame of reference? We saw earlier that the risen Lord is in clear continuity with the Jesus of the public ministry, but that he is also changed, transfigured. Thus, the new state of affairs will be, in a way, the same earth and the same heavens, but now lifted up to a condition of perfection. We might suggest that the new creation is to the old as a sphere is to a circle, or a pyramid to a triangle, or a box to a rectangle. In each of those cases, the more primitive shape is preserved, but it is enhanced, raised literally to a new dimension.

Having assured that the cosmic aspect of this reconciliation is sufficiently emphasized, I should like to return to the particularly human arena, for the Creed says that the principal work of Christ, having come in glory, is "to judge the living and the dead." I wonder whether, within the horizon of our cultural assumptions, there is any article of the Creed more objectionable than this one. I say this because we, at least in the secularized West, are massively uncomfortable with the idea of judgment—at least we say we are. When practically every other moral value is relativized and subjectivized, we assume, as a sort of default position, that nonjudgmentalism is an objective and universal desideratum. We have become expert in the art of self-exculpation. The bad feelings and negative self-image that follow from judgment strike people today as so extraordinarily dangerous that practically no effort is spared to undermine it. That an outside agent would pronounce negatively on what a person says, does, or claims to be is construed as an inexcusable act of violence.

If all of this is true in regard to the judgment offered by one's fellow human beings, how much more problematic it becomes in regard to a judgment offered by God—which is to say, one that is definitive and that carries everlasting implications. By way of an initial response, I might point out the contradiction involved in most of the opposition to "judgmentalism." Those who are most vocal in protecting themselves and others from judgment are typically all too willing to judge, even harshly so, those who are not in agreement with them, a phenomenon all too familiar in the often brutally exclusive advocates of radical inclusion. We should simply face the fact that something like judgment is more or less unavoidable, no matter what position we take, for to set one's face is, necessarily, to set one's back. I will confess that it is with some amusement that I direct those who see Jesus as *the* model of inclusivity and nonjudgmentalism to the stark judgments that are found, fairly regularly, on the lips of that same Jesus. And when we turn to the judgment of God, we should see that this divine discrimination should be, in fact, a source of vindication and comfort rather than dread. First, to say that God is the judge of truth and falsity, of right and wrong, of beauty and ugliness is to acknowledge that God is the true, the good, and the beautiful in their properly unconditioned form. Thomas Aquinas' fourth argument for God's existence in the *Summa theologiae* hinges upon this insight.[52] Thomas says that we evaluate things as relatively good or just or beautiful, precisely in relation to some ultimate criterion recognized as supreme goodness and supreme beauty. If this unconditioned element were removed, all such judgments would be invalidated, subjectivized. This ultimate and metaphysically objective determinant of value is what all people, Thomas concludes, call God. If this grounding criterion were removed, all values—moral, aesthetic, and rational—would become unmoored, and we would not be finally capable of determining and ordering what is objectively true or good. And as history makes painfully and abundantly clear, in that sort of epistemic and moral chaos, the will to power prevails and a strong man imposes order, following his own whim or fear. Within the Gospels, Pontius Pilate, indifferent to the truth, is the archetype in this regard.

Though secularists are tempted to read it as decorative boilerplate, the language concerning God in the prologue to the American Declaration of Independence is of crucial significance. "We hold these truths to be self-evident, that all men are created equal and are endowed by their creator with certain inalienable rights."[53] The moral truths that Thomas Jefferson is describing, in other words, find their grounding in a transcendent source, and hence government is not their *fons et origo*, but rather their guarantor. George Will has trenchantly remarked that the most important word in the Prologue to the Declaration is "secure," as in "in order to *secure* these rights, governments are instituted among men."[54] Government serves certain objective goods and hence is constrained by them. Though the full development of the argument would take me far beyond the confines of

52. Thomas Aquinas, *Summa theologiae* 1.2.3.

53. Thomas Jefferson, "The Declaration of Independence," in *Basic Documents in American History*, ed. Richard B. Morris (Malabar, FL: Krieger, 1965), 27.

54. George F. Will, *The Conservative Sensibility* (New York: Hachette Books, 2019), 22–23.

this book, I would reiterate that the presence of God as judge—which is to say, delimiting criterion of truth and goodness—is the best protection against tyranny. That the United States declares itself to be a nation "under God" is not to indulge in harmless patriotic piety; it is essential to its self-understanding as a democracy.

So far, we have illumined the judgment of God from a fairly abstract point of view. We can make our analysis more concrete by looking at the disconcerting fact that the world is a dark, violent, and deeply unjust place. Even the most casual survey of history and of the daily newspaper reveals that there have been and continue to be massive assaults on the dignity of human beings: murder, kidnapping, rape, genocide, slavery, human trafficking, pornography, imperialistic oppression, denial of fundamental rights, etc. These outrages quite rightly call forth the ameliorative efforts of decent people: police officers, journalists, judges and lawyers, social activists, military personnel, preachers, and politicians. Sometimes indeed, the interventions of such figures result in the righting of wrongs, the punishment of offenders, and the restoration of violated human dignity. But if we are honest, we must admit that far too frequently, injustice goes insufficiently answered within the lifetimes of the perpetrators or the offended parties. How many murders have remained permanently unsolved, how many broken lives permanently unrepaired, how many war-ravaged societies and psyches permanently compromised? No matter how righteous a political leader or activist might be, she is incapable of responding adequately to all the moral outrages committed within her jurisdiction. No matter how skilled and dedicated a detective might be, he cannot possibly solve every crime he investigates. No matter how eloquent and influential his voice, no religious leader can draw sufficient attention to every type of suffering within his purview.

And so by an altogether legitimate instinct, we say that all of these injustices "cry out to heaven for vengeance." Knowing full well that nothing here below can truly right these wrongs, and knowing furthermore that there is an objective standard for all of our moral judgments, we refer these sins to God, we bring them before God for final adjudication. Precisely because

God is both unconditionally good and outside of the strictures of time, we can hope that all sins, even those lost in the mists of history, can be addressed, and all suffering, even of people long dead, can be soothed. But this conviction is given further support and focus through the dying, rising, and ascending of the Son of God. As we saw, the Crucifixion of the sinless Lord was the greatest act of injustice possible, since it was tantamount to the killing of God. In it, we might say, all of the outrages and injustices of the world were contained, acknowledged, brought into the light. And then, in the Resurrection of the Son of God, all of that darkness was overcome, the *shalom* of the risen Jesus signaling the setting right of what was off-kilter. Finally, the Ascension, which entails the enthronement of that same Messiah, represents Jesus' lordship over space and time, his great ongoing work of reconciliation through his Mystical Body, the Church.

According to the Creed, this magnificent work of the ascended Christ involves, at the end of the day, the judging of the "living and the dead." The presumption is that when he comes—that is to say, when things are finally resolved—there will be some still living on the earth as well as an army of those who have died over the aeons. All will be evaluated in terms of their relationship to Christ; all will be arranged, so to speak, properly under his headship. Will everyone, finally, find his or her place in the heavenly kingdom? Will everyone be "saved?" I know from lots of practical experience in the field of evangelization and apologetics, there is massive interest in the resolution of this question, and fierce opinions are held on all sides of it. To be honest, the scriptural witness is somewhat ambiguous. On the one hand, we have many statements of Jesus himself regarding the reality of hell, or what he usually refers to as "Gehenna." And there is the famous utterance of the Lord concerning the wide road that many take and the narrow way pursued by very few. We also find Jesus' seemingly hopeless evaluation of Judas his betrayer: "It would have been better for that one not to have been born" (Matt. 26:24). Moreover, the book of Revelation seems pretty clear that there is a definite number of the saved and a fairly large contingent who end up in the "lake of fire" (Rev. 20:14).

On the other hand, there are numerous texts in the New Testament that present, at the very least, the possibility that all will, on that great day, find their place in the kingdom. One thinks, for example, of Jesus' bold statement in the Gospel of John that "I, when I am lifted up from the earth, will draw all people to myself" (John 12:32). The epistles of Paul are filled with assertions that are universalist in scope. For example, in Romans chapter 5, we find: "Therefore just as one man's trespass led to condemnation for all, so one man's act of righteousness leads to justification and life for all" (Rom. 5:18). In First Corinthians chapter 15, Paul says, "For as all die in Adam, so all will be made alive in Christ" (1 Cor. 15:22). In the Letter to Titus, there is the straightforward claim, "For the grace of God has appeared, bringing salvation to all" (Titus 2:11). Perhaps most persuasively, in the Letter to the Ephesians, Paul asserts, "With all wisdom and insight he has made known to us the mystery of his will, according to his good pleasure that he set forth in Christ, as a plan for the fullness of time, to gather up all things in him, things in heaven and things on earth" (Eph. 1:8–10). At the close of the famous hymn in Philippians chapter 2, we find these stirring words: "So that at the name of Jesus every knee should bend in heaven and on earth, and every tongue should confess that Jesus is Christ is Lord to the glory of God the Father" (Phil. 2:10–11).

Proceeding from this scriptural ambiguity is an ambiguity in the tradition regarding this matter. Tertullian was the first to argue that part of the joy that the blessed in heaven experience is savoring the suffering of the damned, and in this he was imitated by both Peter Lombard and Thomas Aquinas, who said that seeing the torments of the reprobate would increase the beatitude of the saved. St. Augustine opined that, due to original sin and its effects, there is a *massa damnata* (a damned mass) from which God, in his inscrutable mercy, delivers a relative handful.[55] No doubt influenced by these theological opinions, a number of mystics and spiritual writers have claimed that hell is densely populated indeed. I have heard the phrase attributed

55. Tertullian, *De spectaculis* [*The Shows*] 30 (*ANF* 3:91). Peter Lombard, *The Sentences, Book 4: On the Doctrine of Signs*, trans. Giulio Silano (Toronto: Pontifical Institute of Mediaeval Studies, 2010), 276. Thomas Aquinas, *Summa theologiae* Suppl. 3.94.3. Augustine, *On Rebuke and Grace* 12 (*NPNF*[1] 5:476).

to both St. Teresa of Avila and the visionaries of Fatima, but devotees of a crowded hell love to cite the observation that "souls are falling into hell like snowflakes in a blizzard."

But this point of view represents by no means a universal consensus in the theological tradition. In fact, when we turn to the Fathers of the Christian East, a far different picture emerges. Relying upon many of the Pauline texts cited above, thinkers such as Gregory of Nyssa, Origen, and Maximus the Confessor taught universal salvation, or at least something quite close to it. A central argument of Gregory hinged upon the relationship in God between the act of creation and the end toward which that act was directed. When God made the world *ex nihilo*, he made it for a purpose, and since God is utterly good, that purpose must be utterly good. How, then, could God permit that even one of his creatures come ultimately to the end of everlasting torture? Would not such an outcome tell fatally against the power and benevolence of the Creator? The Eastern Fathers certainly were not blind to the presence of evil in the world or the role that suffering plays in the spiritual development of free agents, but they tended to understand all of this as provisional, something that would eventually be brought to good.

And to be fair, there are plenty of mystics in the Christian tradition who would side with the more universalist perspective. Catherine of Siena, appalled at the prospect of even one person languishing in hell, asks the Lord how he could ever allow someone to slip from his hands. The answer that the Father gives her, which she confided to her spiritual director, is marvelous: "Love cannot be contained in hell; it would totally annihilate hell."[56] Inspired by this knowledge, the saint tells God, "If I could remain united with you in love while, at the same time, placing myself before the entrance of hell and blocking it off in such a way that no one could enter, that would be the

56. Quoted in Hans Urs von Balthasar, *Dare We Hope "That All Men Be Saved"?*, 2nd ed., trans. David Kipp and Lothar Krauth (San Francisco: Ignatius Press, 2014), 172. Balthasar's quotation is an original translation of material from a French edition of Raymond de Capoue's biography of Catherine of Siena, *Vie de Sainte Catherine de Sienne par le bienheureux Raymond de Capoue*, ed. Étienne Hugueny (Paris: n.d.), 479, 481.

greatest of joys for me." St. Edith Stein, martyred at the hands of the Nazis, was certainly not naïve about the twisting and corruption of the human will. Nevertheless, she could speak of the freedom of even the worst sinner being finally "outwitted" by Christ.[57] Most famously, Julian of Norwich, on the basis of her mystical experience, entertained the eschatological hope that "all shall be well, and all shall be well, and all manner of thing shall be well,"[58] a sentiment that T.S. Eliot inserted into his poem "Little Gidding."[59]

So how can we resolve this tension? Or is it perhaps best to leave it unresolved? The Council of Trent warns us off both presumption and despair—that is to say, a too easy confidence that all will be saved and a hopeless sense of the inevitability of damnation for most. Leaving the various and sometimes contradictory biblical, theological, and mystical assertions side by side is perhaps the best way to find the elusive middle ground. For me, the twentieth-century master Hans Urs von Balthasar proved particularly deft at picking his way through the minefield of this issue.[60] A devotee of both Augustine and Origen, he effected in regard to this matter a sort of Origenizing of Augustine. That is to say, without going so far as to embrace Origen's *apokatastasis pantōn* (salvation of all), he also moved away from Augustine's *massa damnata*, defending the proposition that we may *hope* that all people might be saved.

Now, it is crucially important to note that Balthasar's hope is not placed in human accomplishment. If salvation were simply a consequence of a sufficient amount of moral excellence on the part of human agents, then the *massa damnata* theology would be undoubtedly correct. But the hope that he speaks of is not in human accomplishment, but rather in what Jesus accomplished through his dying and rising. Having journeyed to the far country of complete godforsakenness, the Son of God has embraced, at least in principle, even those men and women who have wandered furthest

57. Edith Stein, *Welt und Person: Beitrag zum christlichen Wahrheitsstreben*, ed. by L. Gelber and Romaeus Leuven (Freiburg Herder, 1962), 158ff. Quoted in Balthasar, *Dare We Hope*, 177.

58. Julian of Norwich, *Revelations of Divine Love*, ed. Grace Warrack (London: Methuen, 1901), 56–57.

59. T.S. Eliot, "Little Gidding," in *The Four Quartets* (Orlando, FL: Harcourt, 2014), 56–59.

60. Balthasar, *Dare We Hope*.

from God. He therefore has offered the lively possibility of salvation to all. We spoke earlier, in a Balthasarian vein, of the sinner, running as fast as possible away from the Father, who is running, willy-nilly, into the arms of the Son. To express the same idea in terms of Jesus' famous image already cited, the vast majority of human beings indeed take the wide road that leads to perdition, but Jesus has, out of love, gone precisely to the end of that road in order to head them off. As Paul put it, God "made [Jesus] to be sin who knew no sin" (2 Cor. 5:21) that he might offer the divine mercy to all sinners.

Balthasar observes that all of the talk about hell, even on the lips of Jesus, takes place before the dying and rising of the Lord and that all of the talk of the possibility of universal salvation takes place after the Paschal Mystery. Thus, would it not be permissible to see the first type of rhetoric under the rubric of warning and the second under the rubric of promise and hope? The rejection, even of the acrobatic act of love accomplished by the Son of God, is still a possibility, given the fact of finite and sinful human freedom. In point of fact, Balthasar maintains that hell, properly defined, is a post-Paschal state of affairs, for it signals not just the *Sheol* of the Old Testament but precisely that condition of having turned away from the love offered in Christ. Is such a state of affairs possible? Assuredly yes. May we hope that no one finds himself definitively ensconced in it? Also, assuredly yes. As the *Catechism of the Catholic Church* puts it, "In hope, the Church prays that all men might be saved."[61]

Ultimately, the doctrine concerning hell is a corollary of two more fundamental truths—namely, that God is love and that we are free. Love (willing the good of the other) is all that God is. He does not go in and out of love; he does not change his mind. He is indeed, as Jesus said, like the sun that shines on the good and bad alike. No act of ours can possibly compel him to stop loving us. At the same time, we are free, which means we are not God's marionettes, and hence we can say yes or no to his love. When Jesus urges us to "strive to enter through the narrow door," is he

61. *Catechism of the Catholic Church* 1821.

perhaps suggesting we should stop bickering over how many or few other people will be saved, and as St. Paul put it, work out our own salvation with fear and trembling (Phil. 2:12)?

After affirming that Jesus will come as final judge, the Creed adds the tagline: "And his kingdom will have no end." What is being asserted here is the participation of the new way of ordering things in the very eternity of God. When the new Jerusalem descends from heaven, or to shift the metaphor, when we go out to meet Christ in the air, the two realms of heaven and earth are joined in a kind of marriage. The entire drama of nature and history, which would have unfolded over eons of time, will come, finally, to an end, but not a dead end, not to a condition of stasis, but rather to "rest"—which is to say, a savoring of the supreme good. The Creed is insisting that history is neither pointless nor circular nor dully repetitive. It is decidedly not "one damn thing after another," as the old cliché goes. Instead, it is moving, under the direction of the Holy Spirit, toward a fulfillment beyond what any philosopher or seer could imagine: the kingdom without end.

CHAPTER 4

The Holy Spirit

"I Believe in the Holy Spirit"

It would be worthwhile at this juncture to remind ourselves of the Trinitarian structure of the Nicene Creed. It commences with a relatively brief declaration of belief in the Father. Then it moves to a far longer, more elaborated, declaration of belief in the Son, in both his disincarnate and incarnate state. The section we have just considered is a description of the culmination of the Son's mission to deify the created order. Finally, it articulates the Christian belief in the third person of the Trinity, the Holy Spirit. Like the *Commedia* of Dante, like the *Summa theologiae* of Aquinas, and like Chartres Cathedral, the Nicene Creed is essentially Trinitarian in structure and purpose.

So who or what is the *pneuma ta hagion*, the *Spiritus Sanctus,* the Holy Breath in which we are professing our faith? I suppose the first clarification we should make is that the Holy Spirit is definitely a "who" rather than a "what," despite the rather impersonal descriptor. The reason is that the Creed immediately refers to the Spirit as "Lord." This personalizes him, of course, and also links the Holy Spirit to the Son of God, whom the Creed calls the "Lord Jesus Christ"; and, in one deft move, it unambiguously affirms the deity of the Spirit, for "Lord" is a term used, again and again, of the God of Israel. The Creed gives us another crucially important indicator when it speaks of the Spirit as *Zōopoion* (giver of life). As we saw when considering the Incarnation, the *ruach Yahweh,* the breath of God, is what brooded over the surface of the stormy waters at the moment of creation. All the vitality that came forth from the Creator issued from this ultimate source of life. In the thirty-seventh chapter of the book of the prophet Ezekiel, we find the beautiful and mysterious passage concerning the vivification of the dry bones. The prophet looks out on a field filled with the desiccated remains of soldiers and he is told by God to speak to them: "Prophesy to these bones, and say to them: O dry bones, hear the word of the LORD. Thus says the LORD God to these bones: I will cause breath to enter you, and you shall live" (Ezek. 37:4–5). When Ezekiel speaks, the *ruach* of God stirs the bones and then covers them in sinew, muscle, and skin, and finally breathes life into them, causing them to stand up as a revivified army. So the Holy Spirit operates in and for the holy people Israel.

When the prophet Samuel anoints young David, we hear that the *ruach Yahweh* "comes mightily" upon the boy, thereby equipping him for his military and kingly mission. The prophet Isaiah anticipates the coming Messiah, commenting, "The spirit of the LORD shall rest on him, the spirit of wisdom and understanding, the spirit of counsel and might, the spirit of knowledge and the fear of the Lord" (Isa. 11:2). One of the most lyrical descriptions of the activity of God's Spirit is found in Psalm 104. After exulting in the myriad ways that God brings forth life and fecundity—springs, rivers, birds of the air, trees, young lions, things that move through the waters—the Psalmist comments, "When you hide your face, they are dismayed; when you take away their breath, they die and return to the dust. When you send forth your spirit, they are created; and you renew the face of the ground" (Ps. 104:29–30). There are many more examples I could cite from the Old Testament—in fact, the word *ruach* is used 378 separate times in the Hebrew Scriptures—but this should suffice to show that the Spirit is a divine source of life in multiple senses of the term: physical, moral, intellectual, and corporate.

When we turn to the New Testament, we find a plethora of references to the spirit and the Holy Spirit—indeed, the word *pneuma* is found there 385 times—and these retain their Old Testament sense of life-source, but now they are intensely concentrated around Jesus and the very particular kind of life that comes from and through him. We can see the Spirit's influence throughout the career of Jesus. Thus, in Luke's infancy narrative, we hear the angel tell the puzzled Mary that "the Holy Spirit will come upon you, and the power of the Most High will overshadow you" (Luke 1:35). At the Lord's baptism, the Spirit appears in the form of a dove to John the Baptist, who exclaims, "I myself did not know him, but the one who sent me to baptize with water said to me, 'He on whom you see the Spirit descend and remain is the one who baptizes with the Holy Spirit'" (John 1:33). Similarly, in Mark's Gospel, John the Baptist prophesies regarding the uniqueness of Jesus: "The one who is more powerful than I is coming after me. . . . I have baptized you with water, but he will baptize you with the Holy Spirit" (Mark 1:7–8). After his Resurrection, Jesus appeared to his disciples, breathed on them, evoking thereby the great Old Testament symbol of the *ruach Yahweh,* and said, "Receive the Holy Spirit. If you forgive the sins of any, they are forgiven them; if you retain the sins of any, they are retained" (John 20:22–23). In Luke's narrative of the Ascension, we find the Lord saying to his disciples, "And see, I am sending upon you what my Father promised; so stay here in the city until you have been clothed with power from on high" (Luke 24:49), thereby anticipating the day of Pentecost.

That explosive arrival of the Holy Spirit in the midst of the gathered disciples, which calls to mind so many of the symbols associated with the Spirit in the Old Testament, is described by St. Luke in the Acts of the Apostles. "When the day of Pentecost had come, they were all together in one place. And suddenly from heaven there came a sound like the rush of a violent wind, and it filled the entire house where they were sitting. . . . All of them were filled with the Holy Spirit and began to speak in other languages, as the Spirit gave them ability" (Acts 2:1–2, 4). Those in the upper room were like the dead bones described by Ezekiel, and the Spirit of Jesus stirred them to life, indeed made them a powerful army, ready to go forth.

Then, in the aftermath of Pentecost, the Spirit is unleashed upon the world. He guides, bears witness, prays, teaches, speaks, converts, lifts up, inspires, and directs. St. Paul claims that all of the power and persuasiveness of his preaching comes not from his own wise words or clever rhetoric but from the Holy Spirit: "My speech and my proclamation were not with plausible words of wisdom, but with a demonstration of the Spirit and of power" (1 Cor. 2:4). In a curious passage from the Acts of the Apostles, the Holy Spirit seems involved very personally in the deliberations of the Council of Jerusalem. The protagonists conclude: "For it has seemed good to the Holy Spirit and to us to impose on you no further burden than these essentials . . ." (Acts 15:28). We might go so far as to say that the Holy Spirit is the principal actor in the life of the early Church, always keeping in mind the principle of noncompetitiveness, so that his activity in no way obviates or interrupts the real activity of the disciples of Jesus.

Therefore, we might sum up as follows: the Holy Spirit is the creative, life-giving power of the God of Israel that was involved in a completely unique way with Jesus from the very beginning of his earthly life, which filled him with fire and wisdom, which animated his ministry, and which he was able to give, after his Resurrection, generously to his Church. But what is the nature of this life? What precisely is it that Jesus had in such a distinctively unique manner and that he now offers as a gift to his followers? To answer these questions, we need to turn to the next line of the Creed and to explore it with the help of the theological tradition: "who proceeds from the Father and the Son." We recall St. Augustine's seminal and deeply illuminating psychological analogy for the Trinitarian relations. From before time began, the Father, by a great interior act, knows himself utterly and completely, giving rise, so to speak, to a Word, a Logos, a mirror image. This *notitia sui* (self-knowledge) *is* the Son, who shares in every sense in the being of the Father, with the exception of the Father's fatherhood. Having begotten the Son, the Father looks at the Son with infinite love, for the Son is utterly perfect, and since the Son possesses the same substance as the Father, he looks with the same intelligence and infinite love back at the Father. The shared love, the *amor sui* (self-love)—the "sigh" of love between them, as Fulton Sheen memorably put it—*is* the *Spiritus Sanctus*, the Holy Breath.[1] Recall that to love is to will the good of the other as other. If there is even a modicum of self-interest

1. Fulton Sheen, *The Divine Romance: Falling in Love with God* (Chicago: Biretta Books, 2014), 15–16.

on the part of the one who wills, true love disappears and becomes at least indirect egotism. In point of fact, some postmodern theorists have argued that a real gift, for this very reason, is impossible, for to be authentic it must involve absolutely no expectation of reciprocity. Yet, it appears that any gift has to awaken in the recipient some sense of obligation, even as slight as the obligation of gratitude. But these dynamics do not apply to God, since he is utterly perfect and hence needs nothing. Since the Father and the Son share the one divine essence, neither can possibly "benefit" from the other, and therefore neither can experience self-interest, either direct or indirect. Thus, their shared willing is the purest love possible, the very essence of love.[2]

Once again, lest there be any ambiguity on this score, given the divine simplicity, whatever is attributed to God is identical to the divine essence. Hence, the love proceeding from the Father and the Son is fully divine. He therefore should not be construed along the lines of an act of the will that is but an expression of an underlying consciousness. It is not one thing that God happens to do, but rather God himself. And thus the Creed is correct to specify that the Holy Spirit "with the Father and the Son is adored and glorified." Unlike mere reverence or honor, adoration is uniquely directed to God.

What are we sensing in the rapport between Jesus and his Father but precisely this divine love? In the conversation between the Sender and the One Sent—a conversation that is the Holy Spirit—we find an icon of the love that obtains in God from all eternity. "God so loved the world that he gave his only Son, so that everyone who believes in him may not perish but may have eternal life" (John 3:16). That famous passage from John's Gospel presents the Trinitarian persons admirably, God (the Father) sending the Son precisely out of the love that proceeds from and connects them—namely, the Holy Spirit. And just to make the icon complete, we see that the purpose of this mission is none other than the gathering of the human race into the

2. See Robert Barron, "The One Who Is, the One Who Gives: Derrida, Aquinas, and the Dilemma of Divine Generosity," in *Renewing Our Hope: Essays for the New Evangelization* (Washington, DC: The Catholic University of America Press, 2020), 97–112.

Trinitarian life, into the love between the Father and the Son. That is the life that Jesus shares. That is what he bequeaths to his Church and through his Church to the world: the capacity to love in the utterly disinterested way that the Trinity loves.

Now that these essential elements are in place, we can articulate an at least relatively adequate conceptual account of the Trinity. As we learned from the first line of the Nicene Creed, God is one. At no point does Christian teaching involve a compromising of the fierce monotheism of Israel. The divine essence is one. But because God is all-knowing, he is unconditionally present to himself. He utters an interior Word, completely reflective of his own reality, and therefore, it is appropriate for us to speak of the Father (the Speaker) and the Son (the Word spoken), of the unoriginate and the begotten, both of whom share the one divine essence. And because God's knowledge is unconditioned, he knows himself as good and hence loves what he has understood, and because the Son shares perfectly in the Father's way of being, the Son looks back at the Father and loves what he knows. Therefore, along with the unoriginated and the begotten, we must posit the "spirated"—which is to say, the one breathed back and forth (*spirare* in Latin) between the Father and the Son.

Thus, we have one God and two separate processions, that of the Son from the Father and that of the Holy Spirit from the Father and the Son. And we have identified three within the unity of God—namely, the unbegotten principle of divinity, the begotten internal Word, and the spirated love between them. For want of a better term, we refer to these three realities as "persons." In making what might appear a tossed-off remark, I am imitating St. Augustine who, when musing why we call the Father, Son, and Holy Spirit persons, said that it was so we have something to say when people ask us what they are.[3] In a similar vein, St. Anselm characterized them as *tres nescio quid* (three I don't know whats)![4] Both Augustine and Anselm

3. See Augustine, *On the Trinity* 5.2.9–10, 7.3.8–9, ed. John Rotelle, trans. Edmund Hill (Hyde Park, NY: New City, 1991), 197, 229–230.

4. Anselm, *Monologium* 78 (PL 158:221–222).

realized the serious danger that the word "person" gives the impression of a separately existing and subsistent being. If there are three persons in the room, there are three individuals in the room—and this is precisely what we do not want to communicate in regard to the Trinitarian threesome.

Some nine centuries after Augustine and two centuries after Anselm, Thomas Aquinas engaged in a pretty impressive act of metaphysical poetry and referred to the Trinitarian persons as "subsistent relations."[5] In terms of classical ontology, he was speaking nonsense, for subsistence belongs to substances (those things that exist through themselves) and relations are categorized as accidents (modifications of substances). Therefore, the two terms are mutually exclusive. The one thing that relations do not do is subsist; they inhere in something else. However, the demands of Trinitarian metaphysics compelled Aquinas to break the categories, something in the manner of a physicist saying that light is both wave and particle. The Father, Son, and Holy Spirit are certainly not modifications of the substance "God," for that would compromise the divine simplicity; and yet they are not separate beings, for that would result in tri-theism, compromising the divine unity. They are, we are forced to say, "pure" relations subsisting *as* relations. Thus, the Father is Father only in and *as* a relation to the Son; the Son is Son only in and *as* a relation to the Father; and the Spirit is Spirit only in and *as* a relation to the Father and the Son.

And this allows us to make one more clarification about the Trinity—namely, that there are, within the dynamics of the divine life, four "immanent relations." These are active generation (the relationship of the Father to the Son), passive generation (the relationship of the Son to the Father), active spiration (the relationship of the Father and the Son to the Spirit), and passive spiration (the relationship of the Spirit to the Father and the Son). As I clarified earlier, this "passivity" in God has nothing in common with the potentiality that inheres in creatures—which is to say, the capacity to become more fully actualized in being. All three persons, since they share the

5. Thomas Aquinas, *Summa theologiae* 1.29.4, 1.40.2.

singular divine essence, are utterly simple in their manner of existing. Yet, these dynamics do indeed indicate that something like giving and taking, offering and receiving, breathing in and breathing out, obtains within God.

Perhaps at this juncture, it would be advisable to address the famous (infamous?) *filioque* controversy. I will admit I am reluctant to do so, because I am convinced that there is ultimately nothing to it and that it gives dogmatic theology a bad reputation for logic-chopping and hairsplitting. However, it has figured prominently in the history of the roiled relationship between the Eastern and Western branches of Christianity and continues to be a stumbling block to unification. Exploring the details and intricacies of the debate would be tiresome and would take us way too far afield; therefore, allow me to lay out the matter somewhat economically. In the original version of the great Creed under consideration—that is to say, the Nicene-Constantinopolitan statement of 381—we read that the Holy Spirit "*ek tou patros ekporeuomenon*" (came forth from the Father). This formulation reflects the statement of Jesus in the fifteenth chapter of John's Gospel to the effect that "when the Advocate comes, whom I will send to you from the Father, the Spirit of truth who *comes from the Father* . . ." (John 15:26; emphasis added).

However, others, especially in the Western part of the Church, began to think that many scriptural passages seemed to imply that the Spirit was sent from both the Father and the Son. Time and again, St. Paul refers to the Holy Spirit as the Spirit of Jesus Christ, and even in the citation above, the Lord indicates that he will send the Spirit along with the Father. And according to the principle that dictates that the "economic" Trinity (the missions of the persons in the history of salvation) reflects truths within the "immanent" Trinity (the relations of the persons from all eternity), it seems that the Spirit comes forth from the Father and the Son acting in tandem. And so at the local Third Council of Toledo in 589, the Latin phrase *filioque* (and from the Son) was added to the Nicene-Constantinopolitan formula. When Charlemagne came to power around the year 800, this version of the Creed with the *filioque* became standardized at liturgies throughout much of Western Christianity.

Understandably, many in the East were outraged that a statement of the faith as venerable and ecumenical as the Nicene-Constantinopolitan Creed had been tinkered with by a local synod. More to it, theologians from the Eastern tradition were deeply concerned that making the Son a common source, with the Father, of the Spirit fatally compromised the primacy of the Father within the Trinitarian life. Another concern was that giving the Son the same generating power as the Father vis-à-vis the Holy Spirit would seem to put the Spirit in a position subordinate to the Father and the Son. If one were to insist on a role for the Son in the coming forth of the Spirit, the Eastern theologians were willing to speak of the Sprit coming from the Father *through* the Son.

Rising to the challenge, theologians in the West countered that the *filioque* honored the complexity of the biblical witness and assured the tight link between the Spirit and the Son. Moreover, the great psychological analogy provided by Augustine, the most influential of the Western Fathers, was especially congruent with the *filioque*, since, on his reading, the Spirit is indeed breathed out by both the Father and Son operating in tandem. The Eastern concerns about denigrating the primacy of the Father, Thomas Aquinas argued, are unfounded, in the measure that whatever the Son has, including his capacity to co-spirate the Spirit, came forth in procession from the Father. Finally, a careful reading of such Eastern masters as John Damascene and Maximus the Confessor appears to indicate that everything the West means by *filioque* is implied in the "through the Son" favored by the East.

My personal recommendation is that this controversy, which is at least as much political as theological, should be laid to rest permanently. Both the Orthodox and Catholic traditions believe in the unity of God, the co-equality of the Trinitarian persons, and the unoriginated primacy of the Father. In regard to the *filioque,* the West should say to the East, "What you mean by taking it out, we mean by putting it in," and the East should say to the West, "What you mean by putting it in, we mean by taking it out." Then both sides should declare victory and go home.

Still, under the rubric of determining what precisely this life is that Jesus communicates to his Church, I should like to return to the Bible, in fact to one of the most remarkable passages in the New Testament: the so-called Farewell Discourse offered by Jesus the night of the Last Supper, which culminates in his "high priestly" oration. Covering practically the whole of chapters 14–17 of John's Gospel, this speech constitutes, by far, the longest and most theologically dense utterance of Jesus anywhere in the Gospels—and its focus is the dynamics within the inner life of the Trinity. After clarifying that he himself is the way that conduces to the Father and that the one who sees him indeed sees the Father, Jesus commences to speak of the Holy Spirit: "And I will ask the Father, and he will give you another Advocate, to be with you forever. This is the Spirit of truth, whom the world cannot receive, because it neither sees him nor knows him" (John 14:16–17). The term for "Advocate" that the Lord uses here in the Greek is *Parakletos*, which has the literal sense of "calling to one's side," and hence means something like helper or advocate, someone who will speak on behalf of another, in the manner of a lawyer.

What this advocacy involves is laid out just a few verses later when Jesus declares, "I have said these things to you while I am still with you. But the Advocate [*Parakletos*], the Holy Spirit, whom the Father will send in my name, will teach you everything, and remind you of all that I have said to you" (John 14:25–26). And lest there be any misunderstanding, he specifies in chapter 16: "I still have many things to say to you, but you cannot bear them now. When the Spirit of truth comes, he will guide you into all the truth" (John 16:12–13). We see in these fascinating passages, first, that the Holy Spirit works in tight connection with Jesus, and second, that the truth implicit in the teaching of Jesus requires the ministrations of the Spirit to come to fully developed expression. The Advocate will never work at cross-purposes to Jesus and what is revealed in him, but he does indeed represent an element of freedom and novelty.

In order to understand this operation of the Spirit more profoundly, I should like to call, first, on the greatest Protestant theologian of the twentieth century—namely, Karl Barth. One of Barth's most ingenious insights is that the doctrine of the Trinity can be deduced from the foundational biblical claim that God has spoken (*Deus dixit*).[6] If God has spoken, if he has truly revealed himself, then there must be within God a Speaker. And if God has spoken, there must be a Word spoken, and this Word, if it is truly the Word of God, cannot be less than God. Thus, we have the Father and the Son, two coequal divine persons. However, if the spoken Word of God is to be understood by finite human minds, we require an Interpreter of the Word, who is himself divine. And thus we have the third person of the Trinity, the Holy Spirit, the one who leads us into all truth (John 16:13), the Advocate, who stands by our side enabling us to understand the Word that the Father has spoken to us. Given his Protestant assumptions, Barth undoubtedly understands the Spirit as the one who brings the unchanging Word of God to bear in the hearts of individuals, who makes possible a real act of faith.

I certainly would not want to contest this dimension of the Advocate's activity, but I believe that a more robust account of his work can be found by consulting St. John Henry Newman. At mid-career, just as he was making his transition from Anglicanism to Roman Catholicism, Newman composed a work entitled *An Essay on the Development of Christian Doctrine*. His central argument is that the doctrines of the Church, like any and all ideas, do not exist on the printed page, but rather in the play of lively minds. The mind of an individual never receives an idea dumbly and passively, but instead wonders about it, turns it over, mulls it, compares and contrasts it with similar ideas. And then, almost invariably, he shares his refined version of the idea to another lively mind through conversation, either direct or indirect. That person engages in a similar act of sifting and evaluating, before sending it back to his original interlocutor or to a new conversation partner. Newman compares this process to the gradual revelation of the many facets of a diamond through the turning and tossing of the gem, which exposes it to the light in a variety of ways. Thus, he concludes, in a way that anticipates the

6. See, for example, Karl Barth, "The Triune God," in *Church Dogmatics*, 1.1, *The Doctrine of the Word of God*, trans. G.W. Bromiley (Edinburgh: T&T Clark, 1975), 295–499, esp. 295–296.

phenomenologists of the twentieth century, that "the idea which represents an object . . . is commensurate with the sum total of its possible aspects."[7] An idea dumbly and uncritically passed on will become in short order fatuous and unpersuasive.

This analysis implies that development over time is simply a sign of life, from which comes Newman's perhaps most frequently cited line: "To live is to change, and to be perfect is to have changed often."[8] What most people miss is that Newman's reference here is to the epistemological order. He is most certainly not giving license to unstructured change for the sake of change—just the contrary. The authentic development of an idea is like the unfolding of a healthy tree or the deepening and broadening of a great river: it is a sign of vitality and a guarantee that the developing thing is remaining true to its essential nature. G.K. Chesterton made a remark that is altogether *ad rem* here. The great English controversialist said that the best way to guarantee that a white fence post loses its whiteness is to leave it alone. In short order, the elements will blacken it. Instead, if one wants to keep the post the same, he has continually to clean and paint it, changing it so as to preserve it in its original form.[9]

Thus, the ideas that constitute the faith of the Church are not simply given once and for all and then passed on, like a football, from generation to generation. Rather, they live and grow, commencing as seeds, then growing into trees and continuing throughout history to send off new branches and leaves, responding to the intellectual and cultural environment in which they develop. Newman knew very well that, here below, development is always shadowed by the possibility of corruption—which is to say, an unfolding that compromises that from which it comes.[10] Think perhaps of a cancerous growth on an organ. Thus, the seeds become trees do indeed sometimes give rise to errant branches as well, which need to be cut away if the organisms

---

7. John Henry Newman, *An Essay on the Development of Christian Doctrine* (Park Ridge, IL: Word on Fire Classics, 2017), 28.

8. Newman, 33.

9. G.K. Chesterton, *Orthodoxy* (Park Ridge, IL: Word on Fire Classics, 2017), 114–115.

10. Newman, *Essay on the Development of Christian Doctrine*, 139–169.

are to flourish. And this is precisely why, according to Newman, the entire process of development must be supervised, lest it conduce to a permanent corruption. The first agent of this supervision is the Holy Spirit, the one whom Jesus told us would guide the Church into all truth. The Spirit, to use Barth's language, is the Interpreter of the Word, monitoring its development throughout the course of the Church's life.

Now we can understand more clearly what the Creed means when it says, so simply and profoundly, that the Holy Spirit has "spoken through the prophets." Like Judaism and Islam, Christianity is a prophetic religion—which is to say, a religion that depends not so much on the rational musings of its adepts, but upon the word uttered by certain distinctive figures who made bold to speak, not just about God, but in the very name of God and under his authority. The prophets of the Old Testament were seized by a power beyond themselves and were commanded to speak, very often against their wills. Jeremiah famously protested, "Ah, Lord God! Truly I do not know how to speak, for I am only a boy" (Jer. 1:6), and Isaiah, upon being called, complained, "Woe is me! I am lost, for I am a man of unclean lips, and I live among a people of unclean lips" (Isa. 6:5). This reluctance indicates that the prophet is decidedly not like a philosopher or social activist, operating on his own initiative and according to his own ideas of the good.

The prophet does not necessarily foretell the future, though this can be a function of his fundamental mission. His basic task is, as Yves Congar puts it, to speak God's judgment on things—which is to say, to evaluate the affairs of the world from the perspective of God and God's purposes.[11] What the world tends to treat as ends—power, privilege, wealth, fame, etc.—the prophet sees as, at best, means to an end and, at worst, obstacles to achieving the only end worth achieving, which is doing the will of God. This transvaluation of values is what gives so many of the prophets—think especially of Amos, Hosea, and Zechariah in this context—their cutting, critical edge. It also helps to explain why so many of them ended up persecuted, rejected, or put to death.

11. Yves Congar, *True and False Reform in the Church*, trans. Paul Philibert (Collegeville, MN: Liturgical, 2011), 136.

Abraham Joshua Heschel, one of the twentieth century's great scholars of biblical prophecy, said that the prophet is someone who feels the feelings of God and then speaks out of that experience.[12] In light of this description, one thinks of the way in which these spokespeople for the Lord channeled God's anger, his passion to set things right, his delight, his encouragement, etc. The prophets are frequently ahead of their time, for they see where God is tending and hence they push people and institutions beyond their comfortable status quo. This is what leads to a tension we find frequently in both the Bible and the history of the Church between prophecy and ritualism or institutionalism. Andre Rousseaux, in a work on Charles Péguy, expressed the stress this way: "The prophet always sees the opposite of everybody else: he reverses the apparent order of things that is actually false, and rediscovers the real order."[13] Very much in the same spirit, Chesterton commented that the fool for Christ stands on his head and hence sees everything as upside down. But since this inversion of vision takes place in a world already upside down due to the effects of sin, Christ's fool actually sees things aright.[14]

Now, it is important to note that the tension ought not to turn into a contradiction, for the prophetic perspective, in time and usually after a great deal of struggle and opposition, does become settled teaching. The Gospel of John presents this relationship symbolically in the race of John and Peter to the tomb of Christ on Easter Sunday morning. The prophetic visionary got to the tomb first, but then waited for the official leader to catch up and to verify what the prophet had seen.

Prophecy continues, quite obviously, in the New Testament and in the early Church. Jesus never objected to being called "prophet," and many of his words and actions were congruent with his Old Testament prophetic forebears. The Apostles, filled with the Spirit at Pentecost, certainly preached and wrote in the manner of the prophets, and their teaching came, early on, to be established as authoritative in the life of the Church. And thus it is

---

12. Abraham Joshua Heschel, *The Prophets* (New York: Harper Perennial Classics, 2001).

13. Andre Rousseaux, *Le prophète Péguy*, vol. 1 (Neuchâtel, CH: La Baconnière, 1945), 119. Quoted in Yves Congar, *True and False Reform in the Church*, 138.

14. Chesterton, *Orthodoxy*, 161–163.

not surprising that the doctrine articulated by their successors the bishops became normative for the Christian community. To be sure, up and down the ages, the settled doctrine was sometimes challenged by prophetic figures, some of whom were deemed too extreme, but others of whom were accepted in the Newman-spirit as fomenters of legitimate development and whose critiques, accordingly, were integrated at length into the doctrinal tradition. Newman in fact holds that the prophetic office, broadly interpreted, includes theologians, teachers, writers, and mystics, who sift through the received teaching of the Church and place it in dialogue with the ever-changing cultural situation. It is precisely this open-ended, sometimes chaotic conversation that prompts the development of doctrine—and to be fair, the corruption of it as well. Again, what is required is the refereeing office of the bishops and the pope, which operates, under the Holy Spirit, so as to determine the difference.

It is often commented that the Church is not a democracy, and this is meant in several senses. Under this rubric of prophecy, it means that the teaching of the Church does not emerge as a consensus of the people, as the distillate of the common religious experience. It comes rather from certain very definite and rare individuals who received the grace to speak from the perspective of God. At the risk of proposing a metaphor that will be taken in a purely political sense, the doctrine of Christianity does not come "from below," but rather "from above," from the Holy Spirit who deigned (and deigns) to speak "through the prophets."

CHAPTER 5

The Church

"I Believe in One, Holy, Catholic, and Apostolic Church"

What one should notice first in regard to this article of the Creed is the peculiarity of using the word "believe" when the object of that belief is an institution, the Church. It seems altogether appropriate that we should express our faith in the Father, the Son, and the Holy Spirit, since these are all divine persons. But is it not at least questionable, at worst idolatrous, to be professing *belief* in the Church? It would be, of course, if the Church were nothing but a human institution, nothing other than an aggregation of like-minded people, nothing more than an assembly born of the common will of those who belong to it.

The use of the term "believe" in this context signals perhaps the most fundamental truth regarding the Church—namely, that it is a sacrament of Christ and hence, in a very real fashion, that it participates in Christ's divinity. We saw that the Incarnation involves the eternal Son of God taking to himself a human nature to use as his iconic manifestation, or in the more technical language of Thomas Aquinas, as his *instrumentum*. The glorified and ascended body of Jesus of Nazareth exists now in the realm of God, but the Son of God resolved to take to himself another Body, this one spreading across space and time, made up of all of those grafted onto Christ through Baptism. This Body—and it is St. Paul who first suggested that seminal image to us—would now be the *instrumentum* through which Christ would continue his work in the world. Hence, the Church in which we quite rightly *believe* should not be compared to an organization, though it has, as we shall see, institutional features, but rather to an organism. Summing up much theological speculation from the previous century and a half, the Second Vatican Council, in its document on the Church, entitled *Lumen Gentium,* states, "By communicating His Spirit, Christ made His brothers, called together from all nations, mystically the components of His own Body."[1]

There are, of course, many biblical warrants besides the epistles of Paul for this association. When the risen Jesus speaks to Saul on the road to Damascus, he says "Saul, Saul, why do you persecute *me*?" (Acts 9:4; emphasis added). Saul, of course, was en route to arrest and round up followers of Jesus, and yet the Lord refers to this act as an offense against *himself.* In Matthew chapter 25, we find the famous parable of the sheep and the goats. When Christ the judge determines, at the end of time, who will come with him and who will be excluded, he makes the discrimination on the basis of how each person treated the sick, the hungry, the imprisoned, and the naked. He says to the blessed, "Truly I tell you, just as you did it to one of the least of these who are members of my family, you did it *to me*" (Matt. 25:40; emphasis added). And to the cursed, "Truly I tell you, just as you did not do it to one of the least of these you did not do it *to me*" (Matt. 25:45; emphasis added).

Perhaps the clearest indication of the intimate rapport that obtains between Jesus and his Body the Church is found toward the end of the farewell discourse, parts of which we analyzed in the last chapter, when Jesus offers his high priestly prayer. Addressing his Father directly, Jesus the Son prays for his Apostles and for those who would follow them down through the centuries: "I ask not only on behalf of these, but also on behalf of those who will believe in me through their word, that they may all be one. As you, Father, are in me and I am in you, may they also be in us, so that the world may believe that you have sent me" (John 17:20–21). What is most extraordinary in this passage is the clear implication that, precisely as the Mystical Body of Jesus, the Church is drawn into the inner life of the Trinity, sharing in the oneness enjoyed by the three persons of God. We see now why any account

1. *Lumen Gentium* 7, in *The Word on Fire Vatican II Collection*, ed. Matthew Levering (Park Ridge, IL: Word on Fire Institute, 2021), 51.

of the Church that construes it as a mere human collectivity, as the "Jesus Christ Society," is pitifully inadequate. It would be far more accurate to see it as the prolongation of the Incarnation across space and time.

John Henry Newman makes this point through a lovely reflection on the story of Jesus telling Mary Magdalene on Easter morning not to cling to him. Christ's words, Newman says, should not be seen as an off-putting remonstration, but as an invitation to come into an even more vibrant contact with his Mystical Body: "When I am thus changed, when I am thus present to you, more really present than now, though invisibly, then you may touch Me—may touch Me, more really though invisibly, by faith, in reverence, through such outward approaches as I shall assign."[2]

If Christ Jesus is Head of this Mystical Body, then all those who are members of it through Baptism are cells, tissues, and organs, interdependently related to one another through him. This is why the suffering of any member of that Body is the suffering of every other, and why the triumph of any member is the triumph of every other. What Charles Williams called co-inherence—existing one in the other, each for the other—applies *par excellence* to the life of the Church.[3] It is why such practices as praying for one another or offering one's suffering on behalf of another are metaphysically grounded and not empty pious gestures. Tertullian's famous observation that what attracted so many pagans in the early centuries of the Church's life was the concrete love that believers displayed—"How [these Christians] love one another!"[4]—was made possible by this organic understanding of the Mystical Body.

It is sometimes suggested that Catholics place an obstacle between believers and Christ Jesus since they posit the institution of the Church as mediator. Would it not be better, more spiritually enlivening, to cultivate a

2. John Henry Newman, *Lectures on the Doctrine of Justification* (London: Longmans & Green, 1908), 216–217.

3. *Charles Williams: Essential Writings in Theology and Spirituality*, ed. Charles Hefling (Cambridge: Cowley, 1993), 17–18.

4. Tertullian, *Apology* 39.7, trans. T.R. Glover, Loeb Classical Library (London: William Heinemann, 1931), 177.

direct relationship with the Lord and to construe the Church as indeed a society freely entered into by one's fellow believers, yet altogether subordinate to the personal friendship with Jesus? Again, for Catholics, such an objection is absurd, precisely because we do not understand the Church as "mediating" the relationship with Jesus any more than the body of the historical Christ "mediated" his relationships with Peter, James, John, or Mary Magdalene. In fact, St. Joan of Arc went so far as to say this in response to interrogators at her trial inquiring about her views on the relationship between Christ and the Church: "About Jesus Christ and the Church, I simply know they're just one thing, and we shouldn't complicate the matter."[5]

If the Church is a Body and Christ is the Head, then the Holy Spirit is the soul that animates the Body. We recall the scene described in John's Gospel when the risen Jesus, the night of Easter, breathed on his disciples, saying, "Receive the Holy Spirit" (John 20:22). This is precisely analogous to the Genesis account of Yahweh breathing his *ruach*, his life-giving Spirit, into the lifeless clay of Adam's body. The sending of the Spirit, fully expressed on Pentecost, is what made the Mystical Body into a living organism, and it is the continued presence of the Spirit that vivifies and makes fruitful the life of the Church to the present day. When it teaches, when it governs, when it sanctifies, when it manifests charisms of prophecy and healing, when it leads people to eternal life, the Church is making manifest its inner vitality.

We can discover a good deal about the Church's nature and mission by doing a simple etymological analysis of the relevant Greek word used in the Nicene Creed. What we believe in is the *ekklesia*, a word that in the ordinary parlance of the time designated simply a gathering or a society. It is derived from two terms: *ek* (from) and *kalein* (to call). Hence, an *ekklesia* is a group that has been called out from something into something else, that has been set apart. So in regard to the *ekklesia* under consideration, we have to ask three questions: Who does the calling? What are its members being called out of? And what are they being called into? From the foregoing, it should be clear that the caller is Christ himself. Just as he summoned the original

5. *Acts of the Trial of Joan of Arc*, quoted in *Catechism of the Catholic Church* 795.

Twelve, and gathered in Zacchaeus, Bartimaeus, Nicodemus, Mary Magdalene, and the man born blind, so he continues, up and down the centuries, to call people to himself. We remember Jesus' clear insistence: "You did not choose me but I chose you" (John 15:16). Even those who enter the Church as adults, and who therefore do so as an act of their own will, are choosing to respond to a more primordial invitation.

What are members of the *ekklesia* called from? They are called, if I may use the biblical term, from "the world." This has nothing to do, of course, with a Platonic or Gnostic flight from matter and history. In the scriptural sense that I am using it, *kosmos* (world) designates the set of assumptions and manner of life animated by sin. Hence, "If my kingdom were from this *kosmos*, my followers would be fighting to keep me from being handed over" (John 18:36); and, "This is the Spirit of truth, whom the *kosmos* cannot receive, because it neither sees him nor knows him" (John 14:17). Thus, members of the Church are called out of a fallen way of thinking, feeling, perceiving, and behaving. They are invited to leave a world characterized by self-love and by the worship of false claimants to absolute status, out of the realm of kingdoms that belong to the scatterer (*diabolos*) and the accuser (*Satanas*).

Three Old Testament figures that our tradition has taken as especially emblematic of the Church are Abraham, Moses, and Noah. The first was summoned to leave his home in Ur of the Chaldees and, at the age of seventy-five, and to go in search of a land that God would show him. His obedience, which signaled the beginning of the formation of the people Israel, meant that Abraham entered a liminal space and an extended time of nomadic wandering, precisely when someone of his age would typically savor stability. Abraham's status as pilgrim would set the tone for the holy people, as numerous as the sand on the seashore or the stars in the heavens, that would come forth from him. And so the Church, which is a direct descendant of Abraham, has always been marked by a wandering, pilgrim quality, for it is being called out of sin and toward a land it sees only dimly.

Moses, too, is a man of the in-between. Summoned by the voice from the burning bush, Moses quits his peaceful, bucolic shepherd's life and assumes leadership of Israel languishing in slavery in Egypt. In his dealing with both his fellow Israelites and with Pharaoh, nothing is easy or settled. Then, he undertakes the great mission of conducing the freed slaves from the relative comfort of their lives across a trackless, pitiless desert, to a Promised Land that he himself will never enter. The Church, a descendant of Moses and his people, has accordingly always been marked by this exodus/in-between/journeying-through-the-desert quality. We have indeed left something behind, but we have not arrived yet at our destination; we are, at least in this world, permanently *in via* (on the way), a people on the march.

At a time when the *tohu wabohu* of sin threatened the entire world, God noticed the righteous man, Noah. He commanded this one remaining servant of his to construct a great ship on which Noah's family and representatives of the entire animal kingdom would be invited to weather the storm. The Church Fathers saw Noah's ark as a particularly rich symbol of the *ekklesia*. In the midst of a crisis prompted by sin, God called out a remnant of his good creation and carefully preserved them from destruction. And so he continues to summon a relatively small community and to shape it as a people after his mind and heart. The time aboard that boat—cramped, anxious, unpleasant—evokes the permanent condition of the Church here below, which has not yet completed its voyage through space and time. Picking up on this patristic theme, the builders of the Gothic cathedrals endeavored to design their structures in such a way as to suggest the ark of Noah, making them look and feel like places of shelter in the storm.

So Christ calls his holy people out of the *tohu wabohu* of sin, but he never calls them for their own sake, and the Noah narrative helps us to see this with particular clarity. Once the waters receded, and the Ark came to rest, Noah let out the life, releasing all of the animals, and his own family, to reinhabit the earth and to "be fruitful and multiply." Thus, the election of Noah was not for his own sake, but for the sake of the world. He was singled out not for his own aggrandizement, but rather for mission on behalf of others. The same rhythm can be seen, of course, in the stories of Abraham and Moses—and indeed in the stories of every person ever addressed by God in the Bible. No one—not Samuel, not Joshua, not David, not Jeremiah, not Isaiah, not Daniel—is given an experience of the Lord without being, as a consequence, sent. And thus the Church, the spiritual descendant of all of these figures, the institutional embodiment of Noah's ark, is indeed called *from* the world *for* the world.

And with that clarification, we have essentially answered the third question. The Church is called ultimately into the fullness of life and love that will obtain in heaven, but for the historical moment, it is called into permanent mission. Perhaps the central insight of Pope St. Paul VI's apostolic exhortation *Evangelii Nuntiandi* is that the Church does not *have* a mission alongside of myriad other projects; rather, it *is* a mission, by its very nature.[6] In the language of the Second Vatican Council, it is meant to be the bearer of the *lumen* (the light of Christ Jesus himself) to the *gentes* (the nations). Pope Francis has been particularly eloquent on this score, insisting that a Church that fusses primarily with its own inner life has fallen into corruption. Expanding upon the biblical image of the oil that runs down the beard of Aaron and on to the collar of his robe, Francis says that the oil, which is a symbol of the Holy Spirit, ought to extend to the very fringes of the robe and thereby come into contact with the wider world. When the anointing does not flow out, it becomes rancid, a symbol of ecclesial introversion.[7]

Having examined the *ekklesia*, at least in general outline, let us turn to the four qualities of the Church explicitly mentioned in the Nicene Creed: one, holy, catholic, and apostolic. The Church is one because God is one and God is using the Church to draw the whole human family into the divine life. If there were many absolutes, then we could imagine a variety of equally valid spiritual paths. If there were a plethora of gods, then it would make sense to have a plethora of churches. But that kind of pluralism in regard

6. Pope Paul VI, *Evangelii Nuntiandi* 14–15, apostolic exhortation, Vatican website, December 8, 1975, http://www.vatican.va/content/paul-vi/en/apost_exhortations/documents/hf_p-vi_exh_19751208_evangelii-nuntiandi.html.

7. Pope Francis, "Chrism Mass: Homily of Pope Francis," Vatican website, March 28, 2013, http://www.vatican.va/content/francesco/en/homilies/2013/documents/papa-francesco_20130328_messa-crismale.html.

to the highest truth and goodness is inimical to the Scriptures and to the understanding of God as the unconditioned reality. In the Bible, God is presented consistently as a gathering force, drawing a people Israel to himself so that, through them, he might eventually gather in all the nations. "In days to come the mountain of the LORD's house shall be established as the highest of the mountains, and shall be raised above the hills; all the nations shall stream to it" (Isa. 2:2). Drawing at least implicitly on this Isaian theme, Jesus says in John's Gospel, "And I, when I am lifted up from the earth, will draw all people to myself" (John 12:32). Nowhere is the all-embracing quality of the Church of Jesus given richer expression than in the first chapter of Paul's Letter to the Ephesians: "God put this power to work in Christ when he raised him from the dead and seated him at his right hand in the heavenly places, far above all rule and authority and power and dominion, and above every name that is named. . . . And he has put all things under his feet and has made him the head over all things for the church, which is his body, the fullness of him who fills all in all" (Eph. 1:20–23). This magnificent quotation, which brings together so many themes that we have explored in this book, indicates that the oneness of the Church is a function of the Church's identity as Christ's Body. Since Jesus is the force through which the Father is gathering all of humanity to himself, and since the Church is Christ's very Body, then the Church participates in the "all in all" character of its Lord.

In our postmodern period, this sort of claim, I realize, meets with immediate and intense resistance, for the valorization of pluralism in all things is taken for granted and, concomitantly, the shadow side of unity—namely, imperialistic oppression—is constantly brought to the fore. Any intellectual system, political arrangement, or especially religion that claims absolute or exclusive status is suspected, *ipso facto*, of aggression. The "masters of suspicion"—that is to say, Marx, Nietzsche, and Freud—have taught everyone, from the avatars of the high culture to high school students, to be wary of any ideology that would expect "all things to be drawn to itself."

Permit me to make two basic remarks in response to this concern. First, we must remember that the one who, on the Christian reading, is drawing all people to himself is none other than the crucified Jesus of Nazareth, the victim of an oppressive political and cultural system, who met his persecutors with nonviolence and forgiving love. I believe that a very persuasive argument could be made that the postmodern preoccupation with institutions of oppression is derived, ultimately, from the influence of Christian ethical principles flowing from the extraordinary witness of Jesus himself. Therefore, though it is a rather high paradox, the insistence that all things should be brought under the feet of Christ Jesus is not a power play—just the contrary. It is the privileging of the victim, the implicit criticism of all systems of violence and oppression. That the Church at times throughout its long history has acted at cross purposes to its own nature and imitated the worst of imperialistic regimes goes without saying, but these aberrations should not justify a demonization of the Church as inevitably imperious and domineering.

Secondly, the unity that the Church, at its best, is fostering is not monolithic but assimilating. Even the most cursory glance at the Church's life reveals that it is marked by extraordinary variety. There are multiple schools of spirituality and theology, innumerable orders, congregations, and societies, diverse styles of expression, as many ways of being a saint as there are saints. The Church has been able to take into itself countless forms of life and adapt them to its essential structure. Moreover, as it has made its way through the centuries and across the globe, the Church has assimilated to itself a manifold of philosophies, religious practices, and cultural forms, even as it has resisted others. Thus, Origen, Gregory of Nyssa, Augustine, Anselm, and Bonaventure assimilated the work of Plato; Thomas Aquinas took in Aristotle's metaphysics and epistemology; John Henry Newman used Hume and Locke; Hans Urs von Balthasar relied on Hegel and Barth; Karol Wojtyła took advantage of Max Scheler's ethics; etc. And missionaries to Ireland adapted certain expressions of Irish paganism to Christianity, even as missionaries to Germanic lands did the same with the religious forms that they discovered among the people they evangelized. One of the most splendid Catholic church buildings in the world is Santa Maria Rotondo in Rome, better known as the Pantheon. The Church took what was arguably the most beautiful and best preserved structure from antiquity, a building that perhaps more than any other sums up the glories of classical religion, and assimilated it to itself, not destroying it but raising it up to a higher level. Once again, I am not for a moment claiming that, in its long history, the Church always got this right, but I am indeed insisting that its characteristic instinct has not been to demolish what is other, but rather to draw it, as much as it reasonably can, into its own unity. The master image here is an animal making its way through its environment. If the animal is utterly resistant to what surrounds it, it will, in short order, die; by the same token, if it is utterly acquiescent to what surrounds it, it will also, just as rapidly, perish. The survival of the creature is a function of its ability to resist what it must and take in what it should in order to preserve its integrity and identity. The Church's unity is a function of just that sort of assimilating suppleness.

Relatedly, to say that the Church Catholic is the unique path is not to say that other spiritual disciplines and traditions do not contain elements of truth. That they obviously do is the foundation for conversations both ecumenical and interreligious. Were there no significant points of contact between divergent religious programs, no such discussions would even be possible, much less fruitful. To say this is not to succumb to religious indifferentism; it is merely to appreciate the manner in which participations in the fullness of religious truth obtain. I have long been attracted to Wittgenstein's use of the term "family resemblance" in this context.[8] Somewhere between the extremes of religious exclusivism and religious relativism is the acknowledgement that family resemblances can be found in varying accounts of God, sin, grace, salvation, etc.

The second mark of the Church to which the Nicene Creed draws our attention is holiness. In the Old Testament, *kadosh* (holy) has the sense of "set apart." Thus, the angels that appear in Isaiah's great temple vision sing *kadosh, kadosh, kadosh*, signaling the strangeness and transcendence of the God of Israel. The holiness of the Church follows, then, from its identity as

8. Ludwig Wittgenstein, *Philosophical Investigations*, trans. G.E.M. Anscombe, P.M.S. Hacker, and Joachim Schulte, rev. 4th ed. (Malden, MA: Wiley-Blackwell, 2009), 36.

the vehicle by which Israel's God is gathering people into his distinctive form of life. To put this in more explicitly Christological terms, it is a concomitant of the nature of the Church as the Mystical Body of Jesus, set apart from any other corporate identity. This sense of the holy as the "separate" fits well with the notion that the *ekklesia* has been called out of false forms of community into something altogether new and different.

We saw that the Mystical Body has a soul—namely, the Holy Spirit—and just as we say that it is the soul that makes a person holy, so the Holy Spirit, which dwells perpetually in the Church, is what makes it holy. The Spirit's presence is manifested in the sacraments of the Church, in its official preaching, in its magisterial pronouncements and conciliar statements, in the charisms spread liberally among the faithful, in ordinary acts of love performed in Christ's name, in the witness of the great saints, in the inspired art, poetry, and architecture of the Catholic tradition, etc. This manifold display prevents the holiness of the Church from becoming a mere abstraction or velleity. It can be seen and touched and verified.

The English word "holy" is related, of course, to the word "whole," and indeed, in a variety of other languages, holiness and "wholeness" or good health are closely linked. Thus, *sanctus* and *sanus* in Latin, *saint* and *sain* in French, *santo* and *sano* in Spanish, etc. Therefore, holiness carries the sense of well-being and integration. We might bring these two senses of the term together in this context as follows: the Church is that community that, having been set apart, participates in the distinctiveness and transcendence of God and thereby brings fullness of life to its members.

In regard to this mark of the Church, we confront, once again, a serious objection. How could the Church be described as holy when so many of its adepts have done so many terrible things, often in its name? How could the Church that sponsored the Inquisition, witch hunts, persecution of dissidents, the harassing of Galileo, and the execution of Giordano Bruno possibly be holy? How could the Church that has accumulated massive wealth and been marked, up and down the centuries, by extraordinary institutional corruption and has, in recent days, been guilty of countenancing the crime of the sexual abuse of children possibly be a source of healing and integration? In study after study, the rather manifest unholiness of the Church is cited as a key reason for disaffiliation from Catholicism, especially on the part of young people.

But a distinction is in order. Every single person up and down the centuries who has ever been a member of the Church (with the exception of the Blessed Mother) has been a sinner. Even the greatest of the saints were sinners—and they would be the first to tell you as much, for precisely those who are navigating their lives in the direction of the light are most likely to see smudges and imperfections on the windowpane of their souls. Every single office holder in the history of the Church has been a sinner and thus altogether likely to abuse his power. In point of fact, the doctrine of original sin, which teaches that all of us are members of a dysfunctional family, predisposes us to expect some degree of failure, corruption, stupidity, cruelty, and injustice on the part of everyone at every level. But none of this tells against the holiness of the Church, which is not dependent upon the vibrant sanctity and moral excellence of the baptized, but rather upon the Holy Spirit and those clear manifestations of the Spirit's influence referenced above.

The distinction upon which I am insisting here was the fulcrum on which St. Augustine's resolution of the Donatist controversy turned.[9] The followers of Donatus, an African bishop of the early fourth century, claimed that priests who had apostatized during a time of persecution and who then sought to return to active ministry after the danger had passed could not administer valid sacraments. Against this Augustine raised his voice in strenuous protest, for the Donatist position seemed to give to sin the power to negate the objective efficacy of the Holy Spirit. To be sure, Augustine was really only giving more specific definition to St. Paul's observation in his Second Letter to the Corinthians that the Church holds the treasure of Christ in exceptionally fragile vessels (2 Cor. 4:7). The corruption of the containers should not negate the reality of the treasure.

9. Augustine, *The Writings Against the Manichaeans and Against the Donatists*, vol. 4 of *Nicene and Post-Nicene Fathers of the Christian Church*, First Series, ed. Philip Schaff (Buffalo, NY: Christian Literature Publishing Co., 1887).

The third principal mark of the Church, according to the Creed, is catholicity. The term "catholic" is derived from the Greek *kata holos* (according to the whole) and thus designates something like universal or all-embracing. As such, this ecclesial mark is closely tied to that of unity. Since God wants to draw all people to himself, his outreach is properly all-englobing and so must be the vehicle by which he effects this gathering-in. Accordingly, the Church of Jesus Christ cannot be limited to any one nation, any single region, any particular ethnic group, or the speakers of any one language exclusively. Such a limitation would be repugnant to the catholic trajectory and purpose of the Church. St. Paul saw this with extraordinary clarity within a few years of the founding: "As many of you as were baptized into Christ have clothed yourselves with Christ. There is no longer Jew or Greek, there is no longer slave or free, there is no longer male or female; for all of you are one in Christ Jesus" (Gal. 3:27–28). Paul is choosing here, provocatively enough, some of the most significant fault lines in the society of his time. To know one's religion, ethnicity, social standing, and gender was practically tantamount to knowing who one was. Therefore, blithely to say that none of these finally matters and that an identity more fundamental has emerged was to start a social revolution. That Paul spent a good deal of time in jail proves it.

What put an end to the animosity based on cultural, ethnic, and religious differences was, of course, the cross of Jesus, which represented God's swallowing up of any and all human dysfunction. Paul expressed this idea with unsurpassed clarity in his Letter to the Ephesians. Addressing a contentious Jewish and Gentile community, he says: "But now in Christ Jesus you who once were far off have been brought near by the blood of Christ. For he is our peace; in his flesh he has made both groups into one and has broken down the dividing wall, that is, the hostility between us" (Eph. 2:13–14). Hence, the cross of Christ is the matrix of catholicity, the means by which God overcame the divisions of the fallen world. Once again, this ought to relieve the concerns of those who might see in the catholicizing push toward universality a disguised power play. The only legitimate imperialism within the Church is the imperialism of the one crowned with thorns and reigning from a Roman cross.

I should like to instantiate these more abstract considerations with the example of two English Catholics—namely, John Henry Newman and Christopher Dawson. When Newman was on the verge of converting to Roman Catholicism in the mid-nineteenth century, he read an article by then-Bishop Wiseman on St. Augustine's principle *securus judicat orbis terrarum,* a phrase that might be rendered "the whole world judges securely." Wiseman's point was that, in the determination of the truth of doctrine, the widest, most universal perspective is the best. When a matter of dogma is seen only from the point of view of one nation or people, it will not be interpreted validly. In the wake of that article, Newman could not help but see that the Anglicanism of his time was simply too provincial, too circumscribed ethnically and geographically, to be an authentically *catholic* church.[10] Christopher Dawson, the great culture commentator and Church historian, transitioned from Anglicanism to Catholicism when he was still a comparatively young man. When he told his aristocratic mother of this change, she had no objection on doctrinal grounds, but she did comment disapprovingly, "But now you will be worshiping with the help!" In this case, Dawson was opting for a catholicity that cuts disruptively across class lines.

In all of this we should see something of great practical and pastoral moment—namely, that the Church is not simply a community that in principle welcomes people from all nations, races, ethnic groups, educational backgrounds, etc.; it is most especially the place where the tensions produced by these divisions are actively overcome. The Church is an agent and instrument of reconciliation, within itself and outside of itself. And this is why whenever the Church has contributed to division, ethnic violence, race prejudice, or intercultural animosity, it is operating in a manner utterly repugnant to its own nature.

10. John Henry Newman, *Apologia Pro Vita Sua* (London: Oxford University Press, 1913), 212–213.

Still another dimension of the Church's catholicity is this: it has, in the words of Cardinal Francis George, "all the gifts Christ wants to give us."[11] There is not only a "here comes everybody" quality about the Catholic Church, but also a "here is everything" quality as well, for it includes Scripture, the liturgy, a richly complex theological tradition, sacraments, the Eucharistic presence, Mary and the saints, the apostolic succession of the bishops, papal authority, mysticism, a deep commitment to social justice, etc. The *kata holos* principle powerfully holds sway with respect to the inner life of the Church. A mentor of mine once commented that part of the genius of Catholicism is that "we never threw anything away." In the great storehouse of the Church, the full wealth of Christ can be found. Mind you, none of this implies that other Christian denominations and indeed other religions might not represent some of these qualities better or more fully than the Catholic Church does. For instance, some Protestant communions have a more developed sense of the centrality of the Bible and preaching, and the Orthodox Church might have a more impressively mystical appreciation of the liturgy. But none of them possess the full range of the gifts, the catholic totality.

Perhaps just a word as I draw this section on catholicity to a close regarding a standard objection. Some have maintained that the term "Roman Catholic" is simply incoherent, for the first word designates a very particular place while the second word indicates the *universum*. The one thing, it appears, a Roman church cannot be is catholic. The resolution of this dilemma depends upon the biblical principle articulated earlier, that individuals are always chosen not for themselves but for the world. Israel was indeed the uniquely elect people, but they were elected for the sake of mission. The Church is Roman precisely because Peter was chosen by Christ to be the bearer of the keys and he died as leader of the Christian community in Rome. But Peter (and hence Rome) was chosen for the world, not for his own sake. This creative tension is beautifully expressed in

11. Francis George, *A Godly Humanism: Clarifying the Hope That Lies Within* (Washington, DC: The Catholic University of America Press, 2015), 93.

the Bernini colonnade that reaches out, just like two arms, from St. Peter's Basilica in Rome, in a gesture of universal embrace.

And this observation segues neatly into the fourth and final mark of the Church referenced by the Nicene Creed: apostolicity. The one, holy, and catholic Church is grounded in the small band of twelve men whom Jesus called to himself and shaped according to his own mind and heart. At the root of all of the institutional structure and world-spanning reach of the Church is, finally, this intimate company of Jesus, gathered as apprentices around a master. Once again, this apostolic principle shows that Christianity is not an abstract philosophical system or a spirituality flowing from personal experience; it is a relationship to the very particular Christ, whose first preachers and mediators were the Twelve. When the two disciples of John the Baptist followed after Jesus, the Master turned and asked them, "What are you looking for?" The startled response came: "Where are you staying?" And Jesus said, "Come and see" (John 1:38–39). The Church takes its origins and finds its orientation from the first companions who came and saw, who stayed where the Lord stayed.

But to characterize the Church as apostolic is not simply to make a statement regarding its history and etiology. The apostolicity of the *ekklesia* is evident in what we call the "apostolic succession"—which is to say, the passing on of the Apostles' authority from one generation to the next in the persons of bishops. Through the laying on of hands, bishops across time and space have received, as a charism of the Holy Spirit, the mission and identity of apostles. They have been invited, so to speak, into the same relationship of special intimacy with Christ that was enjoyed by Peter, Matthew, John, Thomas, and the others. It is through the bishops, therefore, that the integrity of the Church's teaching, worship, and pastoral service is guaranteed. This means that those intimately bound to Jesus assure that the Church is not simply teaching according to the evanescent philosophy of a given age, or worshiping a God other than the one Jesus called "Father," or serving the poor out of purely secular motivation or with a purely political purpose. This of course does not mean that the bishops directly perform all of these tasks at the highest level. Thomas Aquinas was a greater theologian than any bishop of his time; Mother Teresa served the poor more effectively and dramatically than any bishop of her time. But it does mean that the successors of the Apostles play a refereeing and supervisory role vis-à-vis all such work in the Church.

One of the most illuminating theological commentators on the role of bishops was the nineteenth-century German theologian Johann Adam Möhler.[12] Reacting against an excessively institutional reading of the bishop's authority, dominant in his time, Möhler interpreted the episcopal role within the context of the organic ecclesiology that we sketched earlier. Every ecclesial community, he argued, requires a living symbol of its unity—that is to say, a person who symbolically expresses and institutionally maintains its integrity. Thus, for example, a parish needs a pastor, a shepherd, without whom it would disintegrate in short order. The same is true of a diocese. Without a bishop, who functions as its head, the diocese would dissolve into bickering and, more importantly, would lose its sense of common purpose. By extension, the same principle holds in regard to the Church universal. Even when many of his colleagues were calling for more democratically configured ecclesial communion, Möhler insisted that the unity of the Church demanded a single head—namely, the Bishop of Rome, the pope. Once again, he was not conceiving of the papal authority primarily along juridical lines, but much more along symbolic lines: the community around the world needed *someone* who would hold it together and draw it toward unity. The book in which Möhler laid out this theology of the episcopacy is called *Einheit in der Kirche* (*Unity in the Church*), proving that the mark of apostolicity is intimately tied to that of unity.

As a coda to this treatment of the Church, the Creed adds, "I confess one Baptism for the forgiveness of sins." We notice the shift from belief to confession, for we are professing here not a core point of doctrine, but rather

12. Johann Adam Möhler, *Unity in the Church; or, The Principles of Catholicism*, trans. Peter C. Erb (Washington, DC: The Catholic University of America Press, 2016).

a practice of the Church, though admittedly one so central that it is the only practice referenced in the Creed. One reason, of course, that Baptism comes in for special treatment is that the Nicene declaration, like the earlier Apostles' Creed, grew up out of confessions made by the faithful in advance of their reception into the Church. "Do you believe in God? Do you believe in Jesus Christ? Do you believe in the Holy Spirit?" etc.

However, there is a deeper reason for its prominence, for Baptism is the *sine qua non* of the Christian life, what the Council of Florence called the *vitae spiritualis ianua* (the door of the spiritual life), that without which none of the doctrines articulated in the Creed would make, finally, any existential difference in the life of a person.[13] By Baptism, one is configured to Christ in such a way that one begins to share the relationship between the Father and the Son. And as we saw when examining the Trinitarian relations, this implies a real participation in the Holy Spirit, who *is* the love between the Father and the Son. Thus, this originating sacrament, which is always performed "in the name of the Father, and of the Son, and of the Holy Spirit," is the means by which an adept commences to share in the inner dynamics of the Trinity, which is the entire point of the spiritual life. Everything else in Christian existence—reading of Scripture, participation in the liturgy, the study of theology, service of the poor, evangelization, the reception of the other sacraments—comes from this or returns to it.

The Creed names as the effect of Baptism "the forgiveness of sins," and indeed this cleansing is a major consequence of the sacrament. We might parse this relationship as follows. When we are drawn into the inner dynamics of the Trinitarian life, we are taken up into an altogether new manner of existence. Since the divine life *is* love, sin is repugnant to it, and hence God's gracious inclusion of someone into the play of the Trinitarian persons must be accompanied by the erasure of sin. We might also say that Baptism entails the forgiveness of sins in the measure that it brings us into

13. Quoted in *Catechism of the Catholic Church* 1213.

the life of the Church—and hence calls us out of the fallen world and into something altogether new.

CHAPTER 6

The World to Come

"I Look Forward to the Resurrection of the Dead"

Death haunts the whole of our life here below. Its inevitability and finality cast a shadow over even the greatest of our achievements and the most intense of our pleasures. Because, at the end of the day, we will die, it can easily appear to us that human life, ultimately, is pointless. Indeed, contemporary cosmologists and astrophysicists have only intensified this sense of meaninglessness by reminding us that the earth will one day be swallowed up by the sun, the sun will eventually burn out, and the universe itself is destined finally to pass into the virtual nonexistence of total entropy. The physical universe is marked by both order and chaos, but there seems little doubt that the latter triumphs, at last, over the former.

But we who have professed our faith in God, maker of heaven and earth, cannot resign ourselves to this cosmic futility. If God has made the entire universe, then he cannot leave it simply to wink out of existence. And he most certainly cannot abandon to oblivion his human creatures, who long for him with all their hearts, whether they know it or not. One of the most impressive Old Testament witnesses to this truth is found in the second book of Maccabees. We read that a pious Israelite mother and her seven sons have been arrested for refusing to eat pork during the time of the persecution of Antiochus IV. One by one, the sons are tortured to death in the most horrific manner and in the presence of their mother. As he is dying, the second son says to his torturers, "You dismiss us from this present life, but the King of the universe will raise us up to an everlasting renewal of life" (2 Macc. 7:9). And the third son, when this was asked of him, willingly put out his tongue and his hands, and said, "I got these from Heaven, and because of his laws I disdain them, and from him I hope to get them back again" (2 Macc. 7:11). This grisly but wonderful passage shows not only the emergence of a belief in life after death among Old Testament Jews, but also how that belief is tied to a keen sense of God's goodness and justice. As we saw earlier, if the righteous who are not vindicated in this world find no vindication in a life to come, then the Lord is not just.

Jesus himself professed the truth of the resurrection when he commented that the God of Abraham, Isaac, and Jacob—three figures long dead—is nevertheless not the God of the dead but of the living. For those who believe in the Creator God, protology (the beginning of things) implies eschatology (the consummation of things). And therefore, we "look forward" to our own resurrection and the life of the world to come. The language of the Creed correctly implies that we do not have anything like an exhaustive knowledge of the state of affairs that will obtain after our deaths or at the end of the spatio-temporal universe. But we look, we wait, we hope.

What precisely does "resurrection of the dead" mean? I will not repeat all that I said just a few chapters ago in regard to Jesus' Resurrection; suffice it to say that this hope is not focused on a Platonic escape of the soul from the body, but rather, as the Maccabees passage shows so vividly, on the renovation, transfiguration, and restoration of the whole person. It strikes biblically minded people as foolish to hold that the God who made the body and the material world would simply give up on all of that as a lost cause and rescue a spiritual element from it. Whatever else final salvation involves, it is, most certainly, a bodily state of affairs. But how do we make sense of this? In the face of death, burial, and decomposition, does not this talk of eternal life and resurrection just seem impossibly far-fetched? Are the critics of Christianity not correct in seeing this as the crudest kind of wish-fulfilling fantasy? The Church does not claim for an instant that it has worked out the details of the transition to eternal life, but it has entertained certain models by which the language of resurrection might be understood.

I realize that, even as I indulged in it a moment ago, the setting up of Plato as a foil is more than a tad facile. The dualism of Plato, which certainly from a scriptural standpoint is finally untenable, nevertheless reveals a rather profound truth about human beings. And Platonic-style thinking to a degree helps us to pick our way through some thorny intellectual ground as we struggle to make sense of what our biblical faith is compelling us to say. The doctrine of the Church is that those who have died, and whose earthly bodies have decayed, will rise bodily on the last day. Therefore, there has to be some continuity between the life that has rather obviously ended here below and the life to come. It is in trying to puzzle this out that the Church has turned to the language of soul and immortality, and Plato has proven to be an important intellectual ally in this respect.

Plato clearly saw that the human mind is capable of considering mathematical truths and pure abstract forms, which by definition stand outside of the realm of passing, contingent things. Therefore, the mind, at least in its higher functions, cannot be reduced to the operations of a material organ such as the brain. Thus, we have Plato's great teacher, Socrates, within moments of his death, calmly explaining to his grieving disciples that his soul will live on in the realm of the forms.[1] Now, Plato's student Aristotle, uneasy with the stark dualism of his master's anthropology, opined that the soul is best understood as the "form" or fundamental animating pattern of the body.[2] This helped to solve the problem of dualism, but it also made the soul essentially as evanescent as the body.

One of the most extraordinary intellectual accomplishments of Thomas Aquinas was to have affected a hybrid of Platonic and Aristotelian anthropology in regard to the soul. In line with Aristotle, Thomas held that *anima* (soul) is best construed as *forma corporis* (the form of the body), and this he did not simply out of devotion to Aristotle but because of his biblical commitments.[3] No reader of the opening chapters of Genesis could ever think

1. Plato, *Phaedo*, trans. David Gallop (Oxford: Oxford World's Classics, 2009).

2. Aristotle, *De anima*, trans. C.D.C. Reeve (Indianapolis, IN: Hackett, 2017).

3. Thomas Aquinas, *Summa theologiae* 1.76.1 (Leon. 5:208–209); *Summa contra Gentiles* 2.68–72 (Leon. 13:198–213), trans. James Anderson (New York: Hanover House, 1955).

that the material body is properly understood as a prison for the soul. That sort of antagonistic dualism is simply repugnant to the Scriptures, which teach that God found everything that he had made very good. At the same time, again for biblical reasons, Thomas knew that the Aristotelian soul, in the measure that it would evanesce with the dissolution of the body, is irreconcilable with the hope for eternal life. Thus, he argued that, remaining the form of the body, the *anima* has a subsistent quality, precisely inasmuch as it possesses the capacity to engage in acts of pure intellection.[4]

By means of the senses, the soul can take in the outside world, and through memory and imagination, it can form pictorial representations of that world, but by the intellect, it can abstract formal patterns from particular sense data and images. Thus, commencing with mental pictures of individual human beings, the mind is capable of distilling and holding the form of humanity—which is to say, the essential pattern that all human beings have in common. Or from seven particular things, the intellect can abstract the sheer idea of the number seven. In both of these cases, the mind is dealing with a reality that cannot be material, since it has to be equally valid of any and all individual instances of either humanity or sevenness. If intellectual activity were simply reducible to brain function, this sort of move would be ruled out, for all that a material organ could possibly manage is the processing of sense data and/or images. This proved to Aquinas' satisfaction that the soul, at least in its higher functions, is immaterial and hence does not disintegrate with the death of the body.

Hence, we can and should speak of disincarnate souls that live on after death, but keeping the Aristotelianism of Aquinas in mind, we should also insist that those disembodied souls retain an orientation to the flesh. In their purely spiritual manner of existence, they have not found the rest they finally seek. What they long for is precisely what the Creed calls "the resurrection of the dead"—namely, their reintegration with materiality—and this will take place at the end of time, or outside of time. The Platonic element within

4. Thomas Aquinas, *Summa contra Gentiles* 2.79–80.

Thomas' treatment provides for the needed continuity between this life and the resurrected life. Ultimately, it is not the literally selfsame matter that guarantees the identity of one's earthly body and one's heavenly body, but rather the enduring sameness of one's soul.

An intriguing variation on the Thomistic solution is found in the speculative eschatology of John Polkinghorne.[5] Like Aquinas, Polkinghorne argues that there must be both continuity and discontinuity between our present world and the world to come. For resurrection is not *ex nihilo* (from nothing) as is creation, but rather *ex vetero* (from the old), which means that it retains something of what came before even as it manifests real novelty. Polkinghorne finds the continuity in the same place Aquinas did, but with a twist. Like Aristotle and Thomas, he happily embraces the characterization of soul as the form of the body, by which he means the organizing pattern that guarantees identity over the course of one's life, even as one's body undergoes extraordinary change. Indeed, when we look at a photograph of a person when he is seven years old and then examine him at the age of seventy-five, we find only the vaguest similarity between the boy and the man. And, in point of fact, absolutely none of the atoms and cells that made up the seven-year-old are present in the body of the elderly gentleman (a fact that no premodern theologian could have known). Yet we confidently affirm that it is the same person, since the selfsame pattern has perdured throughout the changes.

When a person dies, this organizing pattern rather naturally fades away—and here Polkinghorne is closer to Aristotle than to Aquinas—however, he speculates, it is remembered by God and subsequently used as the template for the resurrection of the person at a higher pitch of perfection. This reconstituted person is remarkably new, but the remembered pattern preserved in the mind of God provides the continuity with the person that he was. If this explanation seems inadequately to account for real identity between the person pre- and post-resurrection, we must keep in mind that

5. John Polkinghorne, *The God of Hope and the End of the World* (New Haven, CT: Yale University Press, 2002).

we are dealing not with finite and derivative human memory, but rather with the divine "memory," which is not so much reflective of reality as the creator of reality. The "I" that exists in the mind of God is always the foundation of who I am, either in this world or the next.

Out of what materials does God make the resurrected body? Polkinghorne's answer is that God does so out of elements of the material world that we know. But in the world to come, these, too, are transfigured, raised to a higher pitch. What makes the resurrected body "mine" is, once again, the organizing pattern, the form, which serves as its template. Could this elevated body—both like and unlike the body here below—be what St. Paul refers to, with intentional ambiguity, as a "spiritual body"? To be sure, all of this is highly speculative, and no Christian is obliged to accept in every detail either Aquinas' or Polkinghorne's theory. As I said above, we really do not know the mechanics behind the transformation involved in the resurrection of the flesh. What the Creed demands that we "look forward to" is an embodied life on high with God, which is both a continuation of the life we live here below and something so new that of it we are compelled to say with St. Paul, "No eye has seen, nor ear heard, nor the human heart conceived, what God has prepared for those who love him" (1 Cor. 2:9).

Nevertheless, theologians and spiritual writers have proposed models or images to describe life in the heavenly realm. In regard to all of them, we should apply the principles that we laid out earlier in connection with the divine attribution—namely, the *via negativa*, the *via positiva*, and the *via eminentiae.* In this context, the negative way requires us to remove from our image of heaven anything to do with sin, for heaven must be a place marked thoroughly by the love that God is; the positive way requires us to posit of heaven anything that is good and life-giving here below; and the way of eminence requires us to raise those positive qualities to the highest possible degree.

One of the most fundamental metaphors for the life of heaven is the beatific vision—the awareness, the consciousness, that makes us finally happy. The matrix out of which this comparison comes is intellectual, the "seeing" involved in acts of knowing. The mind seeks the truth and frequently finds it, but every finding opens up a plethora of new questions. And thus the mind moves ever onward, upward, inward, in a relentless quest to see. Inspired by his Thomistic heritage, Bernard Lonergan said that what the restless mind ultimately wants is "to know everything about everything."[6] This all-inclusive seeing—obviously impossible to us in this life—*is* the beatific vision, which will represent the culmination of intellectual actualization in the world to come. It is tantamount to knowing the very essence of God, the source of all being and truth, or to put it in more scriptural terms, to seeing God in the face. But how, we might ask, would this exhaustive knowledge of God ever be possible, even in heaven, to a finite mind? Thomas Aquinas answers that it happens only through a graced and supernatural elevation of the intellect, the gift of participating in God's manner of knowing himself. But even having said that, we must add that, for Aquinas, this could never, even for the elevated mind, amount to total comprehension, but only to the joy of unending exploration into God.

If we apply the *via negativa* hermeneutic to this image, we understand that the knowing we will have in heaven will not be marred by sin the way any and all knowledge here below is. Lonergan helps us to see that self-absorption compromises the four great moves of the mind: attention, intelligence, reasonability, and responsibility.[7] For a variety of reasons, all of them bad, we fall into inattention, we do not allow our minds free play, we do not form good judgments, and we do not follow through practically on the implications of what we have judged to be true. In heaven, all of these wounds of the fallen mind will be healed. Under the rubric of the *via positiva* and the *via eminentiae*, we might posit that the exploration into God will not be a solitary enterprise, but rather something more like a gathering of friends in which a variety of conversation partners, lost in the beauty of their discussion and freed from self-regard, seek and find the truth together.

6. Bernard Lonergan, *Insight: A Study of Human Understanding* (New York: Philosophical Library, 1958), 350–351.

7. Bernard Lonergan, *Method in Theology* (Toronto: University of Toronto Press, 2003).

In seeing God face-to-face, we shall also thereby see all those beings and events that participate in God. Dante expresses this toward the end of the *Paradiso,* using the image of a book. St. Bernard invites Dante to look into the loveliness of God, and Dante says, "I saw how it contains within its depths / all things bound in a single book by love / of which creation is the scattered leaves."[8] In a word, we will see, in God, the great work of art, only hints of which in this life we can possibly spy.

A second model for understanding the nature of heaven is that of a city. The Bible is replete with bucolic imagery—think of the "green pastures" to which the good shepherd will lead us (Ps. 23:2)—and it remains rather suspicious of cities. Think of Cain as the founder of cities and all of the kingdoms of the world belonging to Satan. But when speaking of the consummation of things, the Scriptures utilize an urban image. At the conclusion of the book of Revelation, we read of the arrival of the new heavens and the new earth, and then of "the holy city, the new Jerusalem, coming down out of heaven from God, prepared as a bride adorned for her husband" (Rev. 21:2). The metaphor of vision, as rich as it is, might give the impression that the life of heaven is a solitary, contemplative affair, but to say that heaven is like a city is to signal something else altogether. Cities are places where enormous crowds of people come together for business, for entertainment, for sports, for leisure activity, for the arts, for communication, and for communal living. They are loud, bustling, energetic, full of excitement and rich possibility. To be sure, here below, they are also places of loneliness, exclusion, and violence, but remember that our *via negativa* hermeneutic would dictate that anything of the sinful is removed from heaven. Therefore, the city on high retains the beauty of life in intense communion with none of the dross. Will there be sports, entertainment, creative arts, and business in the heavenly realm? I do not see how people in that city could be truly happy without them, again keeping in mind that such activities will produce neither conflict nor boredom. Mind you, the author

8. Dante Alighieri, *The Divine Comedy,* vol. 3, *Paradise,* trans. Mark Musa (New York: Penguin Books, 1986), canto 33, 392.

of the book of Revelation is keen to communicate to us, above all, the *beauty* of the new Jerusalem: "The wall is built of jasper, while the city is pure gold, clear as glass. The foundations of the wall of the city are adorned with every jewel" (Rev. 21:18–19). We should not interpret this as mere decoration, but rather as an indication that all the activity of the heavenly city is marked by wholeness, harmony, and radiance.

Just after the lengthy description of the new Jerusalem's beauty, we find this extraordinary assertion: "I saw no temple in the city, for its temple is the Lord God the Almighty and the Lamb. And the city has no need of sun or moon to shine on it, for the glory of God is its light" (Rev. 21:22–23). For any Jew of the first century, the temple was the center, the very *raison d'être*, of Jerusalem. Whatever else happened in that capital city was related to the temple and its rituals, and God was seen as, in a practically literal sense, dwelling within the walls of that holy place. If all the tribes of the world came to Jerusalem, it was because of the temple. Therefore, what sense does it make to say that the perfected Jerusalem has no temple?

There is no formal religious edifice in the heavenly city *because the entire city has become a place of right praise*. In our fallen world, temples and churches are vivid reminders to bring our lives, public and private, into alignment with God. As Paul Tillich taught, the very presence of these buildings is hence an indication of the sinfulness of the world. In a rightly ordered society, play, sports, business, finance, family life, and politics are all effortlessly ordered to the worship of God—and hence no temple is needed. Notice that the author of Revelation says that the glory of God is the light of the new city, which would seem to indicate that every activity takes place through divine illumination and for a divinely ordained end.

This connection helps us then to understand a final great image for heaven—namely, the eternal liturgy. I know from a good deal of pastoral experience that this comparison can leave many people uninspired, given the blandness and banality of too many liturgies here below. But we must recall that right praise is perhaps the central theme of the entire Bible, for sin is the falling away from "orthodoxy," and salvation is its restoration. Putting God in the center, making God the highest value, is the essential prerequisite of a properly ordered spiritual and moral life. Hence, what we see in the joyful bustle of the heavenly Jerusalem, that city without a temple, is precisely the effect of right praise. We should not think of heaven as an endless version of liturgy on earth, but rather we should see liturgy here below as a vague indication of the orthodoxy that constitutes the life of heaven. In the new Jerusalem, we shall live in community, sing in harmony, understand the divine truth, commune with the angels, internalize the body and blood of Christ, converse face to face with God, and enter ever more deeply into a life of love. Following the prompts of the *via negativa*, take away from our worship on earth all that smacks of boredom, resentment, or incomprehension, and following the prompts of the *via positiva* and *via eminentiae*, take all that awakens a deeper communion with the Trinitarian God, and we might have some sense of what God has prepared for those who love him.

BIBLIOGRAPHY

Alexander of Alexandria. *Deposition of Arius*. In *Nicene and Post-Nicene Fathers of the Christian Church,* Second Series, vol. 4, *Athanasius: Select Works and Letters,* edited by Archibald Robertson, 68–72. Edinburgh: T&T Clark, 1891.

Anselm. *Anselm: Monologion and Proslogion.* Translated, with Introduction and Notes, by Thomas Williams. Indianapolis, IN: Hackett, 1996.

———. *Cur Deus homo.* In *Patrologia cursus completus,* series Latina, edited by J.-P. Migne, 158:359–430. Paris, 1853.

———. *Monologium.* In *Patrologia cursus completus,* series Latina, edited by J.-P. Migne, 158:141–224. Paris, 1853.

———. *Why God Became Man.* Translated by Janet Fairweather. In *Anselm of Canterbury: The Major Works,* edited by Brian Davies and G.R. Evans, 260–357. Oxford: Oxford University Press, 1998.

Aristotle. *De anima.* Translated by C.D.C. Reeve. Indianapolis, IN: Hackett, 2017.

———. *Physics.* Translated by C.D.C. Reeve. Indianapolis, IN: Hackett, 2018.

Athanasius of Alexandria. *De incarnatione.* In *Patrologia cursus completus,* series Graeca, edited by J.-P. Migne, 25:95–198. Paris, 1857.

———. *Four Discourses Against the Arians.* In *Nicene and Post-Nicene Fathers of the Christian Church,* Second Series, vol. 4, *Athanasius: Select Works and Letters,* edited by Archibald Robertson, 306–447. Edinburgh: T&T Clark, 1891.

———. *On the Incarnation.* Rev. ed. Translated and edited by a religious of C.S.M.V. With an Introduction by C.S. Lewis. Crestwood, NY: St. Vladimir's Seminary, 1996.

Augustine. *City of God.* Translated by Henry Bettenson. London: Penguin Books, 2003.

———. *Confessions.* Translated by F.J. Sheed. Edited by Michael P. Foley. Park Ridge, IL: Word on Fire Classics, 2017.

———. *De civitate Dei.* In *Patrologia cursus completus,* series Latina, edited by J.-P. Migne, 41:13–806. Paris, 1845.

———. *De magistro.* In *Patrologia cursus completus,* series Latina, edited by J.-P. Migne, 32:1193–1220. Paris, 1877.

———. *De trinitate.* In *Patrologia cursus completus,* series Latina, edited by J.-P. Migne, 42:819–1098. Paris, 1845.

———. *On Rebuke and Grace.* In *Nicene and Post-Nicene Fathers.* In *Nicene and Post-Nicene Fathers of the Christian Church,* First Series, vol. 5, *St. Augustin: Anti-Pelagian Writings,* edited by Philip Schaff, translated by Peter Holmes and Robert Ernest Wallis, 471–493. Buffalo, NY: Christian Literature Publishing Co., 1887.

———. *Sermones de scripturis,* 117: *De verbis Evangelii Joannis, 1:1–3.* In *Patrologia cursus completus,* series Latina, edited by J.-P. Migne, 38:661–671. Paris, 1865. English translation available in *The Works of Saint Augustine: A Translation for the 21st Century,* III/4: *Sermons,* edited by John E. Rotelle, translated by Edmund Hill, 209–223. New York: New City, 1992.

———. *Soliloquia.* In *Patrologia cursus completus,* series Latina, edited by J.-P. Migne, 38:869–904. Paris, 1877.

———. *The Trinity.* Translated by Edmund Hill. Edited by John E. Rotelle. In *The Works of Saint Augustine: A Translation for the 21st Century,* vol. 5. New York: New City, 1919.

———. *The Writings Against the Manichaeans and Against the Donatists.* Vol. 4 of *Nicene and Post-Nicene Fathers of the Christian Church.* First Series. Edited by Philip Schaff. Buffalo, NY: Christian Literature Publishing Co., 1887.

Aulén, Gustav. *Christus Victor: An Historical Study of the Three Main Types of the Idea of Atonement.* Translated by A.G. Herbert. Eugene, OR: Wipf & Stock, 2003.

Balthasar, Hans Urs von. *Credo: Meditations on the Apostles' Creed.* Translated by David Kipp. San Francisco: Ignatius Press, 2005.

———. *Dare We Hope "That All Men Be Saved"?* 2nd ed. Translated by David Kipp and Lothar Krauth. San Francisco: Ignatius Press, 2014.

———. *Mysterium Paschale.* Translated by Aidan Nichols. San Francisco: Ignatius Press, 2000.

Barron, Robert. *Arguing Religion: A Bishop Speaks at Facebook and Google.* Park Ridge, IL: Word on Fire, 2018.

———. "The One Who Is, the One Who Gives: Derrida, Aquinas, and the Dilemma of Divine Generosity." In *Renewing Our Hope: Essays for the New Evangelization,* 97–112. Washington, DC: The Catholic University of America Press, 2020.

———. *Renewing Our Hope: Essays for the New Evangelization.* Washington, DC: The Catholic University of America Press, 2020.

———. "The Trouble with Beige Catholicism." In *Bridging the Great Divide: Musings of a Post-Liberal, Post-Conservative Evangelical Catholic*, 11–21. Lanham, MD: Rowman & Littlefield, 2004.

Barron, Robert and Brandon Vogt. "#034: Don't Be a 'Beige' Catholic." *Word on Fire Show* podcast, August 2, 2016. https://www.wordonfireshow.com/episode34/.

Barron, Robert and John Allen Jr. *To Light a Fire on the Earth: Proclaiming the Gospel in a Secular Age.* New York: Image Books, 2017.

Barth, Karl. *Church Dogmatics*, vol. 4.1, *The Doctrine of Reconciliation*. Edinburgh: T&T Clark, 1988.

———. *Dogmatics in Outline.* Translated by G.T. Thomson. New York: Harper & Row, 1959.

———. "The Triune God," in *Church Dogmatics*, vol. 1.1, *The Doctrine of the Word of God*, edited and translated by G.W. Bromiley, 295–499. Edinburgh: T&T Clark, 1975.

Bonaventure. *The Soul's Journey into God.* In *Bonaventure: The Soul's Journey into God · The Tree of Life · The Life of St. Francis*, translated by Ewert Cousins, 51–116. Mahwah, NJ: Paulist, 1978.

Chesterton, G.K. *Orthodoxy.* Park Ridge, IL: Word on Fire Classics, 2017.

Congar, Yves. *True and False Reform in the Church.* Translated by Paul Philibert. Collegeville, MN: Liturgical, 2011.

Dante Alighieri. *The Divine Comedy*, vol. 3, *Paradise.* Translated by Mark Musa. New York: Penguin Books, 1986.

Davies, Paul. "The Nature of the Laws of Physics and Their Mysterious Bio-Friendliness." In *Science and Religion in Dialogue*, vol. 2, edited by Melville Y. Stewart, 769–788. Oxford: Blackwell, 2010.

Dawkins, Richard. *The God Delusion.* London: Bantam, 2006.

Denzinger, Heinrich and Peter Hünermann et al. eds. *Compendium of Creeds, Definitions, and Declarations on Matters of Faith and Morals.* 43rd ed. San Francisco: Ignatius Press, 2012.

Descartes, René. *The Philosophical Writings of Descartes*, vol. 3, *The Correspondence.* Translated by John Cottingham, Robert Stoothoff, Dugland Murdoch, and Anthony Kenny. Cambridge University Press, 1991.

Dostoevsky, Fyodor. *The Brothers Karamazov.* Translated by Richard Pevear and Larissa Volokhonsky. New York: Farrar, Straus & Giroux, 1990.

———. *The Idiot.* Translated by Eva M. Martin. Overland Park, KS: Digireads, 2018.

Einstein, Albert. "Physics and Reality." *Journal of the Franklin Institute* 221, no. 3 (March 1936): 349–382.

Eliot, T.S. "Little Gidding." In *The Four Quartets*, 56–59. Orlando, FL: Harcourt, 2014.

Francis, Pope. "Chrism Mass: Homily of Pope Francis." March 28, 2013. Vatican.va.

George, Francis. *A Godly Humanism: Clarifying the Hope That Lies Within.* Washington, DC: The Catholic University of America Press, 2015.

Girard, René. *The Scapegoat.* Translated by Yvonne Freccero. Baltimore, MD: Johns Hopkins University Press, 1986.

———. *Things Hidden Since the Foundation of the World.* Translated by Stephen Bann and Michael Metteer. Stanford, CA: Stanford University Press, 1987.

Harris, Sam. *The End of Faith: Religion, Terror, and the Future of Reason.* New York: W.W. Norton, 2004.

Hegel, Georg Wilhelm Friedrich. *The Science of Logic.* Translated by A.V. Miller. New York: Humanity Books, 1969.

Heidegger, Martin. *Being and Truth.* Translated by Gregory Fried and Richard Polt. Bloomington, IN: Indiana University Press, 2010.

Heschel, Abraham Joshua. *The Prophets.* New York: Harper Perennial Classics, 2001.

Hildebrand, Dietrich von. *Christian Ethics.* New York: David McKay, 1953.

Hitchens, Christopher. *God Is Not Great: How Religion Poisons Everything.* New York: Hachette, 2007.

Hume, David. *Dialogues Concerning Natural Religion.* 2nd ed. London, 1779.

———. *An Enquiry Concerning Human Understanding.* 2nd ed. Edited by Eric Steinberg. Indianapolis, IN: Hackett, 1993.

Jefferson, Thomas. "The Declaration of Independence." In *Basic Documents in American History*, edited by Richard B. Morris, 26–30. Malabar, FL: Krieger, 1965.

John Paul II, Pope. "Homily of His Holiness John Paul II: Oriole Park at Camden Yards, Baltimore." October 8, 1995. Vatican.va.

Julian of Norwich. *Revelations of Divine Love.* Edited by Grace Warrack. London: Methuen, 1901.

Kierkegaard, Søren. *Concluding Unscientific Postscript to* Philosophical Fragments, vol. 1. Edited and translated by Howard V. Hong and Edna H. Hong. Princeton, NJ: Princeton University Press, 1992.

Kreeft, Peter and Ronald Tacelli. *Handbook of Catholic Apologetics: Reasoned Answers to Questions of Faith.* San Francisco: Ignatius Press, 2009.

Lewis, C.S. *Mere Christianity.* New York: HarperOne, 2009.

Lombard, Peter. *The Sentences, Book 4: On the Doctrine of Signs.* Translated by Giulio Silano. Toronto: Pontifical Institute of Mediaeval Studies, 2010.

Lonergan, Bernard. *Insight: A Study of Human Understanding.* New York: Philosophical Library, 1958.

———. "Metaphysics as Horizon." In *Collected Works of Bernard Lonergan: Volume 4 Collection: Papers by Bernard Lonergan.* 2nd ed., edited by Frederick E. Crowe and Robert M. Doran, 188–204. Toronto: University of Toronto Press, 1988.

———. *Method in Theology.* Toronto: University of Toronto Press, 2003.

McCabe, Herbert. *God Still Matters.* Edited by Brian Davies. New York: Continuum, 2005.

Merton, Thomas. *New Seeds of Contemplation.* New York: New Directions, 1961.

———. *Run to the Mountain: The Story of a Vocation.* Edited by Patrick Hart. San Francisco: Harper, 1995.

Möhler, Johann Adam. *Athanasius der Grosse.* 2 vols. Mainz: Florian Kupferberg, 1827.

———. *Unity in the Church; or, The Principles of Catholicism.* Translated by Peter C. Erb. Washington, DC: The Catholic University of America Press, 2016.

Murray, John Courtney. *An Eight Day Retreat,* unpublished manuscript.

Neusner, Jacob. *A Rabbi Talks with Jesus: An Intermillennial, Interfaith Exchange.* New York: Image Books, 1993.

Newman, John Henry. *Apologia Pro Vita Sua.* London: Oxford University Press, 1913. NewmanReader.org.

———. *The Arians of the Fourth Century.* London: Rivington, 1833. NewmanReader.org.

———. *An Essay in Aid of the Grammar of Assent.* London: Longmans & Green, 1903. NewmanReader.org.

———. *An Essay on the Development of Christian Doctrine.* Park Ridge, IL: Word on Fire Classics, 2017. NewmanReader.org.

———. *Lectures on the Doctrine of Justification.* London: Longmans & Green, 1908. NewmanReader.org.

———. "A Letter Addressed to the Duke of Norfolk." In *Certain Difficulties Felt by Anglicans in Catholic Teaching,* vol. 2. London: Longmans & Green, 1900. NewmanReader.org.

———. "The Nature of Faith in Relation to Reason." In *Oxford University Sermons*, 202–221. London: Longmans & Green, 1909. NewmanReader.org.

Nicholas of Cusa. *Nicholas of Cusa on God as Not-Other: A Translation and Appraisal of* De Li Non Aliud. 2nd ed. Translated by Jasper Hopkins. Minneapolis: Arthur J. Banning, 1983.

O'Connor, Flannery. *Flannery O'Connor Collection*. Edited by Matthew Becklo. Park Ridge, IL: Word on Fire Classics, 2019.

———. *The Habit of Being: Letters of Flannery O'Connor*. Edited by Sally Fitzgerald. New York: Farrar, Straus & Giroux, 1979.

Origen of Alexandria. "The Homilies on Exodus." In *Homilies on Genesis and Exodus*, translated by Ronald E. Heine, 227–387. Washington, DC: The Catholic University of America Press, 1982.

———. *Homilies on Genesis and Exodus*. Translated by Ronald E. Heine. Washington, DC: The Catholic University of America Press, 1982.

Paul VI, Pope. *Evangelii Nuntiandi*. Apostolic exhortation. December 8, 1975. Vatican.va.

Pew Research Center. "In US, Decline of Christianity Continues at Rapid Pace." Washington, DC: Pew Research Center, October 17, 2019. https://www.pewforum.org/2019/10/17/in-u-s-decline-of-christianity-continues-at-rapid-pace/.

Plantinga, Alvin. "Is Belief in God Properly Basic?," *Noûs* 15, no. 1 (1981): 41–51.

Plato. *Parmenides*. Translated by Mary Louise Gill and Paul Ryan. Indianapolis, IN: Hackett, 1996.

———. *Phaedo*. Translated by David Gallop. Oxford: Oxford World's Classics: 2009.

———. *The Republic*. Translated by C.D.C. Reeve. Indianapolis, IN: Hackett, 2004.

———. *The Symposium*. Translated by Alexander Nehama and Paul Woodruff. Indianapolis, IN: Hackett, 1989.

Polkinghorne, John. *The God of Hope and the End of the World*. New Haven, CT: Yale University Press, 2002.

———. "The Trinity and Scientific Reality." In *The Blackwell Companion to Science and* Christianity, edited by J.B. Stump and Alan G. Padgett, 523–532. Oxford: Blackwell, 2012.

Pseudo-Dionysius. *The Celestial Hierarchy*. In *Pseudo-Dionysius: The Complete Works*, translated by Colm Luibheid, 143–191. New York: Paulist, 1987.

———. *The Divine Names*. In *Pseudo-Dionysius: The Complete Works*, translated by Colm Luibheid, 47–131. New York: Paulist, 1987.

Public Religion Research Institute. "America's Changing Religious Identity." Washington, DC: PRRI, September 6, 2017. https://www.prri.org/research/american-religious-landscape-christian-religiously-unaffiliated/.

Ratzinger, Joseph. *Introduction to Christianity.* 2nd ed. Translated by J.R. Foster. San Francisco: Ignatius Press, 2004.

Raymond de Capoue. *Vie de Sainte Catherine de Sienne par le bienheureux Raymond de Capoue.* Edited by Étienne Hugueny. Paris: n.d.

Roman Missal. International Commission on English in the Liturgy, 2010.

Rousseaux, Andre. *Le prophète Péguy.* Vol. 1. Neuchâtel, CH: La Baconnière, 1945.

Rutledge, Fleming. *The Crucifixion: Understanding the Death of Jesus Christ.* Grand Rapids, MI: Eerdmans, 2015.

Sartre, Jean-Paul. *Existentialism Is a Humanism.* Translated by Carol Macomber. Edited by John Kulka. New Haven, CT: Yale University Press, 2007.

Scheler, Max. *On the Eternal in Man.* Translated by Bernard Noble. New Brunswick, NJ: Transaction, 2010.

Sharp, Kimberly Clark. "Clinical Interventions with Near-Death Experiences." In *The Near-Death Experience: Problems, Prospects, Perspectives.* Springfield, IL: Charles C. Thomas, 1984.

Sheen, Fulton. *The Divine Romance: Falling in Love with God.* Chicago: Biretta Books, 2014.

———. *Radio Replies*, vol. 1, by Charles Carty and Leslie Rumble. Charlotte, NC: TAN Books, 2012.

Sokolowski, Robert. *The God of Faith and Reason: Foundations of Christian Theology.* Washington, DC: The Catholic University of America Press, 1995.

Stein, Edith. *Welt und Person: Beitrag zum christlichen Wahrheitsstreben.* Edited by Lucy Gelber and Romaeus Leuven. Freiburg: Herder, 1962.

Taylor, Charles. *A Secular Age.* Cambridge, MA: Belknap Press of Harvard University Press, 2018.

Tertullian. *Apology.* Translated by T.R. Grover. The Loeb Classical Library. London: William Heinemann, 1931.

———. *De spectaculis.* Translated by S. Thelwall. In *The Ante-Nicene Fathers: The Writings of the Fathers down to A.D. 325*, vol. 3, *Latin Christianity: Its Founder, Tertullian,* edited by Allan Menzies, 79–92. Buffalo, NY: Christian Literature Publishing Co., 1885.

Thomas Aquinas. *Commentary on the Book of Causes.* Translated by Vincent A. Guagliardo, Charles R. Hess, and Richard C. Taylor. Washington, DC: The Catholic University of America Press, 1996.

———. *Expositio in symbolum apostolorum.* In *Opuscula theologica,* vol. 2. Edited by Raymundus M. Spiazzi. Turin: Marietti, 1954.

———. *Faith (2a2æ. 1–7): Latin Text, English Translation, Introduction Notes, Appendices and Glossary by T.C. O'Brien.* Vol. 31 of *St. Thomas Aquinas Summa Theologiæ.* Cambridge: Cambridge University Press, 2006.

———. *On Creation [Quaestiones Disputatae de Potentia Dei, Q. 3].* Translated by Susan C. Selner-Wright. Washington, DC: The Catholic University of America Press, 2011.

———. *Quaestiones disputatae de potentia Dei.* In *Quaestiones disputatae,* 2:7–276. Edited by P. Bazzi. Turin: Marietti, 1949.

———. *Questiones disputatae de veritate.* Translated by Robert W. Mulligan. Chicago: Henry Regnery, 1952.

———. *Sancti Thomae de Aquino Opera Omnia.* Leonine ed. Rome, 1882–.

———. *The Sermon-Conferences of St. Thomas Aquinas on the Apostles' Creed.* Translated from the Leonine Edition and edited and introduced by Nicholas Ayo. Eugene, OR: Wipf & Stock, 2005.

———. *Summa contra Gentiles.* Translated by Anton C. Pegis and James Anderson. New York: Hanover House, 1955.

———. *Summa theologiae.* In *Sancti Thomae de Aquino Opera Omnia.* Leonine ed. Vols. 4–12. Rome, 1888–1906. In English as *Summa theologiae.* 2nd rev. ed. Translated by the Fathers of the English Dominican Province. New York: Benzinger, 1947. NewAdvent.org.

Tillich, Paul. *Dogmatik.* Düsseldorf: Patmos, 1986.

———. *Systematic Theology.* Three volumes in one. Chicago: University of Chicago Press, 1967.

Vatican Council I. *Dei Filius.* In *Compendium of Creeds, Definitions, and Declarations on Matters of Faith and Morals,* 43rd ed, edited by Denzinger, Heinrich and Peter Hünermann et al., 3000–3045. San Francisco: Ignatius Press, 2012.

Vatican Council II. *Lumen Gentium: Dogmatic Constitution on the Church.* In *The Word on Fire Vatican II Collection,* 45–149. Edited by Matthew Levering. Park Ridge, IL: Word on Fire Institute, 2021.

Will, George F. *The Conservative Sensibility.* New York: Hachette Books, 2019.

Williams, Charles. *Charles Williams: Essential Writings in Theology and Spirituality.* Edited by Charles Hefling. Cambridge: Cowley, 1993.

Wittgenstein, Ludwig. *Philosophical Investigations.* Translated by G.E.M. Anscombe, P.M.S. Hacker, and Joachim Schulte. Rev. 4th ed. Malden, MA: Wiley-Blackwell, 2009.

Wright, N.T. *The Resurrection of the Son of God.* Minneapolis: Fortress, 2003.

———. *Simply Christian: Why Christianity Makes Sense.* New York: HarperOne, 2006.

———. *Surprised by Scripture.* New York: HarperOne, 2014.

INDEX